The Dark Knight and
the Puppet Master

CHRIS CLARKE

The Dark Knight and the Puppet Master

ALLEN LANE

an imprint of

PENGUIN BOOKS

ALLEN LANE

UK | USA | Canada | Ireland | Australia
India | New Zealand | South Africa

Allen Lane is part of the Penguin Random House group of companies
whose addresses can be found at global.penguinrandomhouse.com

First published as *Warring Fictions* by Rowman & Littlefield 2019
Revised edition published under the current title by Penguin Books 2020
001

Set in 9.25/12.5 pt Sabon LT Std
Typeset by Jouve (UK), Milton Keynes
Printed and bound in Great Britain by Clays Ltd, Elcograf S.p.A.

A CIP catalogue record for this book is available from the British Library

ISBN: 978-0-141-99435-2

www.greenpenguin.co.uk

'The true progressive giants are radicals of the real – those who accept that true democracy implies pluralism, and that a plural society is self-evidently made up of many people and kinds, only a few of them truly exploitative and criminal, most just pursuing their own version of the good life as tradition and conviction has offered it to them.'

– Adam Gopnik, review of Clement Attlee biography, *New York Times*

Contents

Context

ABOUT THIS ARGUMENT

Differences between pro- and anti-Corbyn wings have been the subject of painful tensions in the British Labour Party in recent years. *The Dark Knight and the Puppet Master* traces these tensions – and similar divisions in Europe and the US – to their source. It suggests they're thanks to profound differences in the narratives governing our politics. The resulting divide, between the two sides of Labour, is between conflicting perspectives, not conflicting values.

To make this argument, the book sets out two outlooks on the left:

- **Left populism** is a style of progressive politics based on the idea that only left-wing ideas can be moral, that most problems are deliberately imposed from above, and that society is in a right-wing decline. Most common on the Corbynite 'far left' (though not unique to it), left populism deploys stories of conflict, insurgency and crisis.
- **Left pluralism** is an egalitarian politics more common among non-Corbynites. It rejects the idea that the political spectrum is a moral spectrum, and accepts a diversity of values. Left pluralists see social problems as organic, complex and the product of conflicting demands – not as authored. They also tend to be more upbeat about increased interconnectedness with other nations.

These divergences make cooperation hard, with agreement about the context we're working in close to impossible. They explain why the left often splits, why relationships descend into bitterness, why arguments result in non sequiturs. *The Dark Knight and the Puppet Master* looks to identify the nub of the differences. It explores three narratives, which are believed in by the populist left but not by the pluralist left.

Underpinning my argument are two convictions about British politics. The first is that regaining a rational, civil and democratic debate should be the priority for people of all leanings. Until trust in the motives of others is restored, discourse is based on logic, not conspiracy, and respect for opponents returns, politicians cannot address other problems. So, I'm asking that the left – specifically the populist left – takes the steps necessary to stop Britain being consumed by US-style 'culture wars'.

The second conviction is that the crisis of socialism and social democracy, which has put progressives out of power across Europe, is easier to solve than we think. The adage that we have 'run out of ideas' may be true. But there are answers, electorally and through policy-making, if we want them. Yet this is impossible when every conversation is distorted by sacred falsehoods and an atmosphere that straitjackets debate. The thinking needed to tackle global wealth inequality or address climate change is shut down by the visceral stories which guide left populism.

The book is therefore written from an openly left-pluralist stance, and in opposition to the populist approach. It asks how we on the left can jettison our destructive myths and folklore, in order to achieve an egalitarian society.

I

Left Populism and Left Pluralism

TRUMP AND THE RISE OF POPULISM

W. H. Auden called the 1930s a 'low dishonest decade',[1] and it seems likely we will look back on the 2010s in the same way. We have seen the upending of the conventional spectrum and the rise of populist movements from right and left. The shift is profound enough for some to fear the 'end of democracy', with the rise of 'fake news' and with declining political trust.[2] In the UK this has played out in Scottish nationalism, Brexit and the resurgence of the Bennite left. It has seen both main parties close to splitting at the seams, with a short-lived, non-populist breakaway, The Independent Group (TIG), registering as Change UK and then disbanding. The sudden crisis caused by the COVID-19 global pandemic – occurring at the dawn of the 2020s – makes the future even more uncertain in political and economic terms.

The rise of populism has been driven, in part, by globalisation (technological change, inequality, migration and other consequences of globalisation). This has generated problems which are often transnational and chaotic, and beyond the immediate control of national politicians. The chasm this creates feeds us-and-them dynamics and is exacerbated by twenty-four-hour news and social media. These phenomena magnify and polarise.

The populist movements this has spawned are not driven by rational arguments or policy goals. Because the problems are hard, and demand compromise, they are instead fuelled by gestures, symbolism and anger. It's this that has led to the term 'post-truth politics' – a shorthand for a climate where rational debate is eclipsed by emotion and identity. Donald Trump, for instance, claimed that he could 'stand in the middle of 5th Avenue and shoot somebody' and still would not lose voters.

There are three belief systems which sustain these new movements. The first is the belief in a common enemy – 'us versus them'. Populists rely on a malign foe. The second is an anti-establishment default.[3] Populists imply that omnipotent and self-serving elites block the 'will of the people'. The third is a sense of decline – often expressed through opposition to growing interdependence between countries. This lends urgency to the populist cause.

In the UK this is manifest. Both the populist left and the populist right indulge in an attritional world view that lets their outer fringes feel justified in spitting at Tories or in intimidating MPs outside Parliament (as 'Yellow Vest' Brexit protesters have done on several occasions). Both hold 'elites' culpable – 'global' in the case of the former, 'metropolitan' in the case of the latter. Both see themselves as victims of an institutional bias, on the part of the 'right-wing press' or the 'liberal media'. And both are sustained by nostalgia, for the Keynesian consensus of Attlee or the once-Great Britain of Churchill. They're thus driven by a sense of national decline – caused, in turn, by 'neoliberal' globalisation and culturally liberal internationalism – which they suggest that only their movements can avert. As a result, we have demagogues as varied as Jeremy Corbyn and Jacob Rees-Mogg.

Populist belief systems are destructive, wherever they appear on the spectrum. They indulge a cognitively dissonant, conspiracy theorist's view. And they lead to backward-looking and ideologically exclusive approaches. Worst of all is the lack of perspective they encourage. Populist narratives don't present hard choices or contemplate other viewpoints. They hold to ransom the wider electorate, often inadvertently, and imply that they speak for a larger group than they do. They allow the idea that their views have innate moral superiority to dominate the argument.

For instance, UKIP, the 'People's Army', represented only 4 million voters at their peak. 'No Deal' Brexit ultras were also an electoral minority. This does not invalidate these groups' views or mean they are wrong (although I personally think they are). The problem is that, rather than using logic to promote Euroscepticism, they suggest that anyone who points out contradictions or asks questions is a member of the 'establishment'.

Many on the populist left perform the same trick, claiming that those who disagree are closet Tories, or represent 'elite' interests, or wish to usher in a bleak, 'neoliberal' future. The perspective to see that their views are – like all our views – only supported in full by a minority, is absent.[4]

By adopting the belief systems that prop up populism – and the campaigning approaches that come with them – these movements distort the conversation. They claim to speak for 'the people'. But they lead us away from egalitarian and democratic government and eschew a politics which is rational and honest.

Ultimately, these populist approaches are the thin end of an extremist wedge. They have already poisoned much of the debate and led to policies with no foothold in reality. Taken to their conclusion, they encourage reactionary outcomes, enabling narratives of collective guilt to take hold, or elites to be violently purged. One of the lowest points so far, for example, was the horrific murder of MP Jo Cox in 2016 – sincerely condemned by populists, but nevertheless the product of narratives which caricature and dehumanise the other side.

Until Britain's vote to leave the EU – and Donald Trump's victory – populist movements had largely been consigned to opposition. This was because they knew what they were against but not what they were for. Electorates sensed that populists didn't have the answers.

The situation for some time, therefore, was one where seemingly bloodless 'centrists', cowed by populism, sought to find the mean average of a range pulled tauter and tauter. The surprise wins for Leave and Trump showed that this couldn't sustain itself. The political cord snapped. And it snapped in favour of demagogues from the right.

For some on the left, the answer is simple: get better at populism.

Left-wingers must capture the mood of anti-politics more effectively. We must combat our foe more robustly. We must bang the drum of easy answers more loudly. We must reject the decline more resolutely.

Some had already begun to champion this approach a few years ago, with calls for a Tea Party 'of the left'. But the effort to replicate the rage of conservative ultras has become commonplace since 2016.[5] Disciples of this have suggested, variously, that we should exploit the 'splendid fountain of hate' which is currently gurgling, adopt a 'heads on sticks' mentality or wish death on our opponents.[6]

In some cases, this has led to Eurosceptic and anti-immigrant arguments, with a 'socialism in one country' approach not a million miles from Trump's protectionism. Elsewhere, it's simply about a style of politics which is aggressive, oppositionist and sustained by a feeling of crisis. Even after Labour's 2019 election defeat, one Corbynite commentator said that the answer was a greater 'oppositionality'. She wrote that 'any convincing political narrative requires a hero and a villain', and that Labour should 'construct an "other" in order to woo voters'.[7]

This book is arguing the opposite: that we on the left should go against these populist instincts with every fibre. Some may believe the 2017 election – where Corbyn did better than expected – proves that I am wrong, especially when we look at the plight of social democracy in other parts of Europe. Populism works, they say.

I disagree with this, partly because the right is better at producing demagogues – so it is unwise, as the December 2019 election showed, to fight them on their own turf. Thanks to this approach, the UK now has a right-populist government which rules all that it surveys.

But the electoral viability of left populism isn't really the point. The true problem is the lack of integrity. If we don't have answers to wealth inequality, climate change or post-industrial decline, then we must be serious and open-minded about the solutions. It will help no one to get in on a ticket which suggests that only the venality of those in power has stopped them being solved already.

TITANIC STRUGGLE, BRAVE UPRISING, TRAGIC LOSS

Labour has been consumed by infighting since 2015, and major splits on the left remain, even with Corbyn replaced as leader. There were two ill-tempered leadership contests in consecutive years. From the Syria debate to Haringey Council's high-profile divisions over housing policy, the discourse is fraught with accusations of bad faith.[8] The far left and centre left face an impasse that feels too big to cross.

These divides, which are thanks, in large part, to the party's lurch towards populism under Corbyn, can partly be attributed to the rise of the populist mindset everywhere – with its appetite for catastrophe, its tendency to hunt out culprits and its attraction to conspiracism. But I cannot help feeling that the spirit of populism has come too easily to the left; that we have long had this potential inbuilt.

The phenomenon of 'the left splitting while the right holds' is, after all, as old as politics itself. Likewise, the left's tendency is to feel that the right are immoral (whereas the Conservatives merely think we're foolish). The Labour movement has long embraced a romantic and partisan spirit – often at the expense of objectivity and unity. We have a thirst for myths of titanic struggle, brave uprising and tragic loss.

George Orwell wrote in 1937 that 'Socialism is such elementary common sense that I'm sometimes amazed that it hasn't established itself already.' He blamed the fact it had not on something 'inherently distasteful' in socialists' approach, which drove away 'the very people who ought to be flocking to its support'.[9] Little has changed in the intervening years. Hence the perception that we are the home of sectarian extremists, delusional conspiracy theorists and sanctimonious miserablists carries weight – exaggerated by right-wingers, for sure, but fuelled by our own antics.

This explains why the left is drawn towards the siren calls of twenty-first-century populism. And it explains why, despite our core values being strong enough and rational enough that we should be the natural 'party of government', Labour has ruled for barely 30 of the 120 years since it was founded (with 10 of those coming under a prime minister who the populist left now despises as a closet Tory).

Indeed, the appetite for struggle, uprising and loss creates several problems for those who want a more progressive politics. It means the Labour left adopt 'enemy's enemy is my friend' or 'means justify the ends' positions that are reactionary. We fetishise leaders who cannot win and policies that have ceased to be progressive because we see things in moral absolutes. We're viewed by the electorate as incapable of weighing up dilemmas from the perspective of a would-be government. And when we subsequently lose elections, we kid ourselves that the media or big business have thrown them for us. Suspicion of elites makes us instinctively libertarian when it comes to the state, despite goals like redistribution depending on trust in these institutions. We spend years out of power through unwillingness to accept the basics of electoral compromise or global change, meaning other parties define the agenda. And no sooner have we got our act together and won an election than someone declares that we have sold out, and the process starts all over again. The December 2019 election loss summed up where this process takes you – with the Labour Party on life support, having suffered huge losses across almost every part of its traditional coalition.

Worse than all of the above, we on the left are often incurious about – and intolerant of – those who disagree. After all, ideas of struggle, uprising and loss all rely on a force against which we are fighting – be it an immoral enemy, a shadowy elite or a dystopian future. Energy is spent fighting these forces, with an interest in the people and pressures on the other side lost as a result.

For instance, American psychology professor Jonathan Haidt has carried out roleplay experiments to test how well left-wingers, right-wingers and independents can predict each other's politics.[10] Haidt (using American terminology) concludes that 'the results were clear and consistent. Moderates and Conservatives were most accurate in their predictions ... Liberals were the least accurate, especially those who described themselves as 'very Liberal'. When faced with propositions such as 'One of the worst things a person can do is hurt a defenceless animal,' for instance, liberals repeatedly and wrongly assumed that conservatives would oppose the statement. Research suggests the same is true in the UK.[11] A willingness to give the benefit of the doubt seems to be missing.

Hence, we have two related phenomena here: the recent rise of populism across the board, and the left's historic attraction to romantic struggle. These have combined, on what is conventionally known as the far left, to create the left populism against which this book argues.

This was embodied in the UK by the rise of Jeremy Corbyn, a figure who inspires half of those who are left-of-centre and alienates the other half. But the issue isn't just to do with Corbyn as a man or Corbynism as an ideology. It relates to an entire state of mind.

WHERE DO WE DISAGREE?

What, then, is the alternative to left populism? To answer this, we need to ponder something more fundamental: at what level do the far left and the centre left disagree?

Ever since Corbyn pulled ahead in the 2015 leadership contest, this has been the question asked of Labour 'moderates'. Are we 'centre' because we would like to be 'far' but don't think it is possible? Or are we 'centre' because we believe in something more right-wing?

For many left populists, this question answers itself: the far left believes very strongly in left-wing values of fairness, equality and improving the lives of the poorest, and the centre left believes in these things only a little. An extension of this is left populists' claim to have exclusive rights to the terms 'left' and 'radical' – summed up by their preference for descriptions like 'centrist' and 'the right of the Labour Party'. The implication is that the centre left has diluted its values so much that it no longer deserves to be called 'left'.

'Labour moderates', by contrast, would often say they are no less radical than the far left – and that the difference between the two isn't about degrees of progressiveness. They would say the disagreement is about how to enact our values for the people Labour represents. Hence, they aim to be less doctrinal on policy and take electability more seriously.

I share the latter view, and will explain why later. But quite apart from this, it seems there is something deeper underpinning the difference between the two camps. How, after all, can the far left and the centre left disagree so diametrically about which policies will achieve our values? Or about the necessity of compromising with the electorate?

The core distinction, it seems to me, is to do with *interpretation*. It's about how people from different sides of the left construe things and the world views we have as a result.

This brings to mind the famous Karl Marx distinction: 'Philosophers have only *interpreted* the world; the point is to *change* it.' The quote is occasionally used to justify 'shoot first and ask questions later' approaches. But its intention was the opposite: to articulate the link between accurate perceptions and the ability to improve society.

Differences in interpretation are now the core barrier between far and centre left. In every heated discussion I have had with a Corbyn supporter, for instance, the point of divergence has been at the level of perception. You believe Corbyn is a modern-day Keir Hardie; I regard him as a politer George Galloway. Your interpretation is that New Labour was quasi-Reaganite; I protest that it was social democracy in action. (I only exaggerate slightly!)

In other words, arguments have not occurred because the Corbyn-supporting friend is suggesting a level of equality which I find intolerable, or a degree of social justice which I see as a step too far. I may feel a policy or strategy they advocate is inconsistent with progressive values (and vice versa). But this is not, in itself, enough to spark frustration from either side. The disagreement is usually because I think the way they see the world is faulty, and they view my interpretations in the same way.

An exasperated 'How can you think that?' hangs heavy in the air as a result. How can you possibly believe that the EU is a 'capitalist club', I wonder? Or that the *Guardian* is a 'centre right' newspaper? Or that the 1997–2010 governments were 'neoliberal'?

And supporters of Corbyn no doubt feel I am deluded for not believing these self-evident truths. All that can follow is a set of non-sequiturs. It's the equivalent of talking about a football match with someone and wondering afterwards, 'Were we watching the same game?' In the absence of a shared understanding or premise, communication becomes hard. The values are the same, but agreement is impossible.

So, while the main difference between far and centre left is indeed about how we should engage with the real world so as to implement our values, the point of divergence comes a stage before, on the question of what this 'real world' looks like.

Drilling down, there are three key areas where we perceive things differently. These can be summed up by three myths, which the far left holds dear and the centre left mistrusts.

The first myth is the **Dark Knight,** which concerns morality and the political spectrum. The far left usually believes the right is motivated by self-interest or spite. As a result, they regard as immoral many of the individuals, causes, methods and institutions which they think are closer to the right. The centre left doesn't tend to interpret issues through this lens.

The second is the **Puppet Master,** which concerns power and society. The far left often believes that society's problems are coordinated and deliberately created by those in power. The centre left, by contrast, leans towards chaos-based explanations, and is less suspicious of government.

The third myth is the **Golden Era**. This relates to change, decline and the past. The far left's interpretation is usually that society is becoming increasingly right-wing, and has been for decades. The centre left is inclined to see the positives in globalisation or to feel that Labour has made as many advances as retreats.

Whether we believe in these myths governs our approach and how we try to turn values into strategies and policies. Belief in the myths is a bit like belief in a religious creed. If you don't share the core assumptions, then a whole set of behaviours and attitudes makes no sense.

LEFT PLURALISM

In light of the above, the terms 'far' and 'centre' left – with their implications that there is a values continuum – seem inaccurate. As someone who would be described as 'centre' left, for instance, I'm no less egalitarian than the far left. I disagreed with the *premise* of Corbynism, not the values driving it.

For this reason, I mainly refer to 'left populists' and 'left pluralists' throughout the rest of the text – not to 'far left' and 'centre left' or to 'radicals' and 'moderates'. Simply put, 'left populists' are those who lean towards subscribing to the above myths (the Dark Knight, the Puppet Master and the Golden Era); 'left pluralists' are those who do not.

Left pluralism is not a precise synonym for centre leftism, and nor is left populism an exact byword for far leftism. For sure, the far left is where belief in the myths is most concentrated.[12] But it is *possible* to be a pluralist communist – who refutes conspiracy theories, acknowledges that globalisation has brought some benefits, and does not think Tories are driven by malice. Likewise, it's *possible* to be a mild social democrat, whose view of the world is populist (and it should be said that some Remainers are guilty of this). But it seems to happen less often this way around.

In most cases, the populist narratives are neither believed wholesale nor sidestepped entirely. Rather, left populism and left pluralism are poles at either end of a spectrum. Some people are mildly sympathetic to some of the populist myths; others are true believers; others have no time for them at all.

So, when I refer to left populism I don't refer to Corbynism but to belief in the three narratives. I'm sure there are many pluralists who back Corbyn despite his populism.

Likewise, when I refer to left popul*ists*, as individuals, I don't refer to all Corbyn supporters or to everyone on the far left. I refer specifically to the commentators, activists, politicians and self-proclaimed 'outriders' who promote the three narratives. During his time as leader, I saw Corbyn as the beating heart of this, with his lieutenants and public advocates tending – aside from a few exceptions – to be the most ardent believers in the myths.

I choose the word 'pluralism' as the counterpoint to populism for three reasons.

First, if you are a pluralist, you don't believe the political spectrum is a moral one, comprised of worthy White Knights and wicked Dark Knights. Instead, you think there are a range of ideals people strive for, and you seek to persuade and compromise. Pluralist politics is based on the perception that people are mostly as 'good' as each other – regardless of political values.

Secondly, pluralists don't believe that all or most humans covertly share their politics and that only a Puppet Master elite blocks the will of the people. Instead they think citizens are pursuing a range of ideals which often conflict, and that democratic governments mediate poorly and prioritise wrongly – rather than suppressing wilfully.

Thirdly, pluralists regard cooperation with other nations as broadly progressive. They see compromise as a necessary part of bringing countries with different priorities together. Populists, by contrast, put more emphasis on creating something pure in their own nation (as we were more easily able to do in the past), and then exporting it.

Hence, left pluralism shares left populism's egalitarian ideals but does not share its world view. To be a pluralist is to recognise and embrace a diversity of values. It's to see that navigating this is a necessary part of representative government. It's to be a social democrat or democratic socialist – but to always place democracy over socialism.

An article about Clement Attlee in 2018 summed up the difference.[13] The piece contrasted Attlee's radicalism with Che Guevara's populist belief that 'hatred is an element of struggle', concluding:

> the true progressive giants [like Attlee] are radicals of the real – those who accept that democracy implies pluralism, and that a plural society is self-evidently made up of many people and kinds, only a few of

them truly exploitative and criminal, most just pursuing their own version of the good life as tradition and conviction has offered it to them.

This distinction, between the Attlees and Guevaras of this world, epitomises the true difference between left pluralism and left populism. This book is about the beliefs and assumptions that lead people down one course rather than another.

'LESS HEAT AND MORE LIGHT'

In recent years both the pro- and anti-Corbyn wings of Labour have pleaded for honesty with ourselves, as a precursor to any kind of truce. Jess Phillips MP summed this up when she called for 'less heat and more light'. Phillips was referring specifically to the debate about trans issues, but it was a phrase which sums up the gulf that has opened up on the left. Until there is a common premise – some source of light – then the quarrels will continue.

Often, calls for 'light' involve demands that the populist left 'face up to reality' and accept 'the world as it is'. Barack Obama, for instance, predicted that US Democrats would not imitate Labour's post-2015 mistakes because they were too 'grounded' in reality.[14]

Left populists take these demands as attacks on idealism. Those who discuss 'reality' are viewed as electoral bean-counters or as advocates of the idea that there is 'no alternative' to rampant free markets. As populists see it, the 'reality' they are being asked to swallow involves watering down their values beyond recognition.

But this isn't the case. The problem isn't that left populists are more optimistic about the electoral arithmetic than 'reality' dictates they should be. Nor is it that they are deluded to feel social justice is achievable. Rather, it's that the convictions which govern left populism are based on a set of paper tigers and phantom menaces.

Hence, the true 'reality' which pluralists advocate isn't that left populists should, in the name of electability, surrender their flag to the bloodthirsty financiers and fascists on the blue team. It's not that they must grit their teeth and sign up to the agendas of white-cat-stroking elites. It's not that they should concede that the socialist Arcadias of the post-war years aren't coming back. Rather, it's that these frames are themselves fantasies. They distort our perspective, block a meaningful exchange of views and get in the way of progressive goals. They're the enemies of idealism, not the enablers of it.

For a real-world example, see journalist-turned-activist Paul Mason's commentary on the 2016 Labour leadership contest. In one piece, Mason describes a 'besuited elite' with the full artillery of the corporate state behind them, versus 'a loose alliance of rank-and-file Corbynistas', their 'backs to the river . . . throwing cavalry against tanks'. He describes Corbyn-sceptics in 'shiny tights', determined to 'stop history' and prevent 'the workers, the poor and the young [from] getting a say in politics'.[15]

Left pluralists' disagreement with Mason would not come because our values are closer to the poor-hating and bloodless elite which he describes. Rather, it's because we see Mason's warlike and conspiracy-based interpretation as a fantasy in itself.

If I am wrong about this, and Angela Eagle was the public face of a far-reaching corporate plot, then fair enough: I've been had. (I actually worked on Eagle's short-lived campaign, in an empty office space with limited Wi-Fi, and even then I didn't see it.) But let's be clear that that's the level at which disagreement exists – not at the level of values.

This book makes the case for why each of the myths – the Dark Knight, the Puppet Master and the Golden Era – is counter-productive to progressive goals, and potentially anti-democratic. For each myth I describe what it consists of, speculate as to why it's appealing, and outline why we shouldn't be seduced. I want to engage with these three narratives because I think they are a big part of the reason why bad ideas spread beyond the hard left. It does no good to pretend that everyone attracted to Corbyn's politics is a Stalinist or a Trotskyite. The power of the myths is precisely that they form a bridge between extremists and the Labour mainstream, creating an alternative reality where reactionary policies and damaging strategies make perfect sense. With its membership choosing Keir

Starmer as their new leader in 2020 – a figure from the soft left who is often regarded as a 'technocrat' – the Labour Party of the future has an opportunity to pursue radical policies while jettisoning the myths once and for all.

Ultimately, I am arguing that populist interpretations and socialist goals are incompatible. The best way of achieving a socialist society is by striving for objectivity. As Labour MP Bridget Phillipson puts it, 'it is telling the truth that makes us socialists rather than populists'.

I obviously don't suggest that left pluralists have a monopoly on 'reality', any more than left populists do. But the only way to mediate between two interpretations is by testing them. So, I'm trying to dissect the populist myths and show that they are flawed. The goal is to persuade fellow left-wingers that the pluralist view of the world is the more accurate perspective – the one we should adopt across the left. And the ultimate challenge to the populist left is a simple one: can your politics exist, hypothetically speaking, without a reliance on the three myths? And if so, what does this look like?

If I fail in this, then I hope I can at least help the populist left to understand where the pluralist left is coming from, so that we can debate on the level at which disagreement really exists. Calls for civility between the two sides of Labour will only do so much; the real alternative to infighting on the left isn't the sort of fleeting, artificial unity we have at points achieved since 2015. Instead, it's a genuine argument about the differences in analysis that separate us: an argument based not on winning but on getting to the truth.

2

What Do We Want?

FIRST PRINCIPLES

Part of the 'Where do we disagree?' question is to do with the destinations we are striving to reach. Are left pluralists and left populists trudging towards different castles on different hills? Or are we aiming to get to the same place at a different speed or via a different route?

This book argues the latter. Hence, before considering where left pluralists and left populists differ (i.e. in the nature of their analyses) we should start with what they share: their leftism. There are basic, shared ideals that run across the left in roughly equal measure. Even when it comes to specific policy issues, the differences aren't as large as it sometimes seems.[1]

Establishing that this shared commitment to social justice exists is vital. It's the common root, once policies, strategies, perspectives and approaches are set aside. It's the reason why left populists and left pluralists usually cooperate electorally, or else inhabit the same parties.

Finding a set of shared values is also important for another reason. During the rest of the book we need a barometer, when talking about our two conflicting approaches, to work out which best fulfils egalitarian goals. A common ideal provides a yardstick to measure against.

Indeed, the true reason for pluralists' opposition to Corbyn is that, on countless issues, he falls short of the progressive benchmark, through electoral failure and policy dogma. Yet the public basis of criticism, even after his comprehensive defeat in 2019, remains that Corbynism was an unworkable dream.[2]

The role of this chapter is to look at what a common ideal might be. This goal needs to cast a wide net, so as to potentially be enacted via the multitude of ideologies that different progressives advocate. But it must also be specific, so that it goes beyond 'motherhood and apple pie' statements of intent. It needs to be ambitious in its radicalism, but flexible enough to apply in different contexts.

After all, despite being critical of left populism, this book isn't opposed to an idealistic view of politics. It's opposed to the gestures, stances and self-delusions which stop us getting there.

I will not, in this chapter, sift through the many strains of socialist and social democratic thought. In truth, there are a great many '-isms' that could claim to represent a set of first principles. The list of runners and riders would include, in no particular order, Christian socialism, Marxism (and its variants, such as Trotskyism), collective capitalism, guild socialism, Rhine capitalism (and the Nordic Model of the social market economy), syndicalism, mutualism, communitarianism, idealism, Fabianism, utopian socialism, revisionism/reformism, liberal socialism, republicanism, Keynesianism, welfare capitalism, ethical socialism, eco-socialism and other types of Green politics, libertarian socialism, social corporatism, internationalism, anti-imperialism, and so on.

(The approach I term 'left pluralism' here is not vying to be one of these '-isms'. Left pluralism is a type of mindset, not a doctrine for organising society. In fact, almost any of the '-isms' mentioned could be consistent with the left-pluralist analysis – if they avoided Dark Knight, Puppet Master and Golden Era thinking).[3]

The problem with the list of '-isms' clearly is not that they have nothing to contribute. As long as they sign up to parliamentary democracy, they all sit within Labour's broad church. The issue is that most of the creeds listed have implications for *how* you achieve progressive ideals. Many are, therefore, in conflict. Keynesianism, Marxism and Rhine Capitalism, for instance, propose methods that are incompatible.

We need to go back a stage further, drilling deeper into philosophy, to find a shared vision.

For this reason, I use John Rawls's work on the social contract in the rest of this argument as an umbrella philosophy to which many on the left could plausibly subscribe – pluralists and populists included, and disciples of just about all the '-isms' listed above.

The Rawls view was that society should be organised so that it was satisfactory to a rational individual who did not know their start in life. Rawls was not the first to talk about justice in terms of a detached perspective. But he moved the discussion in a more thorough and egalitarian direction.

Although considered outdated by some, Rawls's writing on social justice is both radical about *what* a fair, progressive society might look like, and flexible about *how* you get there. For this reason, the Rawlsian ideal seems like one that everyone from a New Labour disciple to a quasi-Marxist could sign up to – even if they diverged almost immediately about *how* to achieve it. If we arrived at a state of affairs consistent with Rawls's principles of fairness, many on the left could sleep easy.

Hence, in my view, John Rawls's philosophy works as a rough yardstick for progressive values. Although other thinkers have had an impact on my argument in this book – including Anthony Crosland, Jonathan Haidt, Amartya Sen, Steven Pinker and Thomas Piketty – Rawls is the single biggest influence.

RAWLS: AN EXPLANATION

John Rawls (1921–2002) wrote his magnum opus, *A Theory of Justice*, in 1971. The book is among the most important philosophical contributions of the twentieth century. It was followed by *Political Liberalism* in 1993 and *The Law of Peoples* in 1997.

Rawls revived the tradition of political philosophy and provided one of the most powerful rebuffs of utilitarianism, the dominant philosophy of the Victorian age. He re-engaged with the 'social contract' and 'state of nature' arguments of Locke, Rousseau and Kant.

Rawls's criticism of utilitarianism (a philosophy which promotes 'the greatest good for the greatest number') was that it allows the minority to be punished if the benefit to the majority is big enough. One of the examples Rawls gave was slavery. He pointed out that this obvious moral affront was permitted by utilitarianism – as long as the slave owners and the society benefited significantly enough.

Ultimately, Rawls's philosophy prevents a single group being abandoned by progress or prosperity. It would not, for example, let British seaside towns be left behind by the pace of globalisation, or US inner-city ghettos be created by underinvestment – even if the economic benefits for society made this seem like necessary collateral damage.

The central tenet of Rawls's work was the 'original position' or 'veil of ignorance'. This was a thought experiment where you design the world from the perspective of an unborn child who does not yet know what position they'll occupy within society.

The society designed in this state of detachment would be a genuinely fair one, Rawls said – without partisanship, scapegoats, vested interests and double standards. It would stop majorities from subjugating minority interests, and allow the economy to grow (as long as the proceeds were split fairly). No rational person, after all, would take the risk, under the veil of ignorance, of grossly unequal or bigoted societies, or of radically different life chances – for fear that they would draw the short straw and suffer poverty or discrimination.

You would choose, Rawls argued, with pure logic from behind the veil of ignorance – your judgement clouded neither by altruism or ego. This impartiality would bring about moral ends. He set out two principles of social justice as devised in this way (the second of which has two distinct parts):

1. The first principle is that **basic liberties and rights should be distributed absolutely evenly.** As you would not, behind the veil of ignorance, know your gender, your sexuality, your race, your class, and so on, you would design a society where you were not prevented by things beyond your control from voting, from

avoiding arbitrary imprisonment, from being free to move around or go to school or own property, and so on.

2. The second principle is that **'primary goods' should be distributed evenly.** Primary goods include income and wealth, property, access to information, education, opportunity to fulfil your potential, social efficacy. This means that, not knowing what your own genetic endowments will be (e.g. whether you would be born clever, stupid, artistic, entrepreneurial, strong, weak, and so on), you would design the society in such a way that:

A) There is absolute **equality of opportunity** to fulfil yourself when it comes to life chances.

B) There are **fair outcomes.** Inequalities of outcome should only exist if they benefit the weakest at least as much as the strongest. This emphasis on fair outcomes was referred to by Rawls as the 'difference principle' – an acknowledgement that there are some natural differences between people.

The first principle would come before the second. And the first part of the second principle would come before the second part. Equal rights, equal opportunities, fair outcomes.[4]

Rawls wasn't specific about what policies would best fulfil the original position. It would be hard, he suggested, to deliver it via pure communism or unfettered capitalism. But it could be achieved through a socialist economy permitting some competition, or through a capitalist economy organised in a sustainable, inclusive and egalitarian way.

As this lack of prescription shows, Rawls was an advocate of 'liberal neutrality' – favouring 'the right' over 'the good'. He held no value judgement about what a 'good society' looked like, as long as it fulfilled the requirements of social justice. From behind the veil of ignorance, for example, you would see nothing wrong, in itself, with owning a fleet of sports cars – so long as this did not conflict with more pressing social priorities (which is a big 'if').

Likewise, you would see no immorality in a parent wanting to leave as much money as possible to their offspring. But, not knowing how much money you stood to receive (or whether you stood to receive any), you would probably still support high inheritance taxes, as a means of equalising opportunities.

Rawls called the process of sifting priorities like this 'reflexive equilibrium'. In many ways this is a more detailed enactment of the Nye Bevan view that 'The language of priorities is the religion of socialism.'

Rawls's later writing developed the 'overlapping consensus' model, whereby people can privately hold and practise world views that are incompatible with the original position, as long as they sign up to a public consensus which allows others to do the same. For example, a religious world view which opposes gay marriage is fine as part of a person's private philosophy, as long as it isn't imposed on public policy.[5]

In essence, Rawls thought you could have a pluralist and diverse 'live and let live' society, the important thing being that everyone respected the 'let live' part. The structure of this is like a Venn diagram. There may be several different versions of 'the good society' around the outside, but the overlapping area in the middle – the public, political consensus – must be shared.

Rawls's theory offers a way for Labour to stay radical in the twenty-first century – an era where the principal divides are no longer between the colonised and the imperialists or between the workers and the 'boss class'.

A world designed under the veil of ignorance would, in my view, be much closer to left-wing values than to right-wing ones. From the original position, people would, I think, choose an absolutely equal start in life, meaning private education would be eradicated and unearned wealth taxed much more highly. We might choose Proportional Representation, so we had an equal stake in politics. We would opt for a country which was more geographically balanced, so that living in London did not give you the foot-up it currently does – or create an imbalanced housing market. We would want discrimination of all types outlawed, and we would want to know that if we committed a crime, prison would rehabilitate, not institutionalise, us, while also protecting others from us if we continued to pose a threat. Not knowing what talents we would be born with, we would choose a society where we could live with dignity and fulfil ourselves, whatever our natural attributes. We would plump for free healthcare, full employment, a strong welfare state which helped people find work, a living wage and ultra-progressive maternity and childcare systems. We would like to see open borders and the economic divides between countries closed absolutely, so that being born in South Sudan offered us the same chances as being born in the UK. We would push climate change up the agenda, not knowing which generation we would be born into (and not wanting to suffer from past generations' excesses).

The veil-of-ignorance argument makes these things hard to argue with – even if there are compromises and delays necessary in realising each one.

However, Rawls's ideas are also important because – unlike other theories with a radical end-point – he wasn't prescriptive or dogmatic. A world devised under the veil of ignorance fulfils many criteria of socialism. But perspective, objectivity and context are the vehicles for getting there. Rawls's emphasis on the 'right over the good' is about a society which will benefit everyone, rather than advancing the cause of one group over another.

SHORTCOMINGS

This exposition of Rawlsian philosophy may seem like a diversion. In an era of identity politics, low trust and globalisation, the ultra-rationalism of *A Theory of Justice* seems irrelevant. Indeed, Rawls isn't especially in vogue, and his work is hard to apply to the twenty-first century. There are several reasons for this.

a) An overly clinical approach

The first admission is that there is something ultra-detached about the Rawls approach – like looking down the wrong end of a telescope. At its core is a rational foetus, devising society with impartial logic, as if by mathematical formulae.[6]

THE DARK KNIGHT AND THE PUPPET MASTER

Psychologists like Jonathan Haidt, mentioned in Chapter One, are sometimes critical of Rawls for this reason, suggesting that he makes little effort to understand the moral codes of others.[7] The original-position idea does not tally with how most people engage with the world or how campaigners seek to persuade the public.

There are two sub-arguments here. The first is that Rawlsianism may work in theory but is incompatible with human nature – as Marxism has usually proven to be. The second criticism – that of Haidt and others – is that Rawlsianism does not engage with or reflect different, less 'rational' values.

The first argument seems spurious. Rawls was flexible about methods and provided enough elasticity for individuals to fulfil themselves however they saw fit. The goal was to allow maximum happiness and freedom for each person, the only caveat being that this could not stop the happiness and freedom of others.

The second argument is more valid. There can be no question that Rawlsianism is a poor comms strategy. Asking people to see things with the impartiality of a rational foetus does not speak to the values which guide many cultures.

Yet the Rawlsian approach is based on a non-judgemental and non-dogmatic route to egalitarianism. In this respect it's highly pluralistic (and, in fact, in keeping with the quest for understanding and coexistence proposed by Haidt). No set of values can drive out another.

This doesn't change the fact that it's a hard sell. And I'm not suggesting that we take to the doorsteps with copies of *A Theory of Justice* under our arms, nor even that we pursue Rawls's writing to the letter. I'm just proposing that, if we are looking for a castle on the hill that can unite the pluralist and populist left, a Rawlsian ideal – flexible and impartial but egalitarian and radical – is a good starting point.

b) The lack of 'a good society' ideal

Rawls's 'liberal neutrality' is also an issue for some. He is seen as doing too little to champion a 'good society', rather than just a 'right society'. This argument tends to come from a communitarian perspective,[8] and there is truth in it. The danger is that Rawlsianism becomes an atomised creed, based on contractual relationships, not social bonds.

However, Rawls's emphasis on moral ends by non-moral means is also one of the reasons he is important. His 'good society' comes through a hesitance to assign greater morality to some over others.[9] His 'liberal neutral' approach means saying that someone can fly a Union Jack or an LGBT rainbow flag and incur no judgement in either direction, as long as they do no harm. It allows the boy racers, the students of Proust and the owners of Charles and Diana commemoration mugs to all have a place in society – so long as they respect each other. And it asks that government policies reflect this.

To me, this comes close to a good society ideal in itself. It reflects the 'each to their own' tolerance that people in the average pub or café have for each other. The sources of right-wing populism often come not from a sense that everyone should be supporting the Royal family or celebrating St George's Day, but from a sense – real or imagined – that those who care about these things are scorned.

With this said, it's true that, for a Rawlsian type of politics to be successful, the reciprocity at its core needs to gather widespread support and understanding. So far, Rawls's ideas have mainly been used to think about how the state redistributes, not about civil society. As one writer put it in 2010, there needs to be a shift in emphasis here, from 'what they owe us' to 'what we owe each other'.[10]

After all, low levels of trust at present often occur despite improvements to quality of life. (In local government, this is known as the 'performance paradox': services improve but trust falls, thanks to the 'top-down' way in which improvements are delivered).[11] Only when supported by engagement, reciprocity and transparency can Rawlsianism be enacted.

c) The absence of an answer to globalisation

Rawls wrote *A Theory of Justice* before the modern globalisation process had taken hold. His ideas relied on a single political sphere, i.e. a single society, ruled by a single government. Globalisation has introduced a situation where individuals and companies operate across multiple spheres. A globalised world is a poor platform for putting Rawlsian policies into practice.

Rawls's later efforts to engage with globalisation left some disappointed. He argued that a nation needed to first strive towards internal fairness, and then redistribute globally. In practice, reconciling your own backyard *before* turning outwards isn't compatible with globalisation, the consequences of which influence what's going on in your own nation.

So, it's true that globalisation has made the Rawls ideal harder to achieve, and that his answers to it weren't properly developed. But this does not make the basic veil-of-ignorance principle less desirable, or the goals of rational objectivity and radical fairness less valid.

LEFT POPULISM AND RAWLS

I have looked at Rawls early on because, when thinking through a left-wing project which includes a set of sunlit uplands to strive for – rather than a process of perpetual agitation and dissent – his original position is the thing I keep returning to.

There will never be full agreement about the methods, policy and strategy that will achieve our aims. And there will be disagreements about what Labour's goal should be. As the array of '-isms' shows, there are differences in what people mean by social justice.

But the veil of ignorance provides a common denominator: a question you can ask about any society which progressives arrive at. Are there absolutely equal rights, absolutely equal opportunities and absolutely fair outcomes? No society has ever completely fulfilled these things. But if we are moving towards it, then we're on the right track.

Thus, Rawls gives us a guiding (and uniting) principle, towards which different parts of the left – with their conflicting views about means of delivery – can strive. He presents a philosophy based on logic, objectivity and putting yourself in others' shoes.

a) Rawls and partisanship

Rawls's decision to prioritise the 'right' over the 'good' means that, according to his approach, the political spectrum isn't a moral spectrum. Some interpretations may be more 'right' than others – i.e. more consistent with objective fairness – and some can immediately be dismissed as wrong. But Rawls's theory does not say that one ideal is inherently more virtuous.

Moreover, Rawls's 'overlapping consensus' model guards against the inexorabilities thrown up by a singular view. It is robustly plural, meaning no out-group or scapegoat can be created; no singular view can undermine the rights of another.[12] For instance, if you were designing a society from behind the veil of ignorance, you would want to know that if you were born with business acumen you could fulfil yourself. But you would also want to ensure this did not 'pull the ladder up' or crush others. Likewise, you would want stronger trade unions, so that you were fully protected at work. But your support for unions would not go so far as to support non-inclusive practices like the 'closed shop'.

So, while Rawls's theory of justice would advance the cause of progressives, it wouldn't – prizing objectivity above all else – side with the left as a matter of course.

b) Rawls and government

The economist Will Hutton described, in a 2013 article, 'the decay of power' at the hands of populism. Hutton reminded us that those in power were in a position of unprecedented weakness – not unparalleled strength:

> power devolves to myriad new forces that often exercise [it] with narrow obsessions in mind. Who now speaks for the whole? Who keeps a macro view, mediating competing interests and conflicts and has the courage to make decisions based on a strategic view of all our interests, not just sectional ones?[13]

Rawls's philosophy begins to answer these questions, with the veil of ignorance presenting an alternative to the righteous clarity of a single viewpoint.[14] In an era when each faction is convinced of their rightness, Rawls's focus on detachment is vital.[15]

For the left this is especially important. Rawls's emphasis on neutrality encourages us to weigh up competing needs, putting ourselves in the shoes of a government acting as fair arbitrator. This cuts through oppositionist or populist assumptions.

Indeed, Rawls's theory is an answer to the left's age-old choice between 'power and principles'. This dilemma is often played out between those who say that following the electorate is necessary to enact your principles, and those who ask how far we take this.

The utilitarian argument – which Rawls attacked – could justify almost any concession which was supported by the majority. For instance, if enough people would be made happier and better off by the deportation of all immigrants, it would be the right thing to do.

The Rawls approach, on the other hand, seeks to guarantee that everyone's needs are met – as long as they don't harm others' needs. It does not look to impose a minority interpretation of 'the good' on an unwilling population (where, for example, businesses are pointlessly banned or the national flag is censored for no reason). But it simultaneously limits how far the left should go in meeting the will of the people.

c) Rawls and change

Finally, Rawls's philosophy is fluid, responding to how the world is adapting, rather than clinging to a specific doctrine.

It recognises that the criteria of the original position can be fulfilled in different ways, in different economic circumstances and at different points in history. It can be done in nations that have different raw materials, different histories, different economies and different cultures.

In other words, the routes to Rawlsianism are never the same. Hence, while his answers to the globalisation challenge might be insufficient, his liberal neutral approach lets us navigate a way through.

RADICAL BUT NOT EXTREME

In a 1985 essay, Rawls sought to clarify what he'd meant in *A Theory of Justice*:

> There are periods ... in the history of any society during which certain fundamental questions give rise to sharp and divisive political controversy, and it seems difficult, if not impossible, to find any shared basis of political agreement.[16]

This analysis certainly applies to politics in the 2010s, and to the way in which populist movements prevent the 'fair system of social cooperation' which Rawls believed was essential to democracy.[17]

He went on to say that the role of a political philosopher was to

> examine whether some underlying basis of agreement can be uncovered and a mutually acceptable way of resolving these questions publicly established. Or if these questions cannot be fully settled ... perhaps the divergence of opinion can be narrowed sufficiently so that political cooperation on a basis of mutual respect can still be maintained.

In writing this, Rawls presented his theory 'not as a conception of justice that is true, but [as] one that can serve as a basis of informed and willing political agreement between citizens'.

This is central to the way that I'm using Rawls's work. His views about what a fair society would look like are important. But just as vital is his focus on flexibility, rationality and impartiality as means of getting there: on objectivity, not vehemence.[18]

Indeed, Rawls's concept of 'the right' over 'the good' is probably the most relevant part of his theory, in that it recognises that we can, none of us, see past our own hump. His thought experiment was intended to act as 'a means of public reflection and self-clarification', to help us arrive at 'a clear and uncluttered view of what justice requires'.[19]

So, while Rawls offers a radically fair destination, he champions a means of seeing our way through to it which does not rely on hating an out-group, fearing a big bad wolf or resurrecting outdated policy solutions. This offers the basis for an approach based on compromise but not concession; on ideals but not ideology. It provides a chance for radicalism to flourish without extremism blossoming alongside it.

I won't go further into *A Theory of Justice*. I'm aware that there are different views about what a society created behind the veil of ignorance looks like; that there are ways the original position analysis can be altered to include communitarian elements, or to respond to globalisation.

However, even Rawls's academic critics seem to agree with his basic premise: that impartiality and fairness are inextricably linked.

3
Distorting Myths

THREE STORIES

'Thought corrupts language, language can also corrupt thought,' wrote George Orwell.[1] By using certain language or narratives, even just for expediency, we alter our own understanding of things. Likewise, Hannah Arendt believed that the 'ideal subject of totalitarian rule' is a 'people for whom the distinction[s] between fact and fiction ... no longer exist'.[2]

The comparisons between contemporary populism and 1930s extremism arise because of the way certain stories and explanations have taken hold in recent years, overriding truth and logic. This book attacks three such narratives, which have come to govern – and in my view pollute – the debate on the left. Let's reintroduce them:

- **The Dark Knight.** This refers to the belief in a wicked and selfish enemy, against whom our struggle is destined to play out.
- **The Puppet Master.** This refers to the belief in an all-powerful elite, crushing and brainwashing the people for personal gain.
- **The Golden Era.** This refers to the belief in an idealised past or morally pure founding moment, since when things have steadily declined.

To use the analogy of a football match, the Dark Knight would be a zero-sum belief that the opposition players and fans are scum, and anything goes in order to beat them. The Puppet Master would be a conviction that your failures come because all referees are biased against your club. And the Golden Era would be the belief that the game is not what it used to be ('It's not a man's game any more'; 'It's all about money'; etc.).

These assumptions are central to how the populist left self-mythologises. They're virtually stitched into the lyrics of 'The Red Flag', a battle-anthem built on tales of struggle, uprising and loss, with its talk of 'cowards', 'traitors', 'martyred dead' and 'triumphs past'. And they're present in the conclusions drawn by many contemporary left populists – be it paranoia about the 'mainstream media' or decline narratives about 'neoliberalism'.

But the three myths are not only distorting: they're sustaining. Their effect is to breathe meaning into left populists' efforts. As with our footballing analogy, they justify our continued support. They maintain enthusiasm for our side. And they explain disappointments, without us having to go through the pain of self-examination.

The three myths are easy to confuse or conflate. The Tories, for example, stand for all three: they represent, at once, the immoral enemy and the plutocracy pulling the strings. Their election wins epitomise a society becoming more right-wing.

However, the myths are distinct in character. The Dark Knight, with its tendency to divide the world into good and bad, might be characterised by the Socialist Workers Party (SWP) activists who seek out violent clashes with right-wing opponents. Likewise, those certain enough of their moral superiority over Angela Eagle to throw a brick through her window.

The Puppet Master myth, meanwhile, is a libertarian, anti-establishment narrative, epitomised by those who believe George Bush planned 9/11, or that MI5 were behind the 2016 Labour leadership challenge. Likewise, those who hold Julian Assange up as a hero and a martyr, or who say that the BBC is the propaganda arm of the Conservative Party.

The Golden Era, lastly, is a myopic narrative, exemplified by those who wear T-shirts proclaiming 'Labour: I preferred their earlier work', or who bemoan the materialism of young footballers. Likewise, those who mythologise the post-war years, and share Russell Brand's hankering for an agrarian society.

People usually believe in more than one of our myths. The

narratives frequently act as supporting sides of the left-populist triangle. But it is possible to believe in one and not the others.

These tropes – the Dark Knight, the Puppet Master, and the Golden Era – are the psychological bulwarks of an approach which is oppositionist in its nature, united by what it is against, not what it is for. They are the amplifications and embroideries, in turn frightening and seductive, which cloud perception. They lead to self-defeating, small-tent approaches, and undermine rational leftism.

NARRATIVES AND EXPLANATIONS

As we said in Chapter One, these myths aren't unique to the populist left. Significant elements are shared by movements like the Brexit Party, with their wistfulness for a differently remembered bygone era, or the Tea Party in the US – who rail against 'liberal' elites, not 'neoliberal' ones. However, many on the far left have signed up to our three populist analyses.

Those on the centre left, meanwhile, may not believe in the narratives as often, and may be more consensual and forward-looking as a result. But many have historically turned a blind eye to the myths – or else embraced them a little, for expediency. They have done so to simplify and justify arguments, or because it allowed them an easy shorthand in attacking the Conservatives.[3]

It was only really after the election of Corbyn, once those critical of him were re-cast as the villains of the narratives, that the danger of this became apparent. Because the truth is that all three myths eventually devour themselves.

One Fabian article describes this as the 'rise of the golems'. A reference from Jewish mythology, this refers to the short-term creation of a monster to protect your group, which ultimately ends up destroying it.[4] Trump is described in the piece as a counter-establishment golem, created by moderate Republicans who were trying to develop narratives of insurgency. And Corbyn, likewise, is the consequence of Ed Miliband's willingness to deploy Puppet Master tropes.

Similarly, New Labour commentator Hopi Sen refers to 'one-stepping', a tendency which he describes as the oldest trick in the Labour play-book: 'to see someone saying something you largely agree with, but which others in your party do not, and to stand one step to their left and attack them for their heresy'. The technique is self-defeating, Sen says, creating a false Dark Knight analysis, which takes hold and leads you into the political wilderness.[5]

Hence, left pluralists find ourselves playing on a pitch drawn by populists. Each time we assume the mantle of insurgency by talking about 'elites', the grip of the populists gets stronger. Each time we protest that the Tories are the real force for evil, we turn the screw on ourselves a little more. Each time we join populists in bemoaning 'neoliberal' decline, further ground is lost.

The way out of this is for left pluralists to a) directly challenge the Dark Knight, the Puppet Master and the Golden Era analyses wherever we see them (including when they are used by our own side), and b) identify alternative explanations for why society is as it is, and for how we can change it.

Why do people vote for Tory governments, if not because they are self-interested Dark Knights? Why don't the press reflect the interests of the majority, if there is no Puppet Master controlling them? Why has inequality risen, if not because of 'neoliberal' decline from a Golden Era starting point? Unless we answer these questions, the three myths triumph.

The truth, after all, is that most followers of left-populist movements are well-intentioned, progressive and idealistic people. They are committed to social justice and are worried, especially among younger adherents, about opportunities for the future. With social democracy facing big intellectual challenges, many were attracted to the explanations provided by true believers in the left-populist myths, like Corbyn. To persuade them of the merits of pluralism, we need to engage with the narratives and contest them.

Part of this is about thinking through compelling stories of our own, as well as about finding empirical explanations. French President Emmanuel Macron has called for this more eloquently than most:

Modern political life must rediscover a sense for symbolism . . . We
need to be amenable once again to creating grand narratives . . . Why
can't there be such a thing as democratic heroism?[6]

His point is that the cynical interpretations which underpin anti-
politics have gained traction in the absence of counternarratives. In
a democratic, globalised age, pluralists have become the bean-
counters. Hence, the narratives used by blowhards, malcontents and
armchair critics are now the defining paradigms. On both left and
right, the populist 'dog whistles' are winning.

Establishing truthful and inspiring alternatives to the Dark
Knight, the Puppet Master and the Golden Era is a tall ask. As we
will see when we explore them, a big reason for the myths' success is
that they appeal to something primal, following the grain of human
instinct in its most unexamined form. The link between populism
and social media comes, in part, because the myths chime with
something immediate and intuitive: something that can be boiled
down to 280 characters on Twitter.

We need only to look at fiction to see how the Dark Knight, Puppet Master and Golden Era capture the imagination. Films, books
and TV programmes are packed with storylines which juxtapose
'good against evil' – be it *Independence Day*, *Lord of The Rings* or
East of Eden. They are full of plots which pit the powerless individual against the omnipotent establishment – from *Caleb Williams* and
1984 to *Erin Brockovich* and *Enemy of the State*. And they frequently juxtapose an idealised past against a dystopian future – see
Brideshead Revisited, *City of Men* or *Brave New World*. These are
enjoyable precisely because they deploy our three myths in ways that
create dramatic tension and demand emotional commitment.

Yet politics matters too much to be forced into these narrative
templates. Alternatives based on truth are desperately needed. By
debunking the Dark Knight, the Puppet Master and the Golden Era,
we can start to contemplate what might exist in their place.

The COVID-19 pandemic is a fascinating extra factor here.
It creates a challenge which the different parts of the political
spectrum are united in wanting to address. It will be interesting, in

the immediate aftermath of the crisis, to see whether unifying narratives gain traction or whether society returns to a state of polarisation.

I aim my criticism at *left* populism in this book because I am on the left myself. I would like left pluralists – rather than right pluralists – to create the grand, true narratives that can tackle populism and build something constructive. But whichever side of politics we are talking about, there is an onus on pluralists to contest the populist myths, instead of letting these monsters under the bed become the accepted norm.

4
What is the Dark Knight?

'If only I had met, on this search, a single clearly evil person.'

– Timothy Garton Ash

WHICH SIDE ARE YOU ON, BOYS?

The Dark Knight refers to the idea of an irredeemably selfish and wicked incarnation of the political right, with whom the left must clash. The myth stems from a singular view of what is politically moral, which places those with whom we disagree on the side of immorality – or, at least, on the side of 'less morality' – as Dark Knight to our White Knight. The fable encourages politics to be viewed as a continuum from 'moral' left to 'immoral' right. The refrain of the 1930s protest song, covered by Billy Bragg in 1991, is a classic articulation of this:

> Which side are you on, boys?
> Which side are you on?

By claiming that there is a moral spectrum which the left are at the 'good' end of, the Dark Knight lays the groundwork for an in-group versus out-group dynamic. The transition from spectrum to binary is automatic, occurring as soon as you draw a line across the spectrum by asking, on this policy or that, 'Are you with us or against?' If the other person is against, or even if they are unsure, you can legitimately conclude that they are less moral – an analysis which cuts to the quick of their character. A cleft is created, which can only grow. The image below visualises the journey from spectrum to binary.

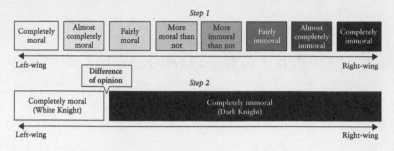

Hence, to recap, the Dark Knight process relies on two consecutive assumptions. The first is that politics is a moral spectrum. The second is that political goals should be fought for on an 'us and them' basis: 'socialism or barbarism'.

The myth is based on this being a *moral* spectrum; on left politics being an articulation of all that's benevolent and selfless. This is a crucial point. The spectrum does not juxtapose one set of legitimate values or priorities against another – from liberalism to tradition, from redistribution to self-reliance, or from equality to growth. It says that the political spectrum runs from altruism to corruption and from decency to callousness.

This is what separates believers in the Dark Knight myth from non-believers. Many people have a conviction that their values represent the best way to run the country. It's almost impossible not to. But not everyone believes that their politics are more moral, or that those who disagree are motivated by self-interest.

One key difference is that morality cannot, within certain parameters, be proven. It's too primal and open to interpretation. Almost everyone *thinks* they're behaving morally or selflessly, even if their actions cause harm. On the other hand, terms like 'fairness', 'effectiveness' or 'sustainability', while open to interpretation, can be discussed with some hope of getting to the truth. People who are overly sure that they're more *right* than others can be unattractive; but people who are overly sure that they're more *good* can be dangerous.

So, I do not, for instance, consider John McDonnell's accusation that anti-Corbyn coup-plotters were 'fucking useless' to be an example of the Dark Knight in action. Nor do I think that John

McTernan's description of the MPs who nominated Corbyn as 'morons' was a Dark Knight sentiment. These comments, although inflammatory, are based on the competence and wisdom of the other side. You could have a sensible discussion about the effectiveness and timing of the 2016 leadership challenge, or the wisdom of endorsing Corbyn. Ultimately, no one is going to usher an opponent into a gulag because they're a useless moron, as they might be tempted to do if they think their opponent represents something wicked.

At any rate, the consequence of Dark Knight thinking is a Manichean view, dividing the world into 'us' versus our political 'other'. There can be no Grey Knight – no area where the goals of White Knight and Dark Knight overlap. It often leads to sanctimony and hatred as a result. And, because it holds that we have morality on our side, it encourages the zealots to believe that anything goes.

At its worst, the Dark Knight narrative permits collective guilt when it comes to upper-class people or Americans or Jews, organising society into hierarchies of those who deserve empathy and those who don't. Likewise, it applies double standards when it comes to conduct, turning a blind eye to our own moral failures on the basis that we are ultimately on the side of good.[1]

In this respect, the Dark Knight draws heavily on ideas of class struggle and on the geopolitics of the Russian Revolution and the Cold War. Indeed, Dark Knight thinking is partly a hangover from the days of picket lines, 'scabs', the space race and the bomb; from an era when conflict and conquest were the route by which most change took place, and when war was the dominating experience for many people.

Because the nature of any 'group' mentality is that supporters need to constantly re-affirm membership, it's easy to shift from in-group to out-group through any activity which puts allegiance in doubt. Hence, the Dark Knight myth is populated by what former Labour speechwriter Phil Collins calls 'One of [the left's] favourite stock characters: the traitor'.[2] These supposed Judas figures have repeatedly been accused of betrayal over the years, and this is part of the reason for civil wars which have frequently raged within the Labour Party. Even a minute overlap with the Conservatives is used to depict someone as a Dark Knight; even a colleague a notch towards the centre can be denounced as 'one of them'; even the mildest concern about Corbyn's electability makes you a Tory.

The process which the Dark Knight feeds is, therefore, inexorable, draining nuance and breeding rigidity. Followed to its natural conclusion, it leads to farce, dogma, defeat, division or extremism.

Of course, most don't follow the myth to its bleak finale. For the majority it's a casual assumption, tacitly endorsed and rarely examined: a 'Tories are lower than vermin' mug sitting in the kitchen cupboard. Yet, as we will see, even a mild version of the Dark Knight – even the view that opponents are *a bit more* malicious – leads us down the wrong path.

POLITICAL CONSEQUENCES OF MANICHEANISM

Readers may feel that I am conflating several traits into the Dark Knight myth: sanctimony, 'us and them' approaches, an alienating political strategy, factionalism and out-grouping, binary thinking on policy, extremism, collective guilt, 'enemy's enemy is my friend' approaches, and so on. How can I put these under one umbrella?

The element that links these phenomena is the role of a singular version of morality. Once I adopt the interpretation that I'm fighting an 'enemy' – one driven at best by greed, and at worst by malice – the whole way I approach politics will change. To see how this Dark Knight thinking spills over, let's consider the following quote, made in 2007 by columnist and comedian Charlie Brooker:

> [The Conservatives are] a force for wrong that appeals exclusively to bigots, toffs, money-minded machine men, faded entertainers and selfish, grasping simpletons who were born with some essential part of their soul missing ... To reach a more advanced stage of intellectual evolution, humankind must first eradicate the 'Tory instinct' from the brain.

Brooker has adopted different positions over time, and the quote is over a decade old. It may have been intended irreverently (although the wider piece does not suggest this), or his view may have changed. Nevertheless, let's take it at face value for a second, and look at the consequences for my politics if I agreed with it.

First, I would feel superiority over Conservative voters, which would translate into sanctimony. How could I not? I am altruistic while they are 'grasping simpletons'. One left-wing blogger in the US embodied this outlook, writing of Republicans: 'I don't know how to convince someone how to experience the basic human emotion of empathy . . . I cannot have political debates with these people.'[3] Hence, the relationship could only begin from a position of contempt.[4]

Secondly, because I believed Tories were malign (with 'some part of their soul missing'), there would be no motivation to address my lack of understanding about them. This would lead to an 'us and them' approach, which saw no potential shared ground. And this, in turn, would lead to bad strategies, because I would see no point in talking to them. How can one win over a 'selfish bigot'? Likewise, I would assume opposing politicians or hostile reporters were approaching things from a place of avarice and spite.

Thirdly, because I saw Tory voters as 'exclusively' driven by self-ishness, I would struggle not to fall down the slippery slope of blanket guilt. Pluralism relies on believing that an individual can be, at the same time, a Tory, an LGBT campaigner, a *Mirror* reader, a Muslim, a Samaritan volunteer, a good father, a welfare claimant, and so on. But the assumption that there is a moral dimension to the Tories' appeal – that only those with a 'part of their soul missing' vote for them – lets you judge the whole on the basis of a part. A real-life example came in 2015, when a Tory-voting woman on *Question Time* broke down in tears because of cuts to tax credits. While some expressed sympathy, there was a feeling that she had got what was coming to her: 'An ally? She'll probably vote for the Tories again!' one person tweeted.[5]

Fourthly, because I viewed the Conservatives as immoral without exception, I would see anyone who conceded anything to them as a traitor. What sort of person, I would wonder, is willing to cave in to the 'faded entertainers' and 'money-minded machine men'? My own political grouping would become sectarian as a result. There would inevitably, after all, be people in the Labour tribe who were closer to the Tories than I was,[6] and this would invite factionalism.[7] Paul Mason's support for deselection comes, for instance, because he wants Labour to be 'a broad church where everybody actually believes in the religion'.[8]

Fifthly, my thinking on policy would become rigid. If the Tories are 'exclusively' a 'force for wrong', then nothing they believe in can be right. Every policy they support must be immoral; every cause they back must be opposed. Quickly, this would lead to rocky territory. I might start categorising things simply by where they sat in relation to the Tories. Before I knew it, I would be siding with anyone the Conservatives opposed, no matter how unsavoury.

The early stages of the COVID-19 pandemic drew this into focus. The crisis in many ways transcended left–right politics. Yet for many on the populist left, ideas like a 'Government of National Unity' were regarded as unthinkable, because they involved working with the Conservatives towards a shared goal.

Lastly, if I believed the above statement – that the left is up against a 'force for wrong' which must be 'eradicated' – then ends would justify means. A whole set of extreme approaches would become legitimate if I believed I was on the side of good against evil. Threats, lies, atrocities and abuse might start to appear necessary and just. Or, at least, I could turn a blind eye to these things, knowing the perpetrators were ultimately the good guys. (Indeed, Corbyn's lifelong adherence to this 'No enemies to the left' mantra has got him into all sorts of trouble when it comes to his past associations.)

By using the Brooker quote, we can see how countless left-populist vices – from quiet disdain through to dangerous extremism – stem from the same source.

THE 'SOCIAL FASCISM' ACCUSATION

Historically, one of the most striking examples of the Dark Knight is the concept of 'social fascism'. The phrase dates to 1924, when it was coined as a term of abuse by the Communist International and directed at others on the left. The allegation was that democratic socialism – and any non-communist form of left politics – was interchangeable with fascism.[9] Stalin himself wrote that 'social democracy is objectively the moderate wing of fascism . . . They are not antipodes, they are twins.'[10]

The 'social fascism' accusation was levelled at non-communist left-wingers in many countries.[11] However, the idea came to real prominence in Germany in the early 1930s. Led by Ernst Thälmann, German communists refused to unite with other left-wingers. They maintained that the German Social Democratic Party were 'social fascists': identical to Nazism in their goals, only better disguised. When Leon Trotsky pointed out that the social democrats were a 'lesser evil' who communists could tolerate and cooperate with,[12] he was himself accused of closet fascism.

The 'social fascism' concept sat alongside another element of communist thought at the time, which was the notion of 'class on class' combat – with those who didn't support communism seen as enemies of the working classes. Because most of Europe's working classes were members of social democratic or socialist parties, not communist ones, this approach split the left, 'consigning to an enemy class the organisations which contained the vast majority of workers' (as historian and former communist Theodore Draper puts it). Trotsky himself complained of the 'shrill and empty leftism' which stopped the communists from reaching out to working-class social democrats.[13]

The consequence was that German communists focused so much on undermining social democrats that they largely ignored the Nazis, even after Hitler's 1933 capture of power. In fact, a few supported the rise of Hitler, believing undisguised fascism would be more straightforward to combat than 'social' fascism.[14] The net outcomes for leftism, once the Nazis took control, were disastrous. Theodore Draper sums up what happened:

> The Communist party was officially outlawed on March 31st; the trade unions were smashed in May; the social democratic party was banned on June 22nd. Thereafter, Hitler made no distinction

between communists and social democrats; he took their lives, cast them into concentration camps or, if they were lucky, drove them into exile.

Despite this, German communists continued to maintain that fascism and social democracy were interchangeable. In June 1933 they passed a motion which said that:

> The complete exclusion of the social-fascists from the state apparatus, and the brutal suppression even of social democratic organizations and their press, does not in any way alter the fact that social democracy is now, as before, the chief support of the capitalist dictatorship.

It was not until two years later, when experiencing the enormity of fascist rule, that this line was abandoned.

There were several ideas wrapped up in the 'social fascism' concept. For starters, there was the belief that social democracy was a legitimising 'front' for fascism and all things right-wing. Hence social democracy was actually *worse* than fascism, because it disguised what it was; you had to defeat social democracy before you could defeat fascism. This escalated further, to the view that fascism was *preferable* to social democracy,[15] because you at least knew where you stood with it.[16] The logical end-point was the 1939 Molotov–Ribbentrop Pact of non-aggression between Stalin and Hitler.

The 'social fascism' accusation held not just that the consequences of fascism and social democracy were the same, but that the aims were interchangeably evil. In the process, the concept grouped together creeds which were very different, conflating social democracy, fascism and industrial capitalism. Thus, as Draper puts it, 'social fascism' came to be little more than 'a catch-all for Communism's enemies and opponents from moderate Left to far Right'.

The rise and fall of the 'social fascism' allegation shows how self-defeating moral binaries are. The 'social fascism' idea started from the assumption that communism was the only political articulation of moral goodness (the White Knight). It amalgamated everything non-communist into a single embodiment of evil (the Dark Knight).

Its basis was that politics is a battle of us and them ('class on class'), and that if you were not with us to the letter, then you were with them.

This occurred, of course, at a point where the stakes had never been higher. A handful of evil individuals were loitering in the wings, primed to seize power. By casting a wide net, the left might have done a better job of combatting Nazism.

This is, of course, one for the writers of alternative histories. And the behaviour of the social democrats is not without its own issues. Those on the left point out the violent suppression, by the social democrats, of a communist protest in 1929.[17]

But there can be no doubt that the 'social fascist' did immense harm. However well-meaning German communists were, their willingness to impugn the motives of political neighbours meant that working-class anti-fascists were out-grouped and their political spokespeople trashed.

There are other instances, in communist doctrines, of the Dark Knight myth letting the best defeat the good, or even of it becoming the ally of the worst ('impossibilism, 'accelerationism', and opposition to charity are good examples).[18] But this book is not a critique of communism itself, so we won't go into these. The 'social fascism' accusation merely offers, as we start to investigate the Dark Knight, the starkest of cautionary tales.

In his 1998 memoir *Things Can Only Get Better*, John O'Farrell humorously describes student discussions about the 1980s Labour leadership, where he was trying to impress a left-wing crowd:

> There had been me thinking Jim Callaghan was one of the good guys, when it turned out he was just a TOR-y. The word 'Tory' had its own pronunciation back then – the 'TOR' part lasted about three seconds. Merlyn Rees? TOR-y! Denis Healey? TOR-y! David Owens? TOR-y! Whenever a Labour politician's name was mentioned I would pause to see which way the wind was blowing.
>
> 'Yeah, I wonder what would happen if they had Tony Benn as leader?' I volunteered, before pausing to see where he fitted into the scheme of things . . .

'Tony Benn?'

'TOR-y?' I asked nervously.

'Tony Benn? A Tory? What are you talking about?'[19]

O'Farrell's account recalls 1980s politics at its loopy nadir. Yet as the 'social fascism' example shows, the thinking behind the 'TOR-y' accusation wasn't a one-off. The belief in a moral in-group has often afflicted the left, returning with a vengeance in recent years.

Let's take, as a case study, left-populist writer Owen Jones. Jones has written two bestselling non-fiction books, *Chavs* and *The Establishment*, both of which became set texts for a generation of leftist millennials. His backing of Corbyn in 2015 gave others the confidence to do the same.

Jones's books are characterised by a determination to prove that the 1997–2010 Labour governments were not just closer to the centre than Jones's own position – nor that they failed in many of their goals – but that their intentions were as right-wing (and thus, in Jones's eyes, as immoral) as the Tories'.

The Establishment pushes home the idea that New Labour was 'on a collision course with the party's traditional values', populated by those who 'believed in little – except, in some cases, money'.[20] The top 'New Labour' listings in the index are 'Kowtowing to big business from', 'Embrace of Thatcherite agenda by', 'Privatisation of the NHS by' and 'Fawning over The City by'.

In *Chavs*, meanwhile, politicians from the last Labour government are described as 'steeped in middle-class triumphalism'. They were, Jones tells us, determined to prove that the working classes were 'on the wrong side of history',[21] and many would have been more at home in the Tory party.[22] He claims that Labour ministers sought to prove 'people are poor because they lack moral fibre',[23] and describes Alan Johnson's supposed eagerness to blame working-class boys for their own failure.[24]

There is no positive mention of the 1997–2010 governments in either book, with Labour policies presented as interchangeable with those of the Tories.[25] When mentioning Labour achievements is unavoidable, Jones suggests they were accidental, insufficient or window-dressing for a reactionary agenda. On the minimum wage, for instance, he argues that Tony Blair opposed it in secret.[26]

One technique is to choose a soundbite by – or about – a former minister, and to use it as a catch-all for the policy platform. The first part of Peter Mandelson's rhetorical (and foolish) claim to be 'intensely relaxed about people getting filthy rich as long as they pay their taxes' is used in both books, as a proxy for the entire New Labour approach to redistribution – despite having long ago been retracted by Mandelson. It comes instead of a nuanced analysis of Labour's mixed record on inequality, and in lieu of suggestions for how they might have tackled the problem better.[27]

Meanwhile, New Labour politicians are represented, almost without exception, as corrupt and personally malign.[28] Centre leftists of the period are invariably slick, perma-tanned and clad in shiny suits, with expense claims or black marks against their integrity mentioned as an aside. Moral lapses by those who share Jones's politics are ignored, by contrast. They are presented as soft-spoken and unassuming, with good deeds and humble backgrounds alluded to in parentheses.[29] The argument is that everyone bar the far left is driven by interchangeably malign intent, be they David Blunkett, Nick Clegg, Michael Gove or Nigel Farage.

Of course, there are many reasons to criticise the 1997–2010 Labour governments. A constructive left-wing appraisal – one which does not rely on our myths – would be welcome.

And it is obviously important to flag corruption in high places – as long as this is consistent and does not ally one ideology with moral purity and the rest with naked venality.

Yet *Chavs* and *The Establishment* do neither of these things, and instead present the centre left as White Knights who've joined the Dark side.[30] New Labour are vain sell-outs and spiteful charlatans, according to Jones – with all personal failings attributed directly to their politics. When describing three MPs caught exchanging money for influence, Jones writes that it was 'hardly a coincidence' that they were 'Blairites'.[31] One wonders how he'd feel if Tony Benn's exploitation of tax loopholes was used in the same way, to suggest that the far left are inherently self-interested.[32]

Having championed the Dark Knight approach, what is striking about the Owen Jones story is that – for a period – he was pushed into the very out-group he'd helped create. Having blamed every criticism of Corbyn on treachery and self-interest, he began to have doubts of his own. He outlined his reservations in a 2016 blog, which began with the following lament:

> It has become increasingly common in politics to reduce disagreements to bad faith. Rather than accepting somebody has a different perspective because, well, that's what they think, you look for an ulterior motive instead. Everything from self-aggrandisement to careerism to financial corruption to the circles in which the other person moves: any explanation but an honest disagreement. It becomes a convenient means of avoiding talking about substance.[33]

He complained, 'I've spent my entire adult life in socialist politics ... and I'm now being attacked as a Blairite, crypto-Tory and Establishment stooge.'

Despite this reminder that 'Blairites' were the real enemy, many left populists ignored this, accusing him of self-interest, spinelessness or closet conservatism.[34] He was eventually granted readmission to the in-group a year later, thanks to a flurry of anti-'centrist' articles.

Owen Jones's approach here is inconsistent, to say the least. He has done more than most to suggest that others in Labour lack progressive values and basic morals, yet he asks to be immune from such accusations himself. But the deeper point is about the Dark Knight dynamic. The accusation that Jones is a right-winger shows (like the accusation that Trotsky was a fascist) how farcical the myth can be.

Indeed, the parallels with 'social fascism' are real. The sustained use, by left populists, of morally pejorative, catch-all terms for everyone they disagree with – 'centrist', 'neoliberal', 'Blairite', 'establishment politician', 'Tory lite' – played the same role, during the Corbyn years, as the 'social fascist' allegation.[35] All that these words do is provide a shorthand to suggest neighbours are enemies. At a point when some genuinely dangerous authoritarians again hold or seek office, the risks of this are real.

Indeed, the footage after the December 2019 election of well-spoken Corbynites denouncing working-class voters' 'lack of empathy' is where the Dark Knight mentality leads.[36] The UK must now endure a Boris Johnson–Dominic Cummings government with a large majority, thanks in part to the alienating form of politics which the myth encourages.

Life-long Labour activists – who have been cast by Jones as self-serving and right-wing – might have felt a stab of pleasure upon seeing Jones get a dose of his own medicine in 2016. But the Dark Knight phenomenon does not end here. The far left may be steeped in Dark Knight sectarianism, but the truth is that milder Dark Knight assumptions permeate far beyond the Owen Jones clique. Many of us have, at points, played a role, indulging in Manichean approaches which, as we are now seeing, have the capacity to eat themselves. Instead of simply objecting when the Dark Knight myth is turned on us, we must recognise that the idea of politics as a moral continuum is wrong wherever it is applied.

ISSUES, METHODS, INSTITUTIONS AND CAUSES

The Dark Knight is at its worst when applied at the individual level. But there is also a policy or issue-based element to Dark Knight thinking. The populist left instinctively sides with certain 'good' professions, nations, causes, methods and institutions, and against 'bad' ones. Parts of the left will, for example, need little encouragement to side against the police or with the teaching profession – even without knowing the substance of the debate.

This comes from a belief that politics is a moral continuum, with sectors, religions, professions, policies and organisations placed on a spectrum from good to bad. (Teachers might be placed closer to the good, left-wing pole than the police, for example.)

Where organisations and causes are distributed is based on a range of factors. But the effect is that, if a conflict arises between one and another, we have a ready-made answer to the 'Which side are you on?' question. If, hypothetically, there was a funding conflict between teachers and the police, the White Knight to Dark Knight spectrum would help frame the issue in moral terms. We could quickly, in good conscience, back the teachers. (Indeed, the 2020 campaign to 'defund the police' followed roughly this logic. The implication of the slogan was that the British police were an immoral entity, beyond reform, who should not, rightly, exist.)

In effect, this is the same process as forms of Dark Knight thinking aimed at individuals. The first step is that a moral spectrum is created. The second is that, whenever a choice arises, we can pick our side.

As a consequence, support for certain causes becomes inexorable, leading to contradictory and inconsistent outcomes. In a complex world, where divides occur between the lesser of two evils or the greater of two goods, we find ourselves ill-equipped. On the issue of immigration, for example, do you side with migrants or with older voters in the least well-off areas? These are two White Knights which often end up in opposition to each other. Likewise, support for Islam and other faith groups can come up against support for LGBT groups.[37]

A good case study is the 2015 London tube strikes. Tube drivers work unsociable hours in unpleasant jobs, but the starting salary is about £50,000, with capped hours and good holidays. Even allowing for the changes their union, the RMT, were striking against – a small rise in the number of night shifts, in return for a small pay rise[38] – this is a rate you might be happy with from behind Rawls's veil of ignorance.

The instinct of the left is to side with trade unions. And in most cases this is correct. But the reason for doing so is that unions protect people in economically precarious positions. By seeing them as de facto moral, we are presented with tricky questions about how far our support goes. What if unions were representing those on £100,000? How about £1 million?

This sounds ludicrous, but the point is that backing any cause or institution unwaveringly can become non-progressive. Because that cause is usually coming at things from a partial viewpoint, their motives will eventually clash with other egalitarian goals.

In the case of RMT strikes, after all, the Dark Knight in the situation was not a profiteering fat cat but a public sector organisation, Transport for London, funded through the taxes and fares of passengers paid less than the strikers. The issue was a White Knight versus White Knight scenario. Fred Jarvis, a leader of the Trades Union Congress during the 1980s, reminds us that this is often the case:

> The bulk of [present trade union members] are in the public sector and public services, which means that when they strike they cause more difficulties for their fellow citizens, who depend on their services, than damage to any bosses' profits.[39]

The 2015 tube strikes were complex, and the drivers may have been right. But the point is that opposition to the tube strikes cannot be unsayable on the left. From a Rawlsian perspective, there might come a point where siding *against* the tube unions would be progressive. That juncture is not necessarily now. But it's worth pausing to consider when it would be. The idea that being on the left amounts to a limitless support for our chosen White Knights means we risk backing the very forces we set out to oppose.

Another example is social class. This is central to how the left views society, and provides clues about the origins of the Dark Knight. The ultra left's continued attraction to 'class war' is an example of how class provides, for many, a theory of change and a set of signifiers along which battle lines can be drawn.

Left pluralists, while committed to equal rights, equal opportunities and fair outcomes, usually regard social class itself as a barrier – pigeonholing people by where they come from and feeding resentment. Of course, class can play an important role in personal identities. But the goal for pluralists is that it does not and should not matter – and that it is a good thing if class identifications become less binary. When left pluralists talk about class, it tends to be descriptive, not partisan – a shorthand for jobs or income brackets.

Left populists, by contrast, focus on holding together class groupings – as a means of withstanding oppression from other classes. The mantra that you should 'rise with your class, not out of it' is still sometimes quoted approvingly.[40] And social classes are often seen, by some left populists, as existing in opposition to each other. This state of mind, based as it is on side-taking, allows other social groups to be seen as the enemy, and those that cross class divides to be cast as traitors.

This difference explains the many non-sequiturs on this issue between pluralists and populists. Left populists, for example, see those who aspire to a classless society as opponents of the working class – rather than of the class system per se. They see the fact that fewer people do working-class jobs as a sign that the working classes have been crushed by people that hate them.[41] Those who say it is a good thing that more of the population now do non-manual occupations are seen as 'sneering' at the working classes.

Labour must always reduce inequality and deprivation – missions which involve supporting those described as working class. But we should be wary of holding together class structures for their own sake.[42]

For one thing, class ties you to the circumstances you were born into, and to group identifications that might not matter to you. Better, surely, for people to fulfil themselves however they like, not to rise or fall with a pre-determined bloc. Indeed, the left-populist view of class is one of the reasons working-class people often vote 'against their interests' for individualistic forms of Toryism. Individualism may, in policy terms, mean the ladder is pulled up. But its willingness to judge people as separate entities, not as members of a tribe, explains its appeal. The sense is often that the left wishes to maintain the class structure, holding people to the trappings of birth.[43] While largely flawed as a critique, the idea that Labour wants a stratified society will continue to carry traction until left populists stop seeing class as a set of battle-lines people must not cross.

Moreover, the increasingly complex nature of the class system means that the left-populist version of class conflict is less and less relevant. In 2013, for example, a group of London School of Economics (LSE) sociologists came up with a new analysis, to replace the model of working, middle and upper class. The resulting framework comprised seven segments.[44] So, whereas Dark Knight views about class were once, at least, allied with economic reality, they increasingly put people into boxes they don't belong in.[45]

This links to another question which is raised by Dark Knight ideas about class: what if the struggle is won? If a 'classless' society isn't deemed a victory, what is? Presumably, it would be one of two scenarios. Either, the working classes close the gap, but some sort of economic stratification or cultural distinction remains. Or, the working classes are victorious, rising so high 'as a class' that they sit at the top of society. The former scenario suggests some social division must always exist. The latter poses the question of whether, once the working classes have 'won', we on the left then switch allegiances and side with the beleaguered middle and upper classes, who are now Britain's underdogs? Or do we abandon our claims to egalitarianism and continue to side with the working classes? At a time when class identification relates less and less to economics, these questions aren't entirely hypothetical.

A purer ideal is a society with neither snobbery nor inverted snobbery; where economic equality is the goal, not a cultural attachment to class. After all, class identifications came about thanks to the cultural differences caused by profoundly unequal societies. It is reasonable to assume that, if progressive goals around economic equality are one day met, a byproduct will be that class stops mattering. The Dark Knight approach blocks this, suggesting that the outbreak of peace in the 'class war' is the same thing as a defeat.

ANTI-SEMITISM AND THE DANGER OF SIMPLICITY

Let's turn to Labour's anti-Semitism problem. There are countless manifestations of this, and although the issue came to prominence after Corbyn won the Labour leadership, there is no doubt that anti-Semitism has long lurked in some 'anti-imperialist' groups. Research into UK anti-Semitic attacks between 2013 and 2016 found that the political motives of perpetrators were perceived by the victim to be left-wing rather than right-wing by a 2:1 ratio.[46]

Some of this stems from left populists' attraction to conspiracy theories (which is explored further in the Puppet Master section).

However, let's think first about politics and side-taking. Most on the populist left are not anti-Semitic. Yet there is clearly a correlation of some kind, with racist attitudes to Jews more widely tolerated – not least by Corbyn himself. A blind eye has long been turned, in a way that it is not turned to other forms of prejudice.

How can the Labour left, which prides itself on tolerance, have reached this position? No doubt there are a few true bigots, but the answer does not lie in straight racism. Rather, it stems from the moral continuum at the heart of the Dark Knight. Politics, the myth tells us, is a case of looking at your left–right spectrum and seeing where a cause or country or religion sits. When a conflict arises you can then, in good conscience, back whichever side sits closest to the 'good', left-wing pole.

Through this Dark Knight process, you end up placing Israelis closer to the 'bad' pole than Palestinians, and Islamophobia closer than anti-Semitism. You believe racism against Jews is wrong, but conclude that racism against Muslims is worse. You end up unable to sympathise with Jews who felt vulnerable or stateless following the Holocaust without fearing that you undermine your compassion for displaced Muslims in Palestine.[47] And as soon as the debate becomes heated, you double down, certain that you're on the side of 'good'.

Corbyn's defence against suggestions that he's anti-Semitic – which is that his mother fought Oswald Mosley's Blackshirts in the Battle of Cable Street – is an example. In the fight between Jews and Muslims, the latter are closer to the 'good' pole. But in the fight between Jews and fascists – as Cable Street was – this is reversed.

Dark Knight believers' difficulty in positioning Judaism on the spectrum stems from the fact that Israeli 'Zionists' are seen as imperialist oppressors of Palestine.[48] The fact that the US supported the creation of Israel, and the way Israel has conducted itself as the occupiers, is sufficient to render Jewish Israelis closer to the Dark Knight pole than Muslim Palestinians (with the word 'Zionism' often acting as the point of conflation between a global Jewish identity and political support for Israeli policies).[49]

Historically, the root of left-wing anti-Semitism also lies in the fact the Jewish community tends to be better off, unlike other minority groups. This means they are easier to conflate with business, property and private sector 'interests'.

Hence, while the Jewish community has been subject to appalling persecution, it also falls into categories deemed right-wing and immoral by the populist left ('the West', 'the rich').[50] Part of Corbyn's difficulty in condemning left-wing anti-Semites like Jackie Walker or Ken Livingstone stems from the fact that he believes they are ultimately, like him, the good guys.[51]

Hence, like most racism, anti-Semitism on the left does not start off as a genuine hatred of an ethnicity. Instead, it tells a story about how Dark Knight ideas of collective guilt and moral singularity can spiral out of control. Because, ultimately, the process of picking sides encourages double standards. Just as, within our metaphorical football match, a fan might cheer when an opposition striker is injured, anything goes once you have entered the realm of Dark and White Knights. You can burn effigies of Margaret Thatcher upon her death but balk when the *Daily Mail* attacks the deceased Ralph Miliband. You can ignore intrusions into the lives of Nigel Farage's children but complain when Seb Corbyn's Tinder account is hacked. And you can condemn Boris Johnson's Islamophobia but defend Corbyn's anti-Semitism.

Before you know it, your enemy's enemy is your ally, and the suffering of 'the other side' has become relativised. You're turning a blind eye to Holocaust denial or calling Hamas your 'friends'. You have moved, with alarming speed, away from what you first considered 'moral'. How far you go down this course varies. But it all starts with the Dark Knight assumption that politics is a battleground between good and evil.

5
The Appeal of the Dark Knight

The Dark Knight does not spring from nowhere. All soldiers, it is said, go into war believing they have 'God on their side'.

There are three 'allures' which draw people to the myth: identity, virtue and simplicity. These explain why morally sophisticated people are susceptible to Manichean thinking when it comes to politics.

THE ALLURE OF IDENTITY

In-group thinking describes wanting to belong to a collective, defined against an enemy out-group.[1] The phenomenon exists at every level of life. Exclusivity and exclusion are powerful reinforcing dynamics, especially when times are uncertain. In the playground children form cliques, and in countless Hollywood films a happy few unite against an evil invader.

At a more severe level, identity politics leads communities to feel suspicious of the 'other'. It can cause xenophobia and bloodshed. It allows rational arguments to be blocked out if they come from members of the out-group. In extreme cases, like terrorist cells, this allows tiny but ultra-robust in-groups to dehumanise their enemies entirely.

The appeal of right populists like Nigel Farage is based on an in-group/out-group dynamic. Their out-group is different to the left-populist one, comprising immigrants, London politicians, feminists, Muslims, *Guardian* readers, Tory Europhiles, BBC journalists, and so on. These outsider threats work to reinforce the UKIP, Leave or Brexit Party identity, with legitimate criticisms dismissed as liberal propaganda.

The allure of identity is especially powerful in the case of a group which feels downtrodden or outnumbered.[2] In the areas Nigel Farage targeted, for instance, economic decline and cultural change had strengthened the sense of an enemy to fight against.

The same thing happens on the left, with feelings of marginalisation reinforcing a group mentality. Indeed, the Dark Knight myth often comes as a direct result of new challenges – Thatcherism in the 1980s, for instance, which left populists of the period responded to by circling the wagons.

In 2015, similarly, the threat had been realised, with the Tories securing an overall majority. Renewed venom towards the out-group felt essential to sustain the Labour in-group. The subsequent rise of Corbynism – with its rallies for the converted and accusations of treason – is arguably the most acute example of a group dynamic that the British left has ever seen.

The paradox is that, because in-groups are exclusivity machines, dependent on the expulsion of insufficiently loyal members, forging an 'us and them' mentality is the worst thing you can do when you're trying to rebuild. This is where the intersection between the Dark Knight and the Golden Era (which we look at later) is most apparent. A sense of decline feeds a sense of group identity, which shrinks the group and accelerates the decline.

Moreover, the impasse with the 'enemy' will only grow. One 2008 US study, which explored the relationship between threat perception and political identification, concluded that each side will 'never achieve an accurate understanding of the opposing side's platform' while a group identity prevents dialogue. This 'quickly lead[s] to a vicious cycle in which shared values are overlooked and differences exaggerated'.[3]

Some may see the clannishness which the Dark Knight generates as a form of collectivism. However, in my view there is nothing collectivist about, for instance, the RMT's Sean Hoyle telling supporters, 'If you spit on your own they just wipe it away. But if we all spit

THE DARK KNIGHT AND THE PUPPET MASTER

together we can drown the bastards.'[4] It's a form of 'solidarity' defined solely by hatred of others.

Although this sort of quote reflects the tone adopted by populists like Len McCluskey, I don't claim that it is representative of most Corbyn supporters. Many – even those who engage in milder Dark Knight assumptions – dislike this rhetoric. But it nevertheless shows the alienating denouement which the allure of identity takes us towards.

THE ALLURE OF VIRTUE

The second allure is the allure of virtue. This is the temptation to feel we are more moral than others.

This might sound similar to 'virtue signalling' – the pejorative phrase which burst into usage in 2015. 'Virtue signalling' described the supposed moral posturing of Corbyn supporters. They seemed indifferent to electability and were thus – it was alleged – less concerned with helping the poorest than with massaging their own egos.[5]

However, 'virtue signalling' is different from the allure of virtue. The former is about feigning compassion to look good (hence why it is offensive, and slips into Dark Knight approaches of its own). The latter is about assuming you're more decent or caring than others – a trait which academics sometimes call 'moral self-regard'. All of us are prone to it (although it is least pronounced in the political centre).[6]

The sentiment in the quote below, from a Corbyn supporter on social media, is an example of what people mean by 'virtue signalling':

> In my case and probably for others too [winning elections] is not the goal. My goal is to be able to vote for someone who I believe in and trust, someone who cares about the people and not themselves . . . I care that [Corbyn] cares and that's good enough for me. Finally, I feel there is someone that has principles and sticks to them. If that's not enough to win an election, then who cares?[7]

You can see why people would attach the term 'virtue signalling' to this. However, I would say that, even in this quote, moral self-regard is the real problem. The Corbyn supporter in question clearly feels that valuing compassion puts him in the lonely minority. And he believes he has found, in Corbyn, a political articulation of this, when everyone else wants callous machine men. He has fallen for the idea that he and his politicians of choice have a firmer grasp of basic decency than others.

The allure of virtue has a psychologically powerful basis. Almost no one, in the history of the world, has believed themselves to be bad. This applies even to the evillest dictators. And it certainly goes for many ordinary people who are trying to do what is right.

Some would counter that it is no bad thing to overestimate your morality. They would say that a sense of personal virtue leads to higher moral standards. But evidence suggests this is not the case.[8] High moral self-regard means we don't check our own behaviour. And it alienates everyone else. One study, which explored what works in persuading political opponents, concluded that

> morality contributes to political polarization because moral convictions lead individuals to take absolutist stances and refuse to compromise.[9]

Indeed, the perception that the left is morally self-regarding is the best recruiting sergeant the right could hope for. In a 2015 article by columnist and author Tony Parsons, he explained why, as a 'reluctant Conservative voter', he could never vote Labour again because of the party's sanctimony. He describes seeing the words 'Tory Scum' graffitied on a memorial to women who had died in the Battle of Britain (an act which was defended by some left populists).[10] Parsons writes:

> Well, that's me, I thought. They are definitely talking about me. Because whatever these people believe, I know that I will always be on the other side ... A total of 11,334,576 people voted Conservative not because the Tories are cruel, stupid or evil.

Parsons concludes: 'The big lie of our time is that the liberal left is morally pure and the Tories are filth.'

The extent to which Parsons is doing some politicking of his own is hard to gauge. But the perception of 'moral self-regard' has either lost us a friend or given ammunition to an opponent. And, while most left-wingers don't talk about 'Tory scum', even a milder impression of moral self-regard can have a similar effect.

Another study, finally, looks at whether there is a 'tendency to escalate commitment more frequently to failing prosocial initiatives than to failing egoistic initiatives'. In other words, do people throw good money after bad when the cause taps into their moral self-regard, more than when it taps into their self-interest? The results found that, on the positive side, people were more likely to give their all to altruistic causes than to self-interested ones. But they were also less likely to give up on these causes if their efforts proved counterproductive.[11]

This is a powerful endorsement of Rawls's belief in 'the right over the good'. It illustrates that overcommitting to the side of 'good' can lead to worse outcomes. And it shows how the allure of virtue ties in with the combative, 'never say die' attitude of the White Knight – with its willingness to battle to the death rather than fight another day.

Through these studies and others, we can see how Corbyn supporters like the one quoted above can be so blasé about electability. And we can understand why Labour's membership persistently sticks with ineffective policies and unelectable leaders, thus failing millions of poorer voters.

THE ALLURE OF SIMPLICITY

The final allure – simplicity – describes the Dark Knight myth's ability to help us understand the political debate, and to choose which side we sit on. It stems from the fact that policy questions are hard. Even trained economists struggle to digest the budget as it's announced. And experienced professionals argue about the viability of a sugar tax or the consequences of fiscal devolution. What hope is there for those of us who do not have the time to go through every policy with a fine-toothed comb?

The allure of simplicity pre-dates 'alternative facts' and 'fake news'. The 'Which side are you on?' refrain may be divisive, but it has always, to some degree, governed how we vote. Writing in the wake of Labour's 2015 election loss, the author Alan Bennett explains that ideas of good and bad appealed to him precisely because the debates were complex:

> I wanted a Labour government so that I could stop thinking about politics, knowing that the nation's affairs were in the hands of a party which, even if it was often foolish, was at least well-intentioned.[12]

Which of us hasn't felt this way? We need to know who is on the side of the angels, so that politics doesn't feel overwhelming and meaningless. The Dark Knight helps us to digest issues, offering the framework of two opposing poles. From this, we can work out where we stand.

The Dark Knight prism often calls this correctly. Yet in a world becoming more complex, the allure of simplicity can be a hindrance. In the EU referendum, for instance, the left–right seesaws were in disarray, meaning a campaign where no one knew who to believe.

In this context, a 2012 study entitled 'The Double-edge Sword in Social Judgments' is interesting. The research looked first at how those with a heightened sense of morality addressed simple questions, and then at how they addressed complex ones. In the simple situations, those who attached more moral weight to decisions acted most ethically. They saw things in clear terms and took the correct side. When evaluating ethically complex dilemmas, however, individuals with a heightened sense of morality imposed their own unequivocal moral framework all the same, leading them to become 'rigid and biased in their social judgment[s]'. In other words, a strident moral compass actually left people ill-equipped to evaluate complex dilemmas – even though they had been the most ethical when it came to simple ones.[13]

This explains how the allure of simplicity fuels the Dark Knight. On a simple issue – i.e. a choice between a fat-cat private-sector employer and a minimum-wage workforce – those seeing things through a clearly defined moral prism might take sides boldly and quickly. But when the situation became more finely balanced – as with the tube strikes discussed earlier (which pitted better-paid public-sector employees against transport users) – they would wander into trouble. A vehement moral compass doesn't work when there is no obvious north and south.

The response to the post-crash economy is another example. From 2008 onwards, there were a series of complex decisions for Labour: how to retain investment while protecting the poorest and making the financial sector pay its way; how and whether to cut the national debt, and whether reducing the deficit was the way to do it (and if so, what balance of cuts and tax rises was fairest); what Keynesian social democracy might look like in straitened times, and so on.

But the allure of simplicity meant that this was interpreted by the populist left as a no-brainer: spending on the poorest versus 'neo-liberal' austerity. The public suspected that the issue was more complex than this, and left-populist narratives inadvertently fed the idea that Labour couldn't be trusted with weighty trade-offs.

Ultimately, simplicity is the most sympathetic of the Dark Knight's allures, and the hardest to unpick. Unlike identity and virtue, which are negative instincts within us all, to be tempered, the allure of simplicity is necessary for democracy. Most people do not have the time to think through every policy issue, but should still be able to feel engaged and passionate.

The challenge for our politicians is to break complex issues down into honest pros and cons, so that there is less need for the compass provided by the Dark Knight myth.

6

The Case against the Dark Knight (People)

To understand why it is necessary to jettison the Dark Knight, let's look at the myth on an issue-by-issue, group-by-group basis. The table below shows some oppositions which feature in the populist-left mindset – a series of White Knights (which are regarded as moral by the left), and their corresponding right-wing Dark Knights. They are divided into a) identities people are born with, b) behaviours and roles people adopt, and c) issues, causes and institutions.

For some, being 'on the left' is about siding with the entities in the White Knight column, whenever they come up against their counterparts in the Dark Knight column.

There are oppositions listed which, for some on the populist left, are articles of faith. Others might be fiercely rejected (e.g. jihadist terrorists). The idea obviously is not to say the populist left are tub-thumping supporters of everything in the left column or seething opponents of everything in the right. (Nor, of course, is it to correlate being a woman with being a *Guardian* reader with supporting nationalisation). The point is about how the populist left regards these oppositions. The instinct, in many cases, is to sympathise more with the entities in the White Knight column, and give them more of the benefit of the doubt than their Dark Knight equivalents.

Imagine we saw a newspaper story about a jihadist suicide bomber who'd killed ten people in an attack on Wall Street, and then we saw on the adjacent page a story about a white supremacist who'd killed ten people in an African-American church. Would our responses be different? There is no reason they should be. Both crimes are equally heinous. Both caused similar amounts of misery. Both perpetrators were brainwashed or unstable. We can try to understand the mentalities, to prevent future attacks, but we cannot excuse one more than the other. The same goes for many of the oppositions below, even on topics less incendiary.

Table 6.1.

	White Knights (regarded as more moral)	Dark Knights (regarded as less moral)
a) Identities	Young	Old
	Working classes	Upper and middle classes
	Scottish	English
	Northerners	Southerners
	Women	Men
	Ethnic minority	White
	Gay	Straight
	Europeans	Americans
	Muslims	Jews
b) Behaviours and roles	Nurses and teachers	Soldiers and policemen
	Guardian readers	*Mail* readers
	Welfare recipients	Bankers
	Irish Republicans	Irish Unionists
	Green voters	Brexit Party voters
	Jihadist terrorists	White supremacists
	Original inhabitants of area	Gentrifiers
	Public Servants	Bankers
c) Issues, causes and institutions	Nationalisation	Privatisation
	More immigration	Less immigration
	More economic equality	Less economic equality
	Nuclear Unilateralism	Nuclear Multilateralism
	Non-intervention abroad	Intervention abroad

continued

Secularism	Organised religion
Pacifism	Militarism
Trade unions	Businesses
Cuba and Venezuela	The US
Palestine	Israel
Public sector	Private sector
Russia	The West
Invest more	Invest less

But the Dark Knight myth encourages us – sometimes just to a minor degree, sometimes more stridently – to take sides. And as soon as we make this transition – as soon as we say the jihadist's crime was more forgivable than the white supremacist's, or that corruption in a trade union is marginally better than equivalent corruption in a bank – we depart from Rawlsian egalitarianism and move into the realm of 'us and them'.

I'll continue to refer to the above table as we explore *complexity*, *circumstance*, *depth* and *inexorability*. These describe the four flaws in the Dark Knight myth.

HUMAN COMPLEXITY

Most on the left would agree that humans are complex. Yet it is sometimes unclear what this means.

To unpack the idea, let's briefly return to left-wing anti-Semitism. We have suggested already that this stems from the fact that Judaism disrupts the White Knight/Dark Knight binaries with which left populists are most comfortable. The Jewish community defies the rule that a persecuted minority must also be economically deprived or a victim of 'imperialism'.

In other words, left-wing anti-Semitism is the product of a world view which cannot cope with the idea that a person or group could contain, at the same time, traits associated with the left and traits associated with the right. Hence, they inhabit the realm of singular identities. They take one surface of a multifaceted identity and make assumptions about the whole.

Of course, the left populist who says that an Israeli Jew is bad full-stop is rare. But what a few might say is that Israeli Jews are *less likely* to be decent people than Palestinian Muslims. They might regard the decent Israeli Jew as an exception to the rule.

This prejudice could equally apply to Americans, or wealthy people, or many other groups in the Dark Knight column. And, in most instances, it would be mild. A person might, in the heat of the moment, refer to 'upper-class bastards' and then refine this view, upon interrogation, to 'upper-class people are more likely to be bastards'. But this still denigrates a vast swathe of society based on a single piece of information.

The point is that, while the 'Dark Knight versus White Knight' mentality prevails, there will always be complex people cast as heroes or as villains through a single group allegiance. There will be the working-class person attacked for their 'white privilege';[1] the hard-up pensioner who still uses the term 'half-caste'; the banker donating to charity; the Polish waitress saving to go to Ascot; the *Express*-reading immigrant. These and all the other category-defying people out there are beyond the grasp of the Dark Knight imagination, with its tendency to judge the whole by a part.[2]

Of course, we can believe this is a superior form of prejudice. And perhaps it *is* better to be prejudiced against better-off people than working-class people, or against Americans than Eastern Europeans. But surely it is better still to avoid collective guilt wherever we see it; to object to the term 'toff' as well as the term 'chav'?

Amartya Sen's book *Identity and Violence* makes this case. Sen's premise is that humans have myriad identities, and that to categorise them on the basis of one facilitates extremism.[3] 'Identities are robustly plural, and the importance of one identity need not obliterate the importance of others.' He rejects theories which assume that 'any person pre-eminently belongs . . . to one collectivity'. Even Karl Marx, Sen points out, disliked the word 'workers', due to what

Sen calls its 'crude presumption that any person belongs to one group and one group only'.[4] The real world is anomalous: 'A person can be a British citizen, of Malaysian origin, with Chinese racial character-istics, a stockbroker, a non-vegetarian, an asthmatic, a linguist, a bodybuilder, a poet, an opponent of abortion, a bird-watcher, an astrologer etc – and all at the same time.'

The same goes when applying the above table of oppositions. A person could be a bisexual, Christian BME woman from a working-class background who is employed by the police, reads the *Guardian*, votes Tory and is an inconsiderate next-door neighbour. Judging her morals by who she votes for or the paper she reads would be reductive.

The character in question may be rare. But, thanks to the disrup-tion of many orthodoxies, she is less rare than she once was.[5] Given the countless identities people now hold, a belief in singular, right–left identifications is more redundant than ever. This is one of the central reasons why the recent polarisation into political groups driven by narrow interpretations of 'the good' is so destructive.

The accusation that certain individuals are not 'politically black' is a particularly acute example of this. This was levelled at BME Tories in 2019, who were branded 'turncoats of colour', 'tokens' and 'sellouts' for joining Boris Johnson's first Cabinet.[6] This is an insult which is straight out of the Dark Knight playbook. It assumes that certain characteristics in the White Knight column (such as being black or Asian) should automatically align with other White Knight traits – such as supporting socialism – and that those for whom it does not forgo their BME identity.

Tony Blair describes how, in the 1990s, a sense of an impending multiplicity influenced his politics:

> Sedgefield was a 'northern working-class constituency'. Except that when you scratched even a little beneath the surface, the definitions didn't quite fit ... They drank beer; they also drank wine. They went to the chippy; they also went to restaurants ... There had been an article – usual *Daily Mail* stuff – about how I was a poseur and

fraud because I said I liked fish and chips, but when in London living in Islington it was well-known I had eaten pasta (shock-horror). Plainly you couldn't conceivably like both since these were indications of distinct and incompatible cultures. The Britain of the late 1990s was of course actually one in which people ate a variety of foods, had a multiplicity of cultural experiences, and rather enjoyed it. This was as true 'up North' as it was 'down South'.[7]

Of course, most on the populist left pride themselves on not being judgemental or binary in their thinking. In principle, many eschew collective blame. But it is alarming the extent to which this does not happen in practice.

Hence, when a situation arises like the one discussed earlier, where a Tory-voting benefit recipient cries on *Question Time*, many judge her as a Tory and nothing else. Likewise, the *Mail* or *Sun* readerships are tarred with a single brush, even though a minority, even among these groupings, vote for progressive parties.[8]

A more specific example is Ken Livingstone's suggestion, in 2016, that a donation to Labour MP Dan Jarvis from hedge-fund manager Martin Taylor was like 'Jimmy Savile funding a children's group' – and was proof that Jarvis was not 'genuinely Labour'.[9] Livingstone's Dark Knight mentality meant he used Jarvis's connection to someone from an out-group (a figure from the financial sector) to call into question his membership of the Labour in-group.

In a letter responding to Livingstone, Taylor contested this dichotomy:

> You may find it hard to believe, but I am a hedge fund manager who actively WANTS the amount of tax that I pay to go up ... That is why I have always donated to the Party ... long after it transparently became against my financial interests to do so.[10]

As another example, let's look at a 2013 article by Laurie Penny in which she claimed that 'all men, not some men' are responsible for the abuse of women.[11] The piece is an eloquent defence of collective guilt, suggesting that 'men as a group, men as a structure ... hate and hurt' women. Penny rejects the idea that you shouldn't 'generalise' – which she says is a way of 'getting women to shut up'. She ends her article with a direct address to men as individuals: 'You can choose to stand up and say no and, every day, more men and boys are making that choice. The question is – will you be one of them?' Her argument is that males should have the autonomy to escape their group, but that women retain the right to judge them en masse – even if the men in question are no more misogynistic than Penny herself.

There are many comparisons to be drawn here, of the 'Do we blame X as a group for the crimes of Y as an individual?' kind. And these lead us back to the door of Penny herself, a privately educated Oxbridge alumna. Is she responsible for privately educated people 'as a group'? I would say she is not, and her 2012 article 'Yes, Mr Gove, I Enjoyed an Expensive Education, but I'm Still Not on Your Team' suggests that she feels the same way.[12] Indeed, Penny complains that 'everyone is divided up into warring tribes' based on their background. She rightly argues against judging people by the 'class in which [they] were born'.

So by appraising the Laurie Penny 'polygon' based on one side we can view her as part of the female in-group, against the oppressive male out-group.[13] But by looking at another side we can judge her by her social class and conclude that she is part of the privately schooled out-group (along with Boris Johnson and David Cameron) – juxtaposed against a state-educated in-group which she hates and hurts.

This latter suggestion may be ridiculous. But it's no more so than the idea that 'all men', regardless of their behaviour, hold equal responsibility for the abuse of women.

Human complexity, then, is the view that people are multifaceted, and that it is an error to judge them solely as members of one category. Left-wing responses to this usually centre on ideas such as 'intersectionality', which acknowledge that there are different planes of inequality. However, the way in which theories like this tend to be used on a day-to-day basis continues to rely on the language of persecutors and victims. Hence, rather than breaking up binary categorisations, such ideas tend to reinforce them, rendering certain groups doubly or trebly oppressive, and other groups double or trebly oppressed.

There are clear electoral implications when it comes to these questions. Indeed, left-populist accusations of 'triangulation' (that is, taking your electoral base for granted and moving to the centre to win votes) are steeped in the Dark Knight idea that by broadening your appeal you capitulate.

If we look at two of the most electorally successful progressive campaigns in recent years, Justin Trudeau's in 2015 and Barack Obama's in 2008, both embraced human complexity. Trudeau declared that 'the Conservatives are not our enemies, they're our neighbours'.[14] And Obama's 'more perfect union' speech asked for politics to look for the good in people[15] – even those behaving wrongly. Both based their campaigns on moral pluralism rather than moral tribalism.

The 'big tent' strategies promoted by Trudeau or Obama cannot come about via a 'White Knight versus Dark Knight' world view. They cannot even come about through a dilution of this moral tribalism (i.e. the move from thinking 'All Tories are evil' to just thinking 'Most Tories are bad').

The three spectrums below show three versions of how the 'White Knight versus Dark Knight' dynamic translates into electoral strategy. In each version, the White Knight represents the left-of-centre party.

Strategy 1 is a purist dynamic, with a morally good White Knight 'in-group' and a morally corrupt Dark Knight 'out-group'. Within it,

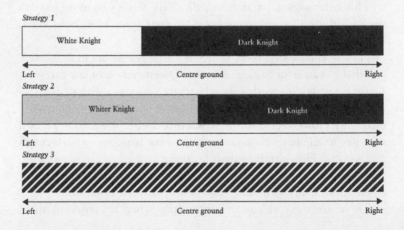

Strategy 1

| White Knight | Dark Knight |

Left   Centre ground   Right

Strategy 2

| Whiter Knight | Dark Knight |

Left   Centre ground   Right

Strategy 3

Left   Centre ground   Right

even a single dividing issue – such as having a different view about water nationalisation – is enough to out-group someone.

Strategy 2 is also a 'White Knight versus Dark Knight' dynamic, but a more moderate one. The White Knight is several degrees less good and the Dark Knight several degrees less bad. This is exemplified by Ed Miliband's failed '35 per cent strategy' in 2015 (mobilising Labour plus attracting Lib Dems), or by the idea of a 'progressive alliance'. In effect, it's a Get Out the Vote tactic, where all the basically good, progressive people line up for one side.

Supporters of Strategy 1 fear that we will have to dilute our in-group too much. Strategy 2 advocates, meanwhile, point to the irrelevance of Strategy 1. Diluting to a darker shade of grey would be better than having the Dark Knight in government, they argue.

The implication of both Strategy 1 and Strategy 2 is that every member of the population has a sort of percentage score for how left-wing they are. The question for a political movement, this logic argues, is simply where you draw the line. True Corbynites might want Labour to rely only on voters with a left-wing score of 80 per cent or more. Soft-leftists might go lower, to 65 per cent and above. 'Moderates', the notion says, would happily go further still – to those with scores as low as 40 per cent or 30 per cent, thus bringing immoral right-wingers into the big tent. Compass chair Neal Lawson's criticisms of New Labour follow precisely this logic: 'The wrong people were voting Labour . . . What meaningful [political] project includes everyone?'[16] Politics, by this rationale, can only be meaningful if it's non-inclusive.

Strategy 3 is different. It's a model where all the individuals in a society are complex – be they rich or poor, black or white, young or old, working or middle class – with some progressiveness and some conservatism within them. The role of left-of-centre politicians is to identify the progressive traits and reassure the non-progressive ones. Tony Blair's success came through the promise that his governments would 'serve people of all ages and backgrounds, including those who didn't vote for us at all'.[17]

This is the Rawlsian approach, rather than the Manichean one. It seeks a settlement with which everyone is satisfied, where the different needs of individuals are fulfilled in a progressive way (so far as they don't come at the expense of others).[18] Pursuing this could involve greater sacrifices from more privileged people. But it wouldn't set out to demonise or outlaw any group.

CIRCUMSTANCE AND LIVED EXPERIENCE

Some readers will feel that the above is stating the obvious. However, they might ask, what about people who *aren't* exceptions to any rule? Of course, there is the odd *Telegraph* reader who bucks the trend and votes Labour, but there are others who fully subscribe to stereotype.

Although these straight-down-the-line Dark Knights are rarer than many think, this is a valid point. It brings us to the role of life circumstance.

As far as the difference between left and right can be summed up, it's that the former errs towards nurture and the latter towards nature. A tendency to believe that social circumstances determine outcomes makes the left favour more equality and education – to level life chances. It makes us lobby for penal reform (because crime is so rooted in social problems and poverty). It makes us disavow nativism or colonialism (realising how lucky we are to be born in the UK) and support the welfare state (because we ourselves might fall on hard times). It leads us to frequently back intervention in the economy, redistribution, unionisation and the public sector, all of which reduce the impact of social luck.

This is founded on John Locke's belief in the 'blank slate'. Writing in the seventeenth century, Locke argued that people are born neither intrinsically good nor intrinsically bad, but are shaped by their environment. His philosophy guided Rawls's view that true fairness can only be achieved by setting aside life experiences.

So it's alarming that we have reached a point where left-wingers feel vindicated in tweeting '#WhyImVotingUkip, because I'm uneducated, uncultured, white and old', or in distributing posters in UKIP target seats, splashing the ultra-Thatcherite message: 'Totally failed at life? Then why not blame a foreigner. It's so much easier than taking responsibility for your own poor choices.'

The view that people are shaped by circumstance is something the populist left applies to crime, education or employment but is less comfortable applying to politics. Many would give the benefit of the doubt to someone caught looting or setting fires in the London riots much more easily than to someone who went on an English Defence League (EDL) march – despite a clear correlation with deprivation in both cases.[19]

The same is true with more general immigration sentiment. Politicians have learned their lesson following the 2010 Gillian Duffy incident, but there remain sections of the left who conflate concerns about immigration with immorality.[20] This seems dangerous, given that these concerns tally so heavily with factors like age, wealth, education and region.

Indeed, studies show how dependent on circumstance views about immigration are.[21] Opinion research, compiled following thousands of interviews, finds that about three quarters of Brits are sceptical about immigration to a greater or lesser degree. The subgroups within this tend to be economically insecure, older and non-university educated, or – particularly in the case of those most hostile to immigration – all three. Interestingly, research often finds fewer differences than we might expect in attitudes between those of white British heritage and those of Asian descent.[22]

Most other evidence backs this up. Fears about immigration are more common among those genuinely fearful of job competition and those who grew up in a different period. Once you whittle away these aspects of life experience, very few are as innately reactionary as the Dark Knight myth supposes.

This should not alter our views on migration policy. But it should change how we see those on the other side of the debate.

Arguing that political attitudes are linked to background is weak on its own, even if it is true. It can lead to patronising approaches and excuse-making. Indeed, left populists are often the guiltiest of misusing this argument – casting opponents of migration as victims of Tory brainwashing. This is effectively a Dark Knight approach of its own. It allows working-class immigration-sceptics to be moved out of the Dark Knight category and into the 'oppressed' White Knight column.

The approach I'm taking here doesn't seek to do this – despite how the previous passage may initially read.

To explain why, let's move to the groups we really struggle to see the good in – the bankers, the Tories, the 4x4 drivers at the gates of private schools, the members of the Countryside or Taxpayers' alliances. We can excuse the morals of the out-of-work scaffolder voting for the Brexit Party, the Dark Knight believer might say. But can we really do the same for the tax accountant voting Tory?[23]

This is the case made by those who oppose the word 'chav' while deriding other demographics such as 'gammon' (a left-populist shorthand for white, lower-middle-class baby-boomers).[24] And it is one which entirely misses the point. My argument is not about pitying people who 'lash out' against immigration when they should be blaming 'neoliberalism'. It's that everyone's values, from the top to the bottom of society, are significantly – often definitively – shaped by circumstance.

Let's take two imaginary people with similar 'natural' characteristics – both intelligent, both conventional. The first comes from a suburban household in the Home Counties. They're private-school educated and go on to work as a corporate solicitor, buying a flat in London using a parental nest-egg. They tend to think the Tories are a safer bet for their future. The second is of Asian heritage and comes from a northern city and a working-class background. They leave school at sixteen and get a job as a mechanic. They rely on in-work benefits and live in social housing, and vote Labour to improve the services they rely on.

These stereotypes are deliberately crude, with all 'complexity' stripped out. Nevertheless, can we make a moral judgement about either character? The first, on paper, sits in the Dark Knight column on most issues: privileged, southern, a gentrifier, a Tory, a private-sector employee. The latter sits on the White Knight side of the ledger. Yet both are products of environment, and live their lives accordingly. They have decent instincts but are also motivated by things which benefit them personally. If they had been switched at birth, they would probably have gone on to live roughly the same lives as each other, and to vote in roughly the same ways.

Of course, the role of Labour is to radically cut the gap between these two hypothetical figures. But this does not require a moral condemnation of one over the other. Someone better off whose interests are served by voting Tory is no more innately selfish than someone worse off whose interests lie in voting Labour.

Evidence backs up the idea that our values are products of circumstance. In 1971, 81 per cent of those brought up in all-Labour households went on to vote Labour – and 75 per cent of those from all-Tory households went on to vote Tory.[25] By 2003 this was down to 62 per cent and 67 per cent, perhaps indicating more autonomy.[26] But the correlations are still strong.[27]

The process is complex, with some 'incorrectly guessing' their family's political stances,[28] or deviating from their parents' views as they mature.[29] Change, when it does happen, is usually gradual.

There are, no doubt, left-wingers from conservative backgrounds who might feel that they have pulled themselves up by their ideological bootstraps. But, like our economy's 'rags to riches' millionaires, these self-made progressives are exceptions to the rule, not proof of it.

There are exceptional people who would have the same ideals regardless of circumstance (and who we like to think we would be among). But life experience plays a defining role for most.

There is still a risk, in writing the above, that we are denying our opponents their autonomy. Yet this is only condescending if it assumes that we progressives are different; that we can see past our lived experience in ways that others cannot. But the obvious truth is that our values also come from life circumstances. We no more have a definitive moral grasp than anyone.

The children of Middlesbrough tyre-fitters are disproportionately likely to grow up with certain politics. The children of Berkshire accountants over-index in other values. And the children of Southwark academics will often have another set, too. Many of those on anti-austerity marches would be card-carrying Tories, had they been born to Berkshire accountants – and vice versa.

Table 6.2.

	Populist-left analysis	Pluralist-left analysis
View of *deprived* reactionaries	Sympathetic – products of inequality, who know not what they do	Products of life experience – thus inconclusive
View of *privileged* reactionaries	Unsympathetic – financially privileged and should know better	Products of life experience – thus inconclusive
View of progressives	Enlightened, definitive and clear	Products of life experience – thus inconclusive

This is why my analysis is different from the patronising idea that middle-class progressives understand working-class people better than they understand themselves. The left-pluralist view should be that *all* perspectives are partial. The table below shows the difference.

Given the strong correlations between values and background, the only alternative I can see is that differences in values are genetic. In other words, that children of Berkshire accountants are inherently more right-wing than those of Southwark academics and that, if the two groups were switched at birth, their politics would switch with them.

This is a worrying view. If we say politics are tied to genetics, then we open the door to views which are more common on the far right than the left. Hence – assuming we reject the idea of genetic primacy – we must accept that moral condemnation of those with different values is, in a sense, at odds with egalitarianism.

Far from censoring progressive values, the pluralist approach is an articulation of them. It asks that we allow for 'nurture' at all levels of society. And it lets Labour become the party of equal life chances, rather than the preserve of certain niche values: magnanimous in social victories, post-materialist in tastes and dismissive of those who feel differently.

One criticism of this is that it is 'relativist', blocking our convictions about right and wrong. If progressive values are skewed by life experience – if we too 'know not what we do' – then how can we believe in anything? Can we oppose Iain Duncan Smith's attitude to unemployment? Is a Nigel Farage wrong to say foreign HIV sufferers should be banned from the NHS? Or is our disagreement with these stances also skewed by circumstance?

There are two considerations in answering this – the first at the level of judging individuals, the second at the level of wider conclusions about right and wrong.

When it comes to individuals, a critique might be that my argument says two people who are clearly morally different are the same. For instance, you could deny Martin Luther King his extraordinariness or excuse Mussolini his heinousness and argue that they are both just products of circumstances.

So, it is important to clarify: I'm not denying that there are more and less moral individuals. I'm merely saying those individuals are distributed across society and the political spectrum. I tend to think there is a mix of morality and immorality in most people – with a few very moral or very immoral outliers. If we look at an individual's life in the whole, we can decide how good or bad they really are. Everything we know about Boris Johnson, for example, suggests he is pretty dishonest and self-serving. But I don't attribute this to his political views.

In other words, the 'circumstance' argument is entirely about *groups* with political, national, ideological or religious allegiances. It's not about individuals. It therefore allows that Mussolini was highly immoral as a single person, but hesitates to say that the millions of ordinary Italians who followed him were also inherently bad. Statistically, we must acknowledge that many of us would have been sucked in if we had lived their lives.[30] Indeed, we need only to look at history to see the truth in this. The prevailing norms in every society 300 years ago involved attitudes and behaviours which would now have you socially outcast or imprisoned.

Moreover, many of the individuals who do the most evil things – be it Mussolini, Stalin, Bin Laden or Anders Breivik – believe they possess a moral vision which justifies significant collateral damage. They often think this vision is singular, pure and absolute, and thus that enemies of it are enemies of all that is good.[31] In other words, the historical figures who behave most immorally are often the most vehement believers in their own White Knight status. Instead of stopping us from 'relativising' bad people, a strong belief in the Dark Knight can lead us to do or tolerate bad things ourselves.

This brings us to the other anti-'relativist' critique of the circumstance argument – namely that it stops us telling right from wrong. If our values are merely products of our experience, how can we recommend them to others in good conscience?

This is where the Rawls distinction between 'right' and 'good' comes in. We cannot say with certainty that our values are good and others' are bad; less still that *we* are good and others are bad. But we can – by looking beyond our own interests and experiences – consider what true fairness looks like, and thus whether one policy or another is objectively right.

From this original position, some arguments can be dismissed in seconds – like Farage's views on HIV sufferers. Others involve more thought – e.g. the balance of public and private sector, or what sorts of taxation are 'fair'. But an acknowledgement of circumstance does not stop us from saying it is right to tax bankers, increase foreign aid or get rid of private education. All it makes us do is argue the case as objectively and logically as we can and remove moral judgements of those who disagree.

7

The Case against the Dark Knight Continued (Policy)

Let's continue to focus on the weaknesses of the Dark Knight fable, looking at the dangers of giving policies and strategies a moral status.

DEPTH: STRATEGY, VALUES AND MORALS

Complexity and circumstance get us so far. But what if somebody's politics are inherently different – if they were *born* with conservative values?

The Dark Knight assumption might be that the right-winger in question has no excuse. To be more conservative is, all things being equal, to be more self-interested and malevolent. For instance, one commentator argued, in 2013, that the Tories were genuinely 'evil'.[1]

This assumption is implicit in almost everything the populist left does. It often takes the form of throw-away mischaracterisations about others' politics – e.g. claims that Tories 'hate the poor' or that Blairites enjoy the prospect of Iraqis dying. These assertions block debate, and make politics toxic. They lead us to the third flaw of the Dark Knight myth, which is that it fails to account for a person or group's moral depth.

The truth is that it is possible to support 'bad' policies despite 'good' values, and to possess 'bad' values despite 'good' morals. The lack of depth within the Dark Knight myth, however, groups these things as one. It allows a relatively superficial aspect of a person (e.g. their views on school funding) to become a proxy for their basic decency.

Historically, this has always been a dangerous attitude, providing an entry point for extremists. As Hannah Arendt wrote, 'One of the greatest advantages of the totalitarian elites of the twenties and thirties was to turn any statement of fact into a question of motive.'

To elaborate, let's look at two approaches to the link between politics and morality – shown in the table below. I have developed these myself, and believe the first is essentially how populists view the relationship, and the second is how pluralists view it.

The first is the two-tier version of political morals. This acknowledges that there is a superficial element of 'politics', which relates to electability (the need to perform in public, and so on). I have called this tier 'image'. Sitting beneath this is a core of essential substance – the bulk of the iceberg – which combines the policies someone supports, their values and even their basic morals. I have called this tier 'principles'. This understanding of the relationship between politics and morality acknowledges that you need style as well as substance. But it sees everything beneath style as the same thing.

Populists adopt the two-tier approach almost without thinking. They use it casually, and occasionally cynically, to pull the debate on to the level they feel most comfortable with.[2] Hence, cutting the welfare bill can only be done because you wish to see poor people die.

The second, deeper way of looking at things is the four-tier model.

'Image' again describes politics at its most superficial. (Do we call our proposed wealth tax a 'silver spoon levy' or a 'strivers' windfall'? Do we need a new logo? Is the messaging right?)

'Policy and strategy' is as it sounds: the policies and electoral strategies chosen in order to fulfil your values.

'Political values' describes what the core ideals look like. If you were designing the planet in a vacuum, without interference, would you want a world that was equal, liberal and community-based? Or would you want one defined by tradition, competition and personal responsibility?

Table 7.1.

Two-tier model (populist)	Four-tier model (pluralist)
Image	Image
Principles	Policy and strategy
	Political values
	Personal morals

And 'personal morals' describes basic questions of the human fabric: would you take pleasure in the suffering of others; would you steal from the charity bucket; would you save a drowning stranger?

I will refer to these as 'image', 'strategy', 'values' and 'morals' from here on. The central idea is that a person's opinions about strategy (or policy) are not a straight proxy for their values, and that their values aren't a proxy for their morals. This allows greater depth and texture than the two-tier model is capable of.

The MP Jo Cox's maiden speech to Parliament contained the famous lines 'we are far more united and have far more in common than that which divides us'.[3] After her tragic murder by a far-right terrorist, the speech came to feel portentous: a source of hope in a fractured post-Brexit climate. So, how do we put Jo Cox's words into practice, given there are political ideologies we vehemently disagree with?

The two-tier model, illustrated below, has no capacity to identify shared ground. It accepts that people have different views about how to win elections or about which leaders come across better. But it presents two monolithic blocs once you get beneath this: left-of-centre people who are good, and right-of-centre people who are bad. (NB: the diagram only uses the two main parties, and deploys rough proxy positions for the image tier. The exercise is primarily about the relationship between the tiers, not the precise definitions.)

This is the thinking we encourage when we describe the Tories as evil – or when we blame every policy divergence on a difference in values. It's an approach which ultimately causes the left monolithic

The two-tier model

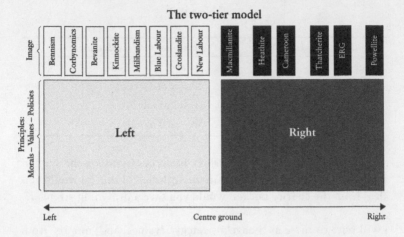

bloc to shrink, as those with different views on policies are deemed immoral and driven away.

By contrast, the four-tier understanding offers a route to the 'more in common' vision. The diagram below shows why. It suggests a right-of-centre person is no more likely to be personally immoral than a left-of-centre person; there can be shared morals, even without shared values.[4]

And it also suggests that two people from different parts of the left (or of the right) still retain the same core values – even if they disagree about policy and strategy. Being a Blairite does not make you any less liberal, internationalist, egalitarian or collectivist than being a Corbynite, for example.

These are controversial claims, to some. So, let's try to back them up. We will look first at how values are different from morals, and then at how strategy and policy are different from values.

Morals run all the way across the political spectrum according to the four-tier model, whereas values are particular to the two wings of politics. But how do values and morals differ? Isn't there a risk that this justifies the selfishness and cruelty of the right?

The first thing to clarify is that, just because morals stretch across the spectrum, this does not mean I am saying that all people have hearts of gold. I am not making any claim about the essence of

The four-tier model

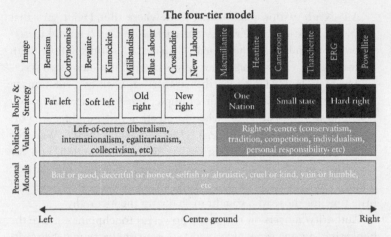

Image	Bennism	Corbynomics	Bevanite	Kinnockite	Milibandism	Blue Labour	Croslandite	New Llabour	Macmillanite	Heathite	Cameroon	Thatcherite	ERG	Powellite

Policy & Strategy	Far left	Soft left	Old right	New right	One Nation	Small state	Hard right

Political Values	Left-of-centre (liberalism, internationalism, egalitarianism, collectivism, etc)	Right-of-centre (conservatism, tradition, competition, individualism, personal responsibility, etc)

Personal Morals	Bad or good, deceitful or honest, selfish or altruistic, cruel or kind, vain or humble, etc

Left   Centre ground   Right

human nature. The argument is simply that those with good morals (e.g. those who don't behave corruptly, or take pleasure in others' suffering) are not found at one end of the spectrum more than at the other, and are not particular to one political leaning.

There is plenty of anecdotal evidence for this. An example is the 2009 expenses scandal, which saw no obvious correlation between misconduct and political leaning. Those over-claiming came from across the ideological range – from members of the Socialist Campaign Group through to the 1922 Committee, and from every point between.

To take this further, let's look at psychological explanations for how people translate morals into values. How can decent individuals hold contrasting views about how to run society, with both believing that their politics are an articulation of morality? A good starting point is Jonathan Haidt's *The Righteous Mind*. This sets out six ways in which people process morality, which Haidt calls the moral 'taste buds':

- Care/Harm
- Liberty/Oppression
- Fairness/Cheating
- Loyalty/Betrayal
- Authority/Subversion
- Sanctity/Degradation

All six are within most of us, somewhere. But Haidt says that people with left-of-centre values concentrate on Care/Harm, Liberty/Oppression and, to some extent, Fairness/Cheating. Those with right-of-centre values spread themselves more thinly, across all six.

The taste buds Haidt identifies are driven both by evolutionary psychology and by culture. For example, the Authority/Subversion taste bud was vital at points when 'protecting order and fending off chaos' was the abiding concern.[5] In the Second World War, for instance, the UK had a strong leader, Winston Churchill, and the war effort was based on everyone fulfilling their role in a largely unquestioning way. At that juncture, many of us would have had little time for those who sought to shake up the hierarchy.

Authority/Subversion remains a powerful touchpoint – hence the hankering, among some older voters, for a simpler time (when Britain ran the world, when the man was head of the family, and so on). It is not an 'immoral' basis for a set of values. And even if we do not see much modern relevance for it, we make a big mistake if we accuse those who do of lacking basic decency.[6]

The same goes for the other taste buds the left struggles with. The Sanctity/Degradation taste bud stems from concern for hygiene and the human body, which was necessary at more uncertain points in history. Culturally speaking, Sanctity/Degradation leads people in divinity-based countries like India to adopt different rituals. In the UK it explains continued intolerance about homosexuality among some religious groups.[7] But the roots of the taste bud are primal to the human species, causing us to invest certain entities or ideas with sacred value, and to fear that those things are being polluted.

The Loyalty/Betrayal taste bud is the impulse that tempts even the most fair-minded people to prioritise friends and family. When it takes on a political dimension it can lead to policy views we are uncomfortable with (e.g. a 'charity begins at home' hostility to foreigners). But anyone who has stuck up for a friend they knew to be in the wrong has accessed this taste bud at some point.

Meanwhile, the Fairness/Cheating taste bud is the impulse that makes us angry at queue-jumpers. It manifests itself in left-wing sentiment, like hostility to unearned wealth, but also in right-wing sentiment about welfare provisions. Middle-class progressives may find anger about benefits inexplicable. But think about the frustration if we felt we were routinely doing the washing-up for a flatmate who did not return the favour.

The emphasis placed on each of Haidt's taste buds determines whether someone comes to hold right-wing or left-wing values. Some of the taste buds have ceased to have much use in peaceful, secular societies. Yet their existence shows how people arrive at different values, via morals no more 'evil' than our own.

Another way of looking at this is the British Values Survey. Developed through polling since 1973, this combines Abraham Maslow's hierarchy of needs with Shalom Schwartz's twenty-one core human values. The model identifies three overarching values' sets:

- *Groupish values* are based on perceived threats and anxiety about change. Those with these values think in ultra-local ways. Groupish values are more common among older people, who often seek familiarity, security and continuity. Politically, this can manifest itself in social conservatism – epitomised by support for Brexit and 'no nonsense' policies on crime – sometimes alongside support for redistribution.

- *Individualistic values* are based on competition and aspiration. Those with a concentration of these values are optimistic and ambitious, driven by achievement and recognition. The values are common among young people and some BME communities, as well as upwardly mobile middle-class groups. Politically, individualistic values manifest themselves in economic pragmatism, and in an emphasis on education, hard work and achievement.

- *Post-materialist values* are based on inner fulfilment and a desire to understand the world and behave ethically. Those with more post-materialist values are often better off and university educated, and seek creativity, stimulation and understanding. Politically, they tend to be socially liberal, and to favour universal fairness, internationalism and sustainability.

As with Haidt's six taste buds, we have aspects of all three values' sets within us, but are driven by one more than another. This explains why two people can see the same thing differently. For instance, deciding to send your child to an inner-city state school with poor exam results could be a sign of moral good, according to post-materialist values. But according to other values, it represents a moral failure to do the best for your family.

The key thing about the three values' sets is that they stem from different needs, not different morals. And this means we shouldn't seek to categorise their worth. Should governments aim to convert the BME 'individualist' to ethical self-sacrifice, or demand that the 'groupish' pensioner becomes a post-materialist? Is the compulsion to write a novel of ideas more moral than the compulsion to own a nice car? Are you a better person for going on a climate-change march than you are if you give up your time for a Neighbourhood Watch scheme? I would be loath to answer yes to these questions. Indeed, post-materialists, with their quest for social purpose and self-realisation, are seeking something no less 'selfish'; they're simply less concerned about money and resources, often because they have less need to be.

Beyond Haidt's taste buds and the British Values Survey, there are other models of how morals translate into values. But what all of these have in common is that they are not pejorative about the moral worth of different ideals. Instead, they accept that everyone is different. Some love novelty; others dislike change. Some want to show they are successful; others shun the finer things. Self-reliance, competence, curiosity and even emotional intelligence are not distributed equally. As long as humans are born with different cap-abilities, needs and preferences, there will be some diversity of values.

Isaiah Berlin, one of the biggest figures in the pluralist tradition, sums this up:

> I am not a relativist; I do not say 'I like my coffee with milk and you like it without; I am in favour of kindness and you prefer concen-tration camps' ... But I do believe that there is a plurality of values which men can and do seek, and that these values differ ... If a man pursues one of these values, I, who do not, am able to understand why he pursues it ... Hence the possibility of human understanding.[8]

The problem, of course, is that the fulfilment of one person's values has implications for another's. The elderly traditionalist in Thanet may want security, but what about the needs of the elderly traditionalist in Syria, for whom UK refuge offers a more pressing form of safety?

Karl Marx popularised the phrase 'From each according to his ability, to each according to his need,' a sentiment which sought to organise society so that everyone could get what they required from it. If we pursue this logic, then there should be ways of fulfilling the population's diverse values' needs without judging those with different needs. Looking at the situation from Rawls's veil of ignorance, not knowing our own values, what type of society would we devise? How would we allow for individualists' need for achievement without undermining post-materialist egalitarianism? How would we fulfil the pro-global impulses of one values cluster, without dismissing the traditionalist instincts of another?

I will not pursue this further now. But, ultimately, much of the above comes down to tolerance and willingness to give the benefit of the doubt. Many supporters of both left and right parties would pass simple ethical tests – helping a young mum carry a pram down a flight of stairs, for instance. We should use this as our moral basis, rather than voting behaviour or political ideals.

Those with differing values may share decent morals. But how can we claim, as the four-tier model does, that different strategies are rooted in shared values?

It is worth clarifying: I am merely saying that those with different strategies and policy positions from across the left have a *common origin*, in the form of their motivations at the ballot box or their inspirations for going into politics. Alastair Campbell and Diane Abbott, for example, have politics which are rooted in similar values – even if they disagree, on almost every point, about how to enact these values.

In the case of left-of-centre values, this means a blend of egalitarianism, internationalism, social liberalism, communitarianism and social justice. For sure, there are small differences: New Labour followers are more comfortable with competition; Blue Labourites are more traditionalist; the Bennite left are less internationalist. But ultimately, unlike right-wingers – whose ideals comprise tradition, authority, competition, individualism, self-reliance, and so on – most who describe themselves as 'left of centre' share these values.

This is reflected in the fact that many of those considered 'centrist' have radically different roots. Left and right populists may treat Tony Blair and David Cameron as identikits. Yet Blair first ran for Labour under Michael Foot, flirted with Trotskyism, and stated in his maiden speech that 'socialism most corresponds to an existence that is both rational and moral. It stands for cooperation, not confrontation; for fellowship, not fear. It stands for equality.' Cameron, by contrast, entered the Tory fold during the high noon of Thatcherism. It was just that they both adapted to political reality, to try and enact their values, hence they compromised and borrowed.

As political psychologist George Lakoff writes, 'There are moderates, but there is no ideology of the moderate.'[9] According to Lakoff, most people frame things using an essentially left-of-centre prism or an essentially right-of-centre one – even if they sometimes use ideas from the other side.

(This is a problem which Change UK, formerly the TIG, failed to appreciate, and which ultimately contributed to their implosion. Other explicitly 'centrist' parties will face the same challenge.)

Values and strategy correspond with the terms 'ends' and 'means', commonly associated with Anthony Crosland's 1956 book, *The Future of Socialism*. In the book, Crosland distinguished between what the left wants (ends) and how it plans to get there (means); between left-of-centre ideals, and policy techniques. His frustration was with those who conflate the two in a way that means socialist values aren't achieved.

Crosland argued that equality is the overriding socialist end; methods like nationalisation are just the means.[10] He thought a property-owning, capitalist economy could be consistent with the values of socialism, if there was low inequality, high social mobility and no poverty, class hierarchy or power imbalances. This may have placed him on the 'right of the Labour Party' at the level of strategy and policy. But he was no less committed to social justice, community, equality, and so on. He just had different ideas about how to fulfil these goals.

If we take the topic of equality, we can see how people with similar values advocate different policies. One might say we should call the bluff of mobile capital, and create a maximum wage. Another might believe 'pre-distribution' is a less clunky tool. A third might sacrifice a high rate of corporation tax and focus on multilateral approaches to global profits. A fourth might wish to cut taxes on earnings and raise them on wealth. A fifth might decide inequality is, for now, too hard to fix through taxes, and that public-sector funding and reform we our best hope of addressing it.[11] And all would have different views about how electorally palatable and technically doable the above policies are, even though their basic goal is the same.

Looking at the Labour civil wars which raged from 2015 onwards, we can see why the two-tier and four-tier models are important. Both of Corbyn's leadership victories were successfully framed by left populists using the two-tier framework.[12] In both, the arguments centred around principles versus image. Corbyn was presented as scruffy, off-message and unelectable, but as personally decent and true to Labour values and policies. His opponent Liz Kendall, by contrast, was seen as slick and palatable to middle England, but as a betrayer of progressive values and – for some – morally bankrupt as a result.

This damaged the debate. Strategy differences were taken as a statement about the values and even the morals of Corbyn's opponents. The choice became one of voting for a good person who couldn't win an election, or for a bad person who could.

Critics of Corbyn hold some responsibility for letting the debate be couched in these terms. Polly Toynbee wrote that, 'Free to dream, I'd be [to the] left of Jeremy Corbyn – but we can't gamble the future on him,' the suggestion being that Corbyn was the only candidate of principle, but didn't have the right image.[13]

Tony Blair, by contrast, admitted that the issue was not one of image: 'I wouldn't want to win on an old-fashioned leftist platform . . . even if I thought it was the route to victory.'[14] Yet he didn't do enough to clarify that the disagreement was down to policy, not values. So, he too operated within the two-tier model, inviting the familiar accusation that he didn't sign up to basic Labour principles – and was not, therefore, a good person.

Only by adopting a four-tier model (which teases apart policy, values and morals) could the real point have been made – which is that Corbyn's policies and strategies would fail to deliver left-wing goals.[15]

An example of the 'two-tier' model at its worst in the 2015 contest was the accusation that those who opposed Corbyn were 'Tory scum'. This gained currency in relation to Liz Kendall, partly thanks to her view that Labour needed to reduce the national debt. Her policy position was that it was actually left-wing to address the debt: 'There's nothing progressive about spending more on debt than on our children's education.' It was also based on the premise that Labour lacked fiscal credibility, and wouldn't deliver progressive goals without changing this. Kendall's view thus reflected major differences with Corbyn's. She saw reducing the national debt as consistent with left-of-centre values and goals. He didn't. If she was wrong – economically or electorally – then she was wrong at the level of policy/strategy.[16]

Instead, Kendall's position was interpreted as a statement about her values – leading to her dismissal as a 'Tory'. And the two-tier model allowed this to become a statement about her morals – hence the 'scum' adage.

Believing the country needs to address the national debt does not, in fact, make you a 'Tory' (John McDonnell adopted precisely the same line as Liz Kendall a few months later).[17] And having Tory values doesn't make you 'scum'. Yet the two-tier model allows these big leaps to be made with ease: debt-cutter = right-winger = scum.

The 'Tory scum' epithet was the preserve of keyboard warriors. However, high-profile left populists fed the two-tier approach that drove it. Many mischaracterised those who didn't support Corbyn as 'neo-cons', closet Tories and inequality enthusiasts, despite widespread evidence that this was not their motivation at all.[18] Others encouraged the idea that Corbyn-sceptics were self-interested, careerist or corrupt. A dog-whistle politics emerged as a result, where every dispute shook down to a clash between basic decency and naked self-interest.

For a more concrete example, let's look at the vote about intervention in Syria in 2015. This set the stage for one of the first battles between the pro- and anti-Corbyn wings of Labour. MPs like Liz Kendall saw intervention in Syria as consistent with their internationalism. Hilary Benn's speech in favour of intervening drew a visibly emotional response from Kendall, not by appealing to flag-waving nationalism, but through invoking the Internationalist Brigades' opposition to fascism.[19]

Corbyn, by contrast, saw intervention as incompatible with internationalist values. He thought it would make the situation worse. Thus, differences between Kendall and Corbyn did not lie at the level of values. The opinions of both were built on a shared commitment to internationalism, but diverged on the question of how this should manifest itself. If Kendall shared Corbyn's perception that intervening in Syria was an act of colonial aggression, she would have opposed it. If Corbyn shared Kendall's conviction that intervention would save Syrian lives, he would have supported it.

Was Kendall placing too much faith in a mode of liberal intervention debunked by Iraq? Was Corbyn seeing things through an anti-imperialist prism which became irrelevant decades ago? Thanks to the two-tier analysis, these questions barely came up. Corbyn said he was 'appalled' by the 'jingoism' of MPs like Kendall, thus pushing the debate down to the level of values.[20] And for other populists it fell further still, and became a case of divergent morals, with those supporting intervention dubbed 'murderers' by Corbyn supporters in Parliament Square. Framing the debate as a struggle between those who want peace and love and those who want violence and death didn't get us any closer to the right outcome.

In a world where very few people are evil, and where most have respectable ideals, all that the conflation of strategy, values and morals does is encourage people to see the worst in others. It creates false divisions and, ultimately, reduces everything to a Manichean struggle.

Arguing for the four-tier model is vital if pluralists of all leanings are to rescue politics from this fate. To win arguments against our opponents, we must engage at the true level where differences exist.

INEXORABILITY OF ARGUMENTS

Some left populists might admit that it's a dead end to obsess over whether supporters of different policies are immoral. However, the argument against taking sides is less obvious when it comes to the policies themselves – causes, interests, institutions, countries, sectors, and so on. Surely, we can at least say that inequality, US foreign policy or the private sector are inherently bad?

The response to this links again to the Crosland distinction between ends and means (ends being the ultimate, unchanging ideal, and means being the way you get there in a given context). By supporting a set of means unswervingly, you can quickly arrive at a point where they clash with your ends.

This is what 'inexorability' means. It describes the part of the Dark Knight myth which breeds not sectarianism but dogma. It is the phenomenon whereby we support a cause, policy, institution, country or method, despite it failing to achieve our ideals, because we believe it is moral *in itself*.

Trade unions are a good example. They are part of the solution to a range of practices – from zero-hours contracts to unpaid internships to the gig economy. Falling union membership is a real concern. Yet as the tube strike case study demonstrated, there is a possibility that we side with them come what may – and that this ultimately undermines both progressive goals and union credibility. With better-off professions now heavily over-represented in the labour movement, this risk is real.[21]

These are the sorts of question that the inexorability issue raises. Is our preference for certain methods infinite? Is our support for nationalisation limitless? Does our opposition to foreign intervention apply regardless? If the 'class war' was won, would we continue to fight it?

If we answer yes to these points, then we end up dragging our policies to the point where they are incompatible with social justice. We move away from Rawls's vision of a society which works for everyone, and towards a politics which is doctrinaire. The best we can hope for, through this approach, is to be right more often than wrong.

The risks of inexorability are serious. For example, the hard left's Euroscepticism – based on opposition to the use of free trade as a means – was maintained even while the EU achieved left-wing ends, like cultural diversity, prosperity and peace for poorer countries, and workers' rights.[22] In some cases, the Dark Knight's inexorability is actively dangerous, such as with the unflinching sympathy it justifies in relation to Russia or Venezuela – long after both countries' policies had become impossible to square with social justice.

Thinking about inexorability involves asking ourselves hypothetical questions. Let's do this in relation to economic equality. This is something which we on the left want more of. If you asked us whether we were pro-equality or anti-, we would of course say pro-. The next question, though, is how much equality we want? We are all in favour of *more*, but at what point would we stop? For genuine Trotskyites the answer might be absolute, total economic equality. And that's fair enough. Most left-wingers, though, are not radical enough to believe in a world with no commerce and no rewards for creativity or social contribution. So, what is optimal equality?

It is hard to put a number on this. Rawls – working on a non-economic basis – argued that unequal opportunities were always wrong, and that inequalities of outcome were only acceptable if they helped the poorest most. In other words, inequality cannot carry across generations, and incentives must benefit everyone.

We can agree that our deeply unequal society is a long way off this, and for now that is enough. However, if we sign up to Rawls's prescription, or something like it, we must accept that there could come a point where we had delivered economic equality so successfully that we needed less of it in order to achieve growth. In this circumstance, progressives would need to do the unthinkable and argue for more inequality.

This is so distant that it is barely worth considering. Yet such thought experiments matter because they compel us to define what we stand *for*. This is more sophisticated than aligning ourselves with a set of causes and interests which we back to the hilt – and against others which we fight unwaveringly.

Another example is gentrification. In London, this is rightly seen as stripping neighbourhoods of their identity, and creating tensions between affluent newcomers and existing communities. It has made it near-impossible for low-income people to buy or rent in the capital. Even if we do not make moral judgements about those moving in, we can surely oppose gentrification itself?

Yet here too there is a risk. One of the left's core aims is that different communities mingle. In a perfect society, the average classroom would be a cross-section of the population at large. So, gentrification is a good thing when it takes the form of those from better-off backgrounds moving to areas where they are under-represented. The problem arises once it goes so far the other way that they are over-represented.

In areas like Lambeth or Hackney, this is now happening. But the role of gentrification is that of means, not end; neither positive nor negative in itself. To support gentrification in the Lambeth of the 1970s would be to favour the middle classes moving to underpopulated areas where they had once have been too snobbish to venture. To favour the same in the Lambeth of 2020 would mean something very different.

Siding inexorably with certain countries, causes, interests and institutions leads to the left losing the argument. There are two reasons why.

For one thing, it prevents us renewing ourselves. Once means become invested with morality, then you cannot adapt your values to changing circumstances. Those who challenge orthodoxy are shouted down; those who raise doubts are cast as traitors; new approaches, which might yield left-wing outcomes, become taboo.[23]

On defence policy, for instance, Jeremy Corbyn is committed to unilateral disarmament on the grounds that it will limit the danger of nuclear weapons being used. Others are committed to multilateral disarmament for the same reasons. Yet a debate is constantly closed down by unilateralists like Corbyn, who invest unilateralism *itself* with morality.[24]

The same goes for foreign policy. Military inaction is just one method to achieve peace, not an ideal per se. But you sense that the populist left now see non-intervention as an 'end' in itself, which they would back regardless of circumstance – be it 2003 Iraq, 1994 Rwanda, 1960s Vietnam, or 1939 Germany.

These approaches characterise what Maajid Nawaz, co-founder of the think tank Quilliam, calls the 'regressive left'. This refers to groups who see the choice between challenging extremism and challenging 'Western imperialism' as a zero-sum game.[25] Organisations like Stop the War allow their support for anti-interventionist policies and anti-West causes to be unconditional. Hence, they find themselves taking reactionary positions because they always back the same side.

As well as preventing discussion, there is an electoral problem with an unswerving support for White Knight causes. A question posed by the novelist Howard Jacobson in 2015 summed this up. Despite agreeing with Corbyn on taxation and welfare, Jacobson asked:

> Why can't we oppose the inequities of a society weighted in favour of wealth ... without at the same time having to snuggle up to Putin, pal out with Hamas, and make apologies for extremists? ... Corbyn's distinction is to have held on to these articles of faith while all about him have been losing theirs. In an age of facing-both-ways, he doggedly faces in one direction only.[26]

Corbyn gives the impression he would support certain sides regardless. For Jacobson, this casts his entire judgement into doubt. Corbyn becomes a stopped clock that is right twice a day, lacking credibility even when voters agree with him.

As a result, while people might agree with Corbyn on some policies, they fear he would pursue lost causes after the facts had changed. Many may back rail nationalisation, for example, but worry that Corbyn's opposition to the private sector is so automatic that he would want to nationalise everything else, too, leading to reactionary outcomes.

This is my interpretation of Jacobson's view. Yet it is backed up by sporadic opinion research suggesting that voters agreed with many Corbyn policies – as long as he was not associated with them.

This type of polling was often circulated by Corbyn supporters to suggest that the only reason he was unpopular was the media smearing him rather than focusing on his ideas.[27] Yet far from showing that voters were pro-Corbyn in spite of how he was presented, these polls actually showed that people were anti-Corbyn in spite of agreeing with him. There is a strong streak of egalitarianism in the British public. But, in the same way as you would trust the football opinion of a neutral over a rabid supporter of one team, the electorate needs to know that left-wing policies will be applied in a restrained and non-partisan way before they will back them.

Public spending is the ultimate arena for this, with the fear being that Labour's enthusiasm for investment will saddle the country with debt.[28] In this area and others, the public is more progressive than they are given credit for.[29] Yet they will not vote for left-wing parties unless they trust that their passion for White Knight solutions is neither fanatical nor limitless.

The 2019 General Election, when Labour's 'red wall' of northern and Midlands constituencies crumbled, was a perfect example. There was deep suspicion in these seats about whether Corbyn's expensive manifesto was the product of pragmatism or of an unconditional preference for higher spending. And policies such as universal free broadband were seen as the result of an inexorable support for nationalisation.

Meanwhile, there was a sense that Corbyn opposed British interests come-what-may, thanks to a lifetime of unfailing hostility to UK foreign policy. At a cultural level, the inability of Corbyn's supporters to take a nuanced position led many voters to feel that Labour was not on their side. John McDonnell's comdemnation of Winston Churchill as a 'villain' in 2019 is just one example. This – along with countless other statements which reduced issues to black and white – gave ammunition to right-wing newspapers and convinced the public that Labour was dogmatic rather than fair-minded.

8

What is the Puppet Master?

'It was much better to imagine men in some smoky room somewhere, made mad and cynical by privilege and power, plotting over brandy. You had to cling to this sort of image, because if you didn't then you might have to face the fact that bad things happened because ordinary people, the kind who brushed the dog and told the children bed time stories, were capable of then going out and doing horrible things to other ordinary people. It was so much easier to blame it on Them.'

– *Terry Pratchett*

THE EVIL FROM ABOVE

Few see themselves in the ways described in the Dark Knight section. No one likes to think they are sectarian or partisan. Many on the populist left pride themselves on finding the good in people. There are large out-groups to whom this benefit of the doubt is not extended. But most wish, at least in principle, to take a kinder view of their opponents than the Dark Knight myth allows.

The problem is that, if 'bad people' on the right are not to blame, an alternative explanation is required for why the world is imperfect. And this leads towards a second myth – sometimes believed in tandem with the Dark Knight, sometimes as an alternative – which is almost as fanciful as the first.

The Puppet Master refers to fears about an omnipotent plutocracy, controlling our lives to protect their interests. This appears within all forms of populism. The Scottish independence and Leave campaigns both relied on the idea of a powerful elite, deaf to the will of the people. And left populism is no different.

In effect, many left populists look across the spectrum, empathise with the people they see – even those voting for Farage or sending their children to private school. They conclude that the evil must instead come from a conspiracy above. We see this in action when Richard Burgon MP proclaims that, rather than siding with Remain or Leave, 'Labour wants to reach out to the 99 per cent.' Likewise, it is present in claims that we should stop discussing left versus right and start talking about people versus elites.[1]

The Puppet Master fantasy is the cornerstone of many left-populist arguments. Corbyn himself frequently spoke in these terms,[2] and Paul Mason begins *Post-Capitalism* by describing a global power base 'cut off in their separate world', which inflicts on the population 'the democracy of riot squads, corrupt politicians, magnate-controlled newspapers and the surveillance state'.[3]

According to this analysis, 'the powerful' subvert or bypass the will of the people through force and propaganda. For example, the left-populist claim is that politicians create anti-migrant or anti-welfare feeling, rather than that they surrender to it. This provides an alternative to the Dark Knight for some and a supplement to it for others, cultivating the idea that we live in a dictatorship, not a democracy – and that those we disagree with are brainwashed. It thus avoids the sticky, Dark Knight issues which a democracy throws up when differences of opinions occur – dismissing them as products of a divide-and-rule strategy dreamed up by totalitarian elites.

Of course, there *is* such a thing as the elite. What are you, if you went to Eton, if not a member of this group? So, let's draw some distinctions. There are deserving elites (e.g. elite athletes or elite surgeons) which we need to exist to cultivate particular skills. And there are undeserving elites (e.g. students at elite schools), which exist but shouldn't.

The problem is that the term 'elite' has become allied with a third set of connotations – to do with the powerful subjugating the masses. The idea is that an undemocratic, unaccountable minority lords it over the population. Elites, according to this, conspire and plot, micromanaging society so as to secure power and reinforce privilege. They are not toffs with a silver spoon, they are Puppet Masters pulling the strings. It is this version of the term with which I am taking issue.

DESIGN AND GOVERNMENT

William Paley's 'watchmaker's analogy' was used in 1794 to back up the design argument for God's existence:

> Suppose I had found a watch upon the ground, and it should be inquired how the watch happened to be in that place ... The inference, we think, is inevitable, that the watch must have had a maker ... [who] comprehended its construction, and designed its use.

For Paley, the world was too well made to have been an accident. Of course, all evidence now suggests that Paley was wrong. But in 1794 his case was compelling.

The Puppet Master myth is rather like Paley's metaphor, except that the watch in the Puppet Master represents not the beauty of the world but its collected ugliness: warfare, inequality, poverty, global warming, refugee crises, and so on. We on the left look at these phenomena – at these ugly watches, these machine guns in the meadow – and conclude that they are too imperfect to have been produced by their surroundings. It cannot be the result of ordinary people like us or our next-door neighbours. One per cent of the population owning half the wealth does not just happen, we say. It's unnatural.

Hence, we decide there must be an architect or Puppet Master. This creator must be malign – or deeply self-interested in ways we are not. And they must hold powers which transcend our humdrum lives.

For the non-religious populist left, of course, the role of Puppet Master falls not to a supernatural force but to a malevolent plutocracy; humans, necessarily, but humans more powerful and calculating than anyone we know. Even if we never see this entity – even if people we encounter from 'elites' seem well meaning but ineffectual, or prone to follies we recognise in ourselves – it holds a grip on the imagination.

The Puppet Master explanation rests on this premise. It says that failures are rarely the result of cock-up, chaos or incompetence. Nor are they down to short-termism or weakness in the face of public opinion. And they are certainly not due to the challenges of a globalised world and an ideologically diverse electorate. Instead, they come from powerful elites: an ugly watch in a beautiful field which some sharp-suited entity has lowered down to wreak its havoc.

This Puppet Master analysis relies on a lexicon which reads agency and design into everything: political coercion; cultural hegemony; social cleansing; state-sponsored terrorism; pre-decided outcomes; oppression by a 'deep state'; the engineering of ascent; the managing of opinion; the rigging of the system; control by the 1 per cent; the construction of an acceptable mainstream, the edges of which are patrolled by a police state, and so on.

This omnipotent force is an intertwinement of 'interests' from the worlds of politics, finance, business, the judiciary, the civil service and the media. These are often referred to simply as 'they': a minority of corrupt individuals who have the power to end the world's problems but find that it serves their interests not to. In the most extreme versions of the myth, this clique of tyrants and tycoons wilfully pursues a carefully planned agenda, deliberately causing harm as a diversion tactic.

As with the Dark Knight, there are variations in how strongly populists believe in the Puppet Master. For some it is a mild suspicion that the BBC supports 'the establishment'. For others, it extends to conspiracies about Zionism and 'false flags'. However, believers in the Puppet Master have one thing in common: they are almost never associated with parties in power. Indeed, the stronger the belief, the further towards the extremes they usually end up. In the 2015 Labour leadership contest, for example, polling found that Corbyn backers were four times as likely as Liz Kendall backers to say that 'the world is controlled by a secretive elite' (and twice as likely as supporters of Andy Burnham and Yuette Cooper).[4] This is a striking finding, given the candidates' respective platforms, suggesting an exact correlation between distance from the political 'centre' and conspiracism.

This correlation is self-perpetuating. The myth leads, inevitably, to an insurrectionist approach, which sees the will of the people as unanimous. The implication is that we need only to break into the control room and we can press the peace button, twist the poverty dial to zero and put the inequality pedal into reverse.

Hence, those in positions of responsibility almost never believe in the Puppet Master. And believers in the Puppet Master almost never hold positions of responsibility. To do so would be to arrive at the mirage they have been chasing all along – to meet the Wizard of Oz.

This is part of the reason why having figures like Donald Trump and Boris Johnson in government is such a shocking development. It explains why these individuals have had to continually find new Puppet Masters to blame for thwarting them, even once in office – a process which will surely, over time, yield diminishing returns.

Generally, Puppet Master believers in office prove a crushing disappointment.[5] This is blamed on their having sold out, not on problems being harder to solve than they thought.[6] The conclusion drawn is that they have *become* the Puppet Master – not that there *isn't* a Puppet Master. Insurgent becomes incumbent, disillusionment festers, and in time the process repeats itself.[7] The present rise in populism is arguably the culmination of lower-level populist rhetoric being deployed for many years, contributing to this vicious cycle.[8]

DEFINITIONS AND CRITICISMS: WHAT CONSTITUTES A CONSPIRACY?

As with the Dark Knight, readers may be confused about where the Puppet Master myth begins and ends. We have already put a range of things under one umbrella, from the unrealistic commitments of opposition parties to the loopiest conspiracy theories. We have taken in, along the way, elements of civil libertarianism, 'opposition for its own sake' and cynicism about politics. Some may feel that, by conflating conspiracism with these other concepts, we reinforce the status quo. They may even feel that, by attacking the Puppet Master belief system we attack radicalism itself – shutting down those who call for change by always pointing out the restrictions on government.

Moreover, some may say that the Dark Knight and the Puppet Master are the same thing. The former, after all, pits strong, immoral villains against weak, moral victims.

To help explain the difference, let's define the Puppet Master. For me, it is *an analysis that underestimates the extent to which those in positions of influence are regulated by short-term pressures, external constraints and public opinion, and which overestimates their organisational, structural and coordinated power to impose an ideology, pursue their 'interests' or override public opinion.*

Unlike the Dark Knight, therefore, the Puppet Master isn't really about morals. It's about social control and how politics works. It isn't based on a 'horizontal' struggle between sides. It's based on a 'vertical' struggle between an omnipotent few and a helpless majority.

There is a moral element to this, because the myth assumes that the motives of 'elites' are self-serving. But the question at the heart of the myth is about whether those in government reflect our society or shape it. Is the power 'they' wield more absolute, coordinated and undemocratic than we realise – or less? Do businesses and the media control and manipulate public opinion – or follow, respond to and reinforce it?

Answers to these questions shape our explanations. And they underpin the list of ways in which the myth manifests itself. If I believed strongly in the Puppet Master, for instance, it would create several overlapping consequences for my politics.

First, if I was in an opposition party such as the pre-2010 Lib Dems – or even if I belonged to a backbench faction of a party in power – then I could convince myself that issues were easy to solve and that only the obstinacy of government stopped progress. Even if I knew at some level this wasn't true, the opportunity to imply otherwise would be hard to resist. Politics professor Ben Jackson describes how, among left-wing intellectuals

> the foibles of the Labour party are portrayed as the result of a parliamentary elite who self-interestedly and stupidly choose to accommodate themselves to the status quo. If only Labour MPs for once resolved to act morally and intelligently, runs the implicit argument, then a truly radical Labour government could at last take office.[9]

Secondly, I might assume that the only thing preventing utopia was the venality of leaders. In line with this, I would become cynical, believing that outcomes were a foregone conclusion. In 2019, for example, the Conservatives won the election fair and square, because their pitch to the country was more successful. Yet the next day many marched on Downing Street, complaining that the outcome was undemocratic. The idea that 'the powerful' rigged the election – aided by the 'mainstream media' – blocked a much-needed examination of why Labour had failed. Much the same thing happened after the 2015 contest, ultimately resulting in the ill-fated selection of Corbyn.

Thirdly, if I saw power as self-serving and far-reaching, I would fear it had the desire or capacity to intrude in my life and micromanage my existence. This would create paranoia about trivial, necessary infringements on my freedom, like CCTV, policing of the internet or ID cards, based on the idea of Big Brother elites desperate to lock up dissenters.[10] Often, this would block progressive causes. And it could have a knock-on effect for how I viewed the state generally, with my concerns turning, in time, from civil libertarian to pure libertarian. Why, after all, would I pay more taxes – let alone hand back control of entire industries – to those I suspected of surveillance and coercion?

Finally, if I felt that the world was bad because those with influence had made it so, then the worse it became, the more they would have to answer for. The end-point would be the view that all harm happens with the blessing of 'elites'. This would lead me down the slippery slope of all-out conspiracism. Corbyn's failure in the Copeland by-election could only be explained as a 'soft coup' by the establishment, otherwise Labour would have won;[11] 9/11 could only be understood as the work of George Bush, otherwise he would have stopped it. Etcetera, etcetera, etcetara.

Going down one of the above roads does not mean going down them all. But they each contain, as their common root, the tendency to overestimate how far-reaching power is.

For some, including those who believe in the myth only mildly, this overestimation is automatic. For instance, the Green MP Caroline Lucas is quoted as saying, 'I feel like I've spent my whole life trying to find out where power is. Wherever I am, it always feels like power is somewhere else and I'm chasing [it].'[12] Yet what if she's chasing a mirage? What if the power she alludes to is, in fact, illusory?

Douglas Jay, Clement Attlee's economic adviser in 1945, made the following observation about his time working in Downing Street:

> My most vivid impression in all these months at No.10 was the falsity of the illusion harboured by journalists, academics and others that something called 'power' resides in the hands of a Prime Minister. The picture drawn, or imagined, is of a great man, sitting down in his office, pulling great levers, issuing edicts, and shaping events. Nothing could be further from the truth in the real life of No. 10 as I knew it. So far from wielding great power, the PM at this time found himself hemmed in by relentless economic and physical forces, and faced with problems which had to be solved, but which could not be solved.[13]

Even after Labour's great landslide, and with many things going for them (such as taxes which were already high, thanks to the war), this was the case. In the fluid, globalised and ultra-scrutinised world of 2020, this is perhaps even more true. Progressives run a huge risk if we suppose that challenges only exist because someone, somewhere, is pulling the strings. The pretence that we live in a dictatorship helps no one.

There are two initial criticisms of my argument here. The first points out that leaders have many material powers – to raise taxes or pass laws – and that suggesting they do not renders politics unimportant. The second also says decision-makers have material powers, and adds that pretending they don't lets them off the hook. By pointing out the constraints on power, aren't we just defending injustice?

These potential criticisms stem from a misunderstanding of the myth. To reiterate, the Puppet Master is an overestimation of how much control we are subject to, not the idea that we are subject to any restrictions at all.

The fact that we have laws about how you must conduct protests, for example, is a clear sign that controls exist to limit freedom.

Likewise, the fact that each newspaper endorses a party before an election suggests a design of sorts. Similarly, lobbying and marketing by businesses aims to influence policy and popular opinion.

So, my critique of the Puppet Master does not say that institutions look on helplessly as events unfold, or are motivated solely by altruism. It just says that they generally have less power than we imagine. It leans towards the belief that the world is complex, chaotic and 'human' (in the best and worst senses), not the product of a synchronised plan. And it takes the view that powers are restrained, much more than left populists believe, by public opinion, competing demands, an interconnected world, human error, and all the technical brakes imposed by the democratic system.

This begs a follow-up question: if the Puppet Master describes the tendency to overestimate the reaches of power, then what is a 'correct' estimation? I obviously don't claim to have a definitive answer here. But what I will say is that the estimation must come through an empirical assessment – not through a hunch that we are subject to more control than is evident.[14]

We need to apply Occam's razor – the principle of going with the hypothesis which contains the fewest assumptions. We should assume that the least contorted option is the most likely. Unless we can observe a shadowy alternative dimension, then we should blame everyday incompetence, short-termism, hard challenges or supply-and-demand economics.

Of course, any 'correct' estimation about the reaches of power will vary, depending on the country and the point in time. There have been occasions where 'elites' genuinely have seized full control, spying on and brainwashing the people, passing whatever policies they pleased, suppressing dissent and controlling information. In Stalin's Russia or Hitler's Germany, you would not be a Puppet Master disciple if you observed these things happening. And indeed, modern democracies still contain elements of unaccountability and top-down control.

But it should be clear to us that, in a democratic and largely transparent place like the UK – with a free press and comparatively low corruption – 'the powerful' have much, much less power than in Kim Jong-un's North Korea or General Pinochet's Chile.[15] Of course, there are enough individual outrages – enough acts of self-interest, enough unpopular laws pushed through, enough miscarriages of justice and efforts by marketers to sway the public mood – that we can find a pattern of control if we want. Like William Paley and his watch, we can put together a dossier of circumstantial evidence and come up with a grand architect. But this doesn't mean that such an analysis would be accurate.

Indeed, in modern Britain, Occam's razor actually invites a decidedly anti-Puppet Master diagnosis. We have low deference to politicians; high scrutiny; complex legal processes and regulatory frameworks; judicial review, data protection and freedom of information; security agencies chasing uncoordinated terrorism carried out by 'lone wolves'; scoop-hungry newspapers with falling readerships; businesses operating in an intensely competitive economic environment; risk-averse civil servants and local authorities; social media and twenty-four-hour news creating an environment for information and misinformation to go viral; globalisation generating chaotic phenomena like mass migration, inequality and climate change. Etcetera, etcetera, etcetera.

All of these elements point to a turbo-charged 'law of the jungle' democracy, creating risk-averse governance – not to quasi-dictatorship. All suggest a world too chaotic to control – not a conspiracy. And, while none of these things neuter political influence altogether (there is evidence everywhere of people *trying* to shape public opinion), they mean that politicians who want to deliver change must use their limited power more cleverly.

The Puppet Master ignores this. It begins with the notion of far-reaching power and works backwards. This is why my criticism of the myth does not represent a brake on radicalism. Refusing to subscribe to a Puppet Master analysis is about trying to grasp why society is as it is. It is not about wanting any less to change things. It achieves nothing to assume, automatically, that all roads lead back to a plot by the establishment. All it does is embolden those who promote easy answers.

To illustrate this, let's take economic inequality. If we believe in the Puppet Master, we might blame rising inequality since the 1970s on efforts by a 'neoliberal' elite to bypass the democratic will.[16] We might see globalisation as the result of an overarching Bilderberg world order, involving collusion between the political, media and business classes. We might say that they have made small strategic concessions to social liberalism in return for full control of the levers of global power. We might say that they have subsequently, with the help of 'friends in the media', promulgated divide-and-rule narratives on immigration and welfare to distract the public. The best route to economic equality, we might conclude, is to take down this 'elite'.

If we do not subscribe to the Puppet Master, the view is different. We might believe that, as the electorate became more affluent in Western nations, the organised working class was replaced by more upwardly mobile voters. We might note that this new group became more socially liberal, self-confident and cosmopolitan, but less reliant on state provision, less likely to unionise and less willing to vote for higher taxes. We might also note the globalisation process, which has made it hard for governments to unilaterally deal with high pay, thanks to the fluidity of capital. For the same reasons, bringing corporations to heel is trickier, especially when there is a countervailing pressure to encourage investment. We might notice jobs moving abroad or being automated – leaving governments with the task, which they have often failed at, of breathing life into communities left behind. You might, of course, agree that this was exacerbated by politicians. In the UK we were unlucky enough to be governed by Margaret Thatcher at the crucial juncture, whose values were very much aligned with the changes happening. But you would not see this as the primary cause.

In short, you could either regard the rise in inequality as an authored process, driven by elites with too much power. Or you could view it as an authorless process, enabled by political weakness and a lack of answers in the face of change. These are different diagnoses. They lead to different critiques of decision-makers, and different solutions. But subscribing to the latter analysis makes you no less keen to see inequality reduced. Indeed, as the above quote from Douglas Jay implied, the successes of administrations like Attlee's came because they engaged seriously with the limits of government.

'MSM' OR FERAL BEASTS

To sketch what the Puppet Master is and isn't, let's look at the media. Conspiracies about the mainstream media (or MSM) have become commonplace in recent years – with sentiment going far beyond the left's traditional disdain for certain publications. This has led to left-populist protests against titles like the *New Statesman*, and to the creation of alternative outlets like *The Canary*.

Perceptions about how news works are central to the Puppet Master. The idea that the press are the comms wing of the elite is embraced by the populist left and the populist right. Both blame the 'establishment' media for the failure of their ideas to cut through. Both feel that the press uphold the ideologies of the other side.

But the truth is that both left and right populists chronically overestimate the extent to which media publications deliberately embed certain opinions. And they underestimate the extent to which the press are responsive entities – who know their audiences and have an incentive to reflect their views.

There have been countless instances of the Puppet Master myth being applied to the media since 2015.[17] Let's take a Crispin Flintoff comment piece in the *Independent*: 'The Jeremy Corbyn Story that Nobody Wanted to Publish'.[18] This was a 2016 article about how the press were refusing to report a poetry and comedy tour by pro-Corbyn celebrities. It begins as follows:

> Yesterday, I wrote a blog about the Jeremy Corbyn tour . . . which the media had failed to cover. I wanted people to know about the existence of the tour, but I also wanted to alert people to the fact that none of the newspapers I contacted were interested in reporting it. Journalist after journalist told me that the story was 'not newsworthy'. 'Not newsworthy' is obviously not a scientific term. It's purely subjective. And it's also plain wrong.

The problem begins with the fact that the tour was in fact covered – in the *Independent* and the *Telegraph*.[19] But the real issue is with the deeper assumptions. The definition put forward by

Jan-Werner Müller – author of *What is Populism?* – is that populists 'claim that they and they alone speak in the name of the "real people" or the "silent majority" '.[20] Flintoff does this (on behalf of Corbyn) throughout. He bases the article on the premise that Corbyn – and, by association, the pro-Corbyn arts tour – has over-whelming popular appeal. And from here he concludes that only censorship from those who want to maintain 'top-down politics' could explain journalists' lack of interest. Even the author's flexible understanding of 'subjectivity' shows this, with its implication that his preoccupations chime exactly with the public's, but are sup-pressed by elites. 'Many in the media may oppose Corbynomics,' he concludes, 'but, in the end, they have to respond to the people's interest.'

Nowhere in the piece does Flintoff countenance the possibility that most of those performing on his tour aren't especially famous, and are usually better known for their left-wing politics than for their comedy or poetry. Thus, there is little 'new' in the story. Nor does he consider the harder truth that the proportion of the popula-tion who like radicl poetry, avant-garde comedy and Jeremy Corbyn is, rightly or wrongly, pretty small. The path of least resistance for journalists – especially those with right-of-centre readerships – is to not write about these things.

So, are we claiming that the print press doesn't give left-wingers a hard time? Of course not. At least two studies have analysed the media around Corbyn and found the content overwhelmingly nega-tive. One concludes that 'the degree of antagonism and hatred from part[s] of the media has arguably reached new heights',[21] and the other points to a 2:1 ratio of negative to positive coverage.[22] Few politicians of any colour are presented positively by the media. But progressives struggle most, and Corbyn has had it especially hard.

The Puppet Master myth provides one explanation for why this is. This analysis says that our MSM propagates deliberate misinforma-tion from 'the establishment'.[23] It regards the media as an instrument of ideological control and sees attacks on Corbyn as part of a drive to discredit socialism, led by people guarding their interests. You only have to spend a few seconds 'below the line' on a *Guardian* opinion piece to find this sentiment (although many now say that even the *Guardian* is a tool of the establishment).[24]

There is an alternative to the Puppet Master assessment, however, which is to see the media not as part of an *immoral* grand design, but as the symptom of an *amoral* process. This interpretation says that papers are in fierce competition, driven by bottom lines and falling readerships. They are sustained by content which titillates, scandalises and gets people nodding along – which brings brand loyalty to the title. In other words, they are institutionally conservative with a small 'c', more than they're ideologically Conservative with a big one.

This perspective sees the press as 'feral beasts', as Tony Blair put it in 2007.[25] It is a vision of chaos, not conspiracy.[26] It regards right-wing coverage as the product of a population at least half of which hold right-of-centre views. And it also observes that right-wing preoccupations are often more visceral – making easier hornets' nests to kick. It's the idea of a media styled on *Big Brother* in the Channel 4 sense (rather than the *1984* sense): salacious, knee-jerk, thoughtless and irresponsible, catering to every whim and impulse.

New Labour's notorious spin operation came from this conviction. The media environment was seen as a free-for-all, characterised by groupthink, cults of personality, a race between titles to expose individuals and an appetite for creative destruction. The Labour press operation – now seen by left populists as an elite conspiracy itself – was an effort, wrong-headed or not, to manage this chaos.

Choosing one or another of the above assessments does not sway how you feel about the media. The 'feral beast', supply-and-demand analysis does not exonerate the press, any more than the fact that people like smoking turns the tobacco salesman into a hero.

Moreover, if we apply Occam's razor, the 'feral beasts' perception seems closer to the truth. The Media Reform Coalition, who authored one of the above reports about the negativity of Corbyn's coverage, provided the following clarification:

> There are no doubt some professional journalists and editors who
> have knowingly and willingly used their platform in an attempt to

discredit Corbyn's leadership from the outset. There are also likely some who have knowingly and reluctantly accepted the editorial 'whip' of their pay masters. But most simply believe that they are covering the stories that matter to their readers or viewers, or to the public at large, and in a way that will resonate strongest with them ... This is important because if we want to try and tackle the problem of media bias, we have to first understand it.[27]

Other research suggests something similar, with a chicken-and-egg interplay. Research by MORI describes a 'complex dynamic system with various points of feedback between media and audiences'.[28] And a study into four decades of immigration rhetoric in the Australian press discovers a sophisticated back-and-forth between government, media and the public, with all three reinforcing and reflecting each other – the result being a race to the bottom. As the author points out, 'divergence from popular opinion by democratically-elected governments is an unsustainable political position'.[29] This does not necessarily excuse the politicians or journalists in question, but the analysis is significantly different to left populists'. It suggests weakness is the problem – not coercion or propaganda.[30]

Indeed, a majority of all journalists consider themselves left- rather than right-wing. The ratio is 3:2 in favour of the left, even among very senior figures in the sector.[31] If there is a right-wing-propaganda campaign at play, rather than short-term editorial decision-making, then it runs against the ideals of the media's top brass.

Columnist Hugo Rifkind describes how, when writing editorials for a Murdoch paper, top-down missives were non-existent.[32] And former Observer political editor Gaby Hinsliff writes that 'newspapers thrive commercially by reflecting, not driving, readers' opinions'. People like reading things they agree with, and successful publications play to this.[33]

Of course, Rifkind or Hinsliff 'would say that, wouldn't they'? Yet looking at the breakdown of readerships, they have a point: the editorial lines of different titles tend to loosely correlate with public opinion. The Mirror, Guardian, Independent and I, for instance, had a combined monthly readership of about 81 million across all platforms, as of summer 2019. The *Mail, Express, Times, Telegraph, Sun* and *Star* had an audience of about 122 million.[34] This is a big difference, but not completely unrepresentative.[35]

The truth is that Corbyn's explicitly far-left brand of politics was only shared by one in ten when he came to office.[36] And he did little at first to increase this, refusing to engage with the press and emphasising how out of step with the rest of the electorate he was (e.g. by refusing to meet the Queen). The path of least resistance for the average journalist being to go with the grain of their readership, Corbyn was a gift.

When he did electorally better than expected in 2017, the hostility reduced considerably for a time. This was not because Corbyn had become less of a threat to 'elite interests' (quite the opposite – all the polling suggested he was closer to power). It was because he'd showed himself to be more attuned to public opinion.

Coverage of policy issues reveals the same thing. Just over a quarter of the populace are squarely pro-migrant, with a quarter strongly anti-. The remaining half (dubbed 'the anxious middle'), have milder anti-migration views.[37] Generally speaking, about three quarters say migration should be reduced to some extent. Papers' editorial lines aren't a million miles from reflecting this.

And if we look at left-wing issues for which there *is* public support, like NHS funding, we find that even the most conservative papers strike a fairly progressive tone. Likewise, the right-wing press's coverage of bankers has been extremely hostile since 2008.[38] This undermines the left-populist idea that the press focus on issues such as welfare so as to distract us from the racket of financiers at the top.[39]

Some might say the issue of causation remains. Couldn't the high proportion of right-wingers or migrant sceptics be a *consequence* of elite propaganda cutting through? With headlines like 'It was *The Sun* wot won it' (a claim the paper rapidly disowned), this is a tempting idea.

However, research finds that 'People who don't regularly read any papers have very similar views ... [to] the whole population, while readers of particular papers show heavy slants.' In other words, those who do not consume print media are not more progressive. They are simply closer to the mean average.[40] The press's chief effect is to magnify and polarise, not to sway.

Indeed, looking at the range of British print titles, it's hard to see anything approaching a pro-establishment, MSM hegemony. Most papers present themselves as voices against the status quo – on vastly divergent grounds to each other – and speak for pockets of strongly held opinion. If the press *are* pushing an agenda, then its ideological content is certainly confused, ranging from *Express* to *Independent*, via *Financial Times* and *Daily Star*.[41] In truth, there is far less evidence of the press colluding in a hegemony than of them competing in a cut-throat market.

Of course, this is not to say there is *no* top-down element. As discussed, the Puppet Master overestimates rather than fabricates the reaches of power. It is clear that at certain junctures publications intervene in ideological ways, and that many owners have political views, which their papers reflect at election time.

Yet even here, the buck usually stops with the reader.[42] The *Express* supported Labour in 2001, sensing which way the wind was blowing.[43] The *Mail*, despite having backed the Tories at every election since the Second World War, was not above serialising *Call Me Dave*, Lord Ashcroft's extended attack on the sitting Conservative Prime Minister. The *Telegraph* broke the MPs' expenses scandal, drip-feeding the revelations about the Tories over a week. The *Sun* backed Nicola Sturgeon in Scotland, and led the campaign against cuts to tax credits.[44]

There are countless other examples, ranging from the *Mail*'s coverage of the Windrush scandal to the *Sun*'s writing up of the 2012 Olympics.[45] The most blatant of all is many papers' support for Brexit. This prioritised the instincts of readers over the recommendations of every 'elite' going.[46]

Another explanation for why a conservative bias exists, meanwhile, is the fact that the preoccupations of the right are often more visceral. The political psychologist George Lakoff describes the difference between left and right as being between 'systemic' and 'direct' causal reasoning.[47] The former is abstract, concerned with the whole ecosystem around an issue. The latter is based on cause and effect. A left-winger might say that there is a systemic link between deprivation and crime, for instance. A right-winger would say that nothing directly forces someone in poverty to offend. This has implications for the media. A 'systemic' argument like 'look at the socio-economic factors that lead people into crime' is harder to build a headline around than a 'direct' one, like 'throw criminals in jail so they can't do it again'.

To the extent that the press are disproportionately conservative, this is a big factor. The right's advantage with the media comes less from Puppet Master propaganda than from a way of thinking which chimes with the needs of headline writers.

Underlying this is a separate argument about what we mean by impartiality. Are we asking the media to represent the full range of opinions? Or are we asking them to present an objective 'truth'? I would say that incontrovertible fact should always override the balance of popular opinion. There is little to be gained by a TV debate about whether climate change is happening, no matter what the public thinks. But the airtime given to different perspectives is harder; there is no scientific fact suggesting that more redistribution is better than less, or that borders should be open, not closed. The most we can hope for, on questions like these, is that media outlets represent the full breadth of different views.

Left-wingers often become believers in the Puppet Master because they confuse these things. A personal opinion, which they regard as self-evident fact (e.g. nuclear unilateralism is the only moral policy) is not held by the general population. Politicians who believe it are not invited by the electorate to run our institutions. Commentators who champion it are not as widely read. As a result, a narrative develops that it is being censored by a Puppet Master.

9
The Appeal of the Puppet Master

The Puppet Master is an article of faith for many on the populist left, and has a strong appeal beyond this. Several instincts draw people to the myth.

INSTINCT TO SPEAK FOR THE MASSES

The first explanation is the desire to feel you are backed by 'the people'. Majority support is something that all politicians and activists want, and which many others crave too. Research in 1977 into the false consensus bias, for instance, concluded that we 'systematically and egocentrically' assume that our own choices chime with others'.[1]

Populist movements rely on this belief far more. They often emerge from the fringes by latching on to widespread fears, claiming to be the only ones who care about them – and to speak for the ordinary, silent majority in doing so. This is despite being in electoral minorities and facing opposition from large parts of the population. They use the idea of an undemocratic, inauthentic elite to make this jump.

Research by Amsterdam University finds that a willingness to believe obvious answers are suppressed by the establishment is clustered at the political extremes, from where populism usually originates. The study's author, Jan-Willem van Prooijen, writes that:

> Our findings establish a link between political extremism and a general susceptibility to conspiracy beliefs. Although the extreme left may sometimes endorse different conspiracy theories (e.g. about

capitalism) than the extreme right (e.g. about science or immigration), both extremes share a conspiratorial mind-set, as reflected in a deep-rooted distrust of societal leaders, institutions and other groups.[2]

This correlation reflects an instinct to speak for the masses which has been frustrated. Those on the fringes feel that their views are self-evidently in the interests of the population. And yet democracy exposes the lack of appetite for their ideas.

This creates a cognitive dissonance, making the idea of a far-sighted Puppet Master appealing. The myth represents an alternative explanation, which says that the rest of the population subconsciously agree, but have been brainwashed or silenced. It lets you satisfy the instinct to speak for the masses, without taking the steps required to broaden support.

This does not mean we should always trust the wisdom of crowds, or that fringe opinions are substantively wrong. It just means they are wrong in their Puppet Master explanation of *why* their arguments haven't become government policy. It requires them to think harder about whether their policies are practical, or how they can persuade the public.

My opinion, for instance, is that private education is harmful. I would never send my child to a private school, and would favour complete abolition. However, I accept that there is a spectrum of opinion, which I am at the far end of. Even if many ordinary people say they dislike private schools, they would often send their children there if they got the chance (or support others' right to do so) – based on values differences, or on ideas about parenthood and free choice. And this is before you get into the practical challenges of abolition. So, I do not think private schools' continued existence is because elites have crushed the people's will – even if I still think I am right that we should get rid of them.

Puppet Master beliefs are attractive to anyone whose ideas are unpopular. However, the instinct to speak for the masses is especially seductive for the left, which sees itself, historically, as being on the side of the majority. Instances where elites are unseated by the people – such as the French and Russian revolutions – are viewed as left-wing events. In particular, we on the left are uncomfortable with being at odds with what the working classes want (hence the patronising idea that poorer people vote for right-wing parties as the result of a 'false consciousness').

This means we often rely on Puppet Master explanations, despite the conditions being very different from 1789 or 1917. Even though we're living in a sophisticated democracy with a complex class structure (as opposed to a despotic monarchy or a society where only a handful can vote), the instinct to unanimously rise up as part of 'the 99 per cent' remains attractive.

INSTINCT TO BLAME THE 'SYSTEM'

The second appeal of the Puppet Master is the instinct to blame 'the system'. This is the left's conflation of a desire to 'blame society' with a desire to blame the Puppet Master who allegedly runs it.

As has been mentioned, one distinction between left and right is between 'systemic' and 'direct' reasoning. Systemic thinkers blame wider, structural factors; direct thinkers hold individuals culpable. The former therefore tend to say problems are 'society's fault', subscribing to John Locke's 'blank slate' analysis, and emphasising nurture over nature. This is central to why many left-wingers – myself included – are drawn to progressive politics. The fact, for example, that those with criminal convictions are disproportionately from certain socio-economic backgrounds – and that high court judges are disproportionately from others – suggests that life chances definitively alter where people end up.

However, it's a short journey from believing that issues tend to be 'society's fault' to believing that they are 'the fault of those who run society'. The preference for structural explanations can mutate into the assumption that every problem is engineered. This transgression is what I mean by the instinct to blame 'the system'. Left populists slip from blaming our socio-economic structure to blaming the plutocracy allegedly controlling it.

An example of this is the writing of Noam Chomsky. An anarcho-syndicalist with a campus following, Chomsky argues that people are receptacles for 'propaganda', with their positive impulses massaged into acquiescence by the powerful. In his 1988 book on the topic, *Manufacturing Consent*, he portrays governments as spoon-feeding their corporate agendas to populations who swallow them whole.[3]

According to Chomsky, 'powerful societal interests' successfully 'influence the public in the desired direction'. They 'fix' the policies we take for granted, and 'shape and constrain' news output. They do this through the 'selection' of 'right-thinking personnel' and the 'provision of experts to confirm the official slant'. They 'allow some measure of dissent from journalists' and even plant occasional negative stories about themselves (which Chomsky calls 'flak') to disguise their pre-decided goals.[4]

Keen not to blame individuals, Chomsky suggests journalists are decent people, oblivious to their role in drip-feeding propaganda. Yet his language constantly stresses wilful intent. Someone, after all, must be 'manufacturing' the consent. And the less people are actually involved – with even senior journalists exonerated – the more ingenious the clique who is responsible must be.

In doing this, Chomsky does not identify a 'systemic' explanation for how society works. Rather, he encourages the 'direct' idea of a far-sighted elite injecting their ideology into an inert populace. Indeed, underpinning Chomsky's work is the notion that Locke's blank slate provides a blank canvas on to which 'elites' impose their agenda. Humans have creative and cooperative latent impulses, he says, but these impulses are currently shaped by decision-makers, for their own ends.

Indeed, 'the powerful' are the only ones immune to external influence. They are not blank slates on to whom society has also imprinted a set of values. Nor do they have creative, cooperative impulses. They simply prey on the malleability of everyone else. Or, if these elites *are* influenced by surroundings, then the difference between how they have turned out (ruthless, autonomous, hyper-competent) and how everyone else has (gullible, incurious, decent) is staggering.

Chomsky's assessment is towards the thicker end of the Puppet

Master wedge. But it shows how the instinct to blame 'the system' inadvertently conflates a systemic, complex analysis ('we're all more heavily influenced by our environment than we realise') with a direct, culprit-driven one ('the masses are influenced by their environment, and are preyed upon by an elite which is not').

INSTINCT TO DECONSTRUCT

The instinct to deconstruct describes the left-populist emphasis on critique. This originates from academia, and from forms of critical theory.[5]

Professional academics tend to gravitate towards left liberalism, as do students.[6] This manifests itself in university towns having, some say, become Labour's new heartlands.[7]

Why exactly is this? It is in artistic and humanities fields like Drama and English where the slant is by far the strongest. So, regardless of whether you believe that left-wing arguments are more logical – which I do – the idea that intellectuals are more left-wing because they're more rational doesn't explain the phenomenon.

Part of the reason comes, again, from the tendency towards systemic causation. Someone drawn to life as a history professor, for instance, would usually be more attracted to systemic analyses.

But beyond this there is a separate factor, which is the instinct to deconstruct. This is especially common in arts subjects, disciplines which build less on evidence or existing consensuses than on using creative arguments to disrupt the mainstream view. This crops up most in the fields that are more predisposed to be left liberal, like Philosophy, Drama and English Literature (the subject which I studied). These disciplines often seek unconventional readings, sometimes using paradigms like new-wave feminism, Marxism, post-colonialism, queer theory or psychoanalysis.

Critical theories like these frequently assume that the authors being studied impose the narratives of the powerful, or that history has been told by the victors. Intellectuals take pride in seeing through these narratives and are rewarded academically for doing so.

This instinct to deconstruct leads them not only to question received wisdom but to play an important political role. Suspicion of the mainstream has at points caused an educated avant-garde to oppose injustices which others accepted, such as during the civil rights process.

Yet this comes with drawbacks. The instinct to deconstruct takes more pride in subverting than in finding alternatives; it is not, by definition, constructive. Viewing society as a 'construct' or 'state apparatus' can lead us away from the truth and converge with Puppet Master thinking. When applied to everyday politics, this can mean society is seen as an 'authored' object to be critiqued, with governments regarded as omnipotent, carrying the same autonomy over their work as Flaubert or Dickens did over their novels.

Of course, there is more to politics than achievable, costed recommendations. Re-examining assumptions is key. But the instinct to deconstruct must itself be interrogated. Conspiracy theories correspond with 'lower analytic thinking and . . . greater intuitive thinking'.[8] Hence, if the desire to cross-examine morphs into Puppet Master thinking for its own sake, it loses its ability to probe. It ends up as little more than a way to affirm that we are part of a critical vanguard, set apart from the 'sheeple' who think what they are told to think.

Developed nations tend to be moving towards the post-materialist ideal of 'a society in which ideas count for more than money'.[9] Cultural capital and the ability to critique will come with increasing social value in the future. The challenge is to create questioning societies, but ones which remain open-minded – rather than being guided by an alternative, Puppet Master orthodoxy.

INSTINCT TO SEE A PATTERN

The final factor is the human willingness to read intent and connection into things. When it comes to politics, we are all inclined to pick out a more coherent pattern of cause and effect than exists; to imagine, as Douglas Jay put it, a prime minister 'pulling great levers, issuing edicts, and shaping events'.

The aforementioned work by Amsterdam University describes conspiracy theories as 'comprehensive explanations for distressing events that are hard to make sense of otherwise'.[10] Others have found that an 'intentionality bias' – a view that bad things are done deliberately – is primal to humans.[11] It is harder to see past these instincts than to embrace them and join the hunt for culprits.

During extreme adversity, this is acute. Andrew O'Hagan's book-length post-mortem of the Grenfell fire, *The Tower*, describes how pervasive narratives of guilt were during the aftermath of the tragedy:

> All over the community, to believe the official figures was to align oneself with the obvious criminals. 'Accident' was a banned word: more than anything people needed to believe there had been a cover-up.[12]

This was a natural response among grieving members of the local community. But it was exacerbated by some on the populist left who – horrified by what had happened – encouraged the idea of deliberate intent and accused the authorities of a numbers cover-up.[13]

Another example of the instinct to see a pattern is the 'omission bias' – the tendency to judge harmful actions more harshly than harmful inactions.[14] For governments, the reality is that inaction is a form of action. But the Puppet Master myth assumes that leaders do harm for no reason, rather than that they choose the negative consequences of doing something over the negative consequences of doing nothing.[15]

This is especially true when the omission bias joins forces with another aspect of cognition, the 'Nirvana fallacy'. This is the tendency to idealise a single, perfect solution – with any outcome that falls short of this blamed on malevolence.[16]

There are countless other biases. 'Pareidolia' means we see shapes where none exist. The 'clustering illusion' means we identify patterns in random sequences. The 'illusory correlation' makes us assume that things are linked. The 'anecdotal fallacy' leads us to extrapolate from a single event.

These demonstrate the human brain's aversion to randomness.

They explain why, for example, left populists see Margaret Hodge's daughter working for the BBC, link this to Hodge's criticism of Corbyn, note that Hodge is Jewish and arrive at anti-Semitic conclusions.

Even at a milder level, the instinct to see a pattern weaves venality into each imperfect fudge. PFI under New Labour was an uneasy compromise, to satisfy a population who wanted 'Swedish-quality public services for American levels of taxation'.[17] But the instinct to see a pattern connects several extra dots – e.g. the fact that Alan Milburn consulted for a private health company many years after – to interpret PFI as a coordinated scam.

Most people, regardless of their leaning, assume a greater level of agency from politicians than exists. This is partly because this is how it's presented to them: those in office take full credit for successes, claiming they were part of a coordinated plan; opponents present all errors as deliberate and gratuitous.

Populists, though, are usually more susceptible because, for all the reasons identified, they rarely make it into government. Hence, they never have their instinct to see a pattern tempered by the arbitrary and incoherent reality of office.

IO

The Case against the Puppet
Master (Government)

The most obvious argument against the Puppet Master is that, by overestimating the reaches of power, we risk crying wolf. If a modern-day Chairman Mao or Senator McCarthy took control, accusations of BBC 'propaganda' or paranoia about the 'database state' would suddenly feel over the top.

Beyond this, however, there are four factors that render the Puppet Master myth flawed. These are *humanity*, *prioritisation*, *self-perpetuation* and *collective responsibility*.

HUMAN DECENCY AND INEPTITUDE

Writing in 2016, journalist Ed Smith described one of the last publicly acceptable out-groups.[1] 'Despite widespread political correctness, there is one group that it is perfectly legitimate to despise: politicians,' Smith wrote. He explains:

> When I worked for a newspaper, I was surprised one day to hear a reporter, usually so fair and mild-mannered, describe her hatred and contempt for politicians – 'the worst people, just disgusting'. This is the kind of comment you hear from normally civilised and balanced people, who usually don't know any politicians personally, but feel quite certain of the truth of their conviction.

In Britain you would find many in agreement with the journalist Smith describes. Our leaders are self-serving; we are pure. They micromanage society; our lives are scatty and unpredictable. These narratives rely on the idea that those with power are a different species – a group of cold-blooded, ultra-competent suits.

This has become a call to arms for all strains of populism. Even those who generally avoid ideas of good and evil fall back on the idea of a malign minority – which finds itself, in almost every country in the world, in the position to run things. George Monbiot, for example, wrote at length in 2017 about the altruism running deep within most humans. Yet he went on to explain that one group doesn't possess this humanity: 'We have been induced by politicians, economists and journalists to accept a vicious ideology . . . A small handful, using lies and distractions and confusion stifle [our] latent desire for change.'[2]

I refer to humanity here in the sense of human decency, but also of human ineptitude. The caricature of the power-politician has both aspects: they're malign and self-serving in ways we would never be, but they're also more cunning and far-sighted than anyone we know.

Some left populists fully embrace the idea of an inhuman, super-human elite.[3] But others are more conflicted and try not to condemn individuals.

At the start of *The Establishment*, for instance, Owen Jones distances himself from the view that 'Britain is ruled by "bad" people, and that, if they were replaced by "good" people the problems facing democracy would go away.'[4] In effect, this ends up being an 'I'm not a conspiracist, *but* –' approach, to which most of his subsequent writing runs counter.[5] Every influential figure in *The Establishment* is portrayed as a bloodless suit – 'the real villains of the piece'.[6] Their 'concerted' goal, he says, is 'to "manage" democracy to make sure that it does not threaten their own interests'.[7]

But it is the reason behind this inconsistency that is interesting. Because Jones and other left populists rely on the Puppet Master idea that all problems come from above, they inevitably end up suggesting that those at the top are personally corrupt – whatever caveats they put in place to begin with.

The truth is that 'establishment' figures can either be malign *and* powerful, or neither; the more they are one, the more they are the other. If the world is deeply imperfect and these figures are powerful, then they cannot be decent. And if the world is deeply imperfect and these figures are decent, then they cannot be powerful.

To explore this, let's assume the Puppet Master is true. Let's say that 'the powerful' coordinate with each other to subjugate the people and line their own pockets. Let's say problems are due to an elite cartel blocking the will of the electorate. Let's say CCTV cameras, police powers or the MSM are the means by which they oppress and quieten us.

Then let's consider why 'the powerful' are so wicked that they behave in these ways. There are three potential reasons:

1. 'The powerful' often come from privileged groups, which are inherently more selfish and immoral.
2. 'The powerful' are born immoral at different levels of society and climb to power from whatever position they're born into.
3. 'The powerful' have been corrupted by their positions (and the human fabric is, at core, corruptible).

Each of these propositions is troubling for a progressive. Reason 1 is especially tricky. If the populist left is saying there is a link between start in life and genetic morality, then we are in dangerous territory. As well as opening a door to extremism – the purging or imprisoning of these groups, for example – this invites the populist right to make similar eugenic arguments. Much of the case against this relates to arguments made in Chapter Six, which I won't repeat here. But Reason 1 is an idea we can discount with relative ease.

Reason 2 suggests we live in a sort of 'malignocracy': good and bad people born at every level of the population, with the most callous and corrupt rising to the top. Again, this is troubling. It effectively means that the MPs or CEOs from the humblest beginnings are also, proportionally, less moral than those born into privilege.

After all, even if malignity rises to the top, start-in-life clearly plays a role – given that 'elites' still come, disproportionately, from privileged backgrounds. It follows, according to the Reason 2 logic, that those in our malignocracy who become powerful without social luck must, all things being equal, be more malign than those born with a dollop of good fortune. State-educated Cabinet ministers would thus, on average, be less innately moral than privately educated ones – with those who claw their way to government from genuine poverty the most diabolical of all. If you pursue the Reason 2 logic, the implication is a venal elite, comprising ultra-malign commoners and mildly malign toffs.

There are, it should be said, traits which politicians over-index in, like extraversion.[8] And there is even evidence that CEOs are disproportionately psychopathic – with 3 per cent displaying psychopathic traits, compared to 1 per cent of the overall population.[9] However, the numbers are so small that this doesn't seem like the central issue. And, either way, it does not change the core point – which is that, whatever inherent traits 'the powerful' have, they're likely to be *least* acute among the Etonians who come to wield influence. The worse we believe these traits are, the more suspicious we need to be of powerful people from poor backgrounds.

It is doubtful that the populist left seriously thinks this. But we should be clear that the end-point of Reason 2 is a gift-wrapped argument against social mobility.

Finally, Reason 3. This says that the moral fabric is the same among 'elites' as among the rest of us, but that 'power corrupts'. This has more to it than Reasons 1 and 2. Power can corrupt – especially if there is little transparency or accountability. Even when heavily limited, power brings hubris. Many who govern become convinced they know best. This is a relatively small factor in a country like ours, where there are democratic checks on this hubris. But it's a factor.

However, Reason 3 comes with big implications of its own. In essence, it says we are all, at some level, self-interested. I don't dispute this entirely, given the atrocities which humans have proved capable of. But the logical conclusion of the 'power corrupts' idea is that we would also succumb to hubris – power would corrupt us. This removes much of our justification for anger at the Puppet Master. All we can do is advocate transparency, scrutiny and regulation to hold back the worse instincts of 'the powerful' – and, by implication, of ourselves.

This begs the question of how corruptible humans are? If, like Chomsky or Monbiot, we believe in a benign populace, preyed on by an ultra-malign elite, then our corruptibility is immense. We ourselves, if we ended up in power, would quickly turn from well-meaning dolts to inhuman superhumans. We would be capable of brainwashing the population, coordinating a network of 'outriders' and subjugating the poor – and would do so for an extra zero on our bank balance. If this is right, then Monbiot's view that most ordinary people are 'socially minded, empathetic and altruistic' is hard to credit.

In other words, if you subscribe to Reason 3, then the more you blame the Puppet Master, the dimmer the view you must take of human nature. Anyone who gets the opportunity to improve the world will, however well meaning they start out, be consumed by ruthless greed. Why would we even want to change things or help people, if this is what the human fabric looks like?

Reason 3 is still the best explanation, among our three, for the behaviour of some powerful people. Despite our positive traits, there is a capacity, in most individuals, to take shortcuts, settle scores or turn a blind eye if it is in our interest. To this extent, power corrupts. Yet by taking this approach, we either concede the limits of *how* powerful 'the powerful' in our society are, or we embrace an utterly misanthropic world view. Unless there is a strain of genuine evil running through everyone, then 'the powerful' can't – according to Reason 3 – be as self-serving as the likes of Chomsky suggest.

An inability to deal with this paradox is, I would argue, the factor which takes extreme Puppet Master believers down the path of anti-Semitism. And it leaves other Puppet Master advocates, such as those among the left-populist commentariat, ill-equipped to address the problem – without renouncing their conspiracism at the same time.

After all, the idea of the all-powerful Jew circumnavigates 'human decency and ineptitude'. Anti-Semitic tropes provide, ready-made, a race of inhuman superhumans. They allow Puppet Master logic to jump the track, into overt racism. This 'socialism of fools' offers an illicit Reason 4, tucked under the counter: a white-skinned and economically successful ethnic group, hiding in plain sight.

The reality is that those in power are cut from the same cloth as the rest of us – some good, some bad, some misguided. A morally average human would behave in roughly the same ways as 'the powerful', were they in their position. The conclusion, assuming we believe most people are fairly decent, is that power is more limited than populists suppose.

The caricature of elites devoid of humanity therefore presents – through being so fanciful – one of the best arguments against the Puppet Master. In reality, those with influence are, as one journalist put it, 'neither wicked nor clever enough to do what they're accused of'.[10]

PRIORITISATION: ELECTORAL AND GOVERNMENTAL

Why, if 'the powerful' are as decent and flawed as the rest of us, don't they just do what the people want? The answer is, of course, that there are competing pressures and priorities in any democracy. The number of levers governments can pull is finite. If they cater to one section of opinion, they often do so at the expense of another. If they advance one policy, it usually has a side-effect.

The electorate often wants the best of all worlds. Pluralist leaders draw decisions into focus for them and advocate the best set of choices. And pluralists on the left advocate the most egalitarian and fair combinations possible, taking the public with them.[11]

Populists, by contrast, believe that priorities are an establishment fiction. The notion of a Puppet Master withholding the riches at its disposal forms an alternative. It lets populists reject the idea that there are pros and cons. Those who challenge this are seen as part of the technocratic 'rot at the top', lacking integrity or ideals.

This creates an inability to take decisions. Corbyn's policies on Europe, immigration, Trident, welfare and Northern Ireland – and on the balance between growth and equality – remained unclear throughout his leadership of Labour, thanks to a lifetime of blaming everything on Puppet Master oppression. Forced to set out how he'd prioritise if he was in power, Labour's 2017 manifesto was a not-especially-radical blend of triangulation, trade-off and duplicity. Indeed, many of the compromises were actually reactionary, compiled by a leadership only just learning the 'language of priorities'.[12] The 2019 manifesto, meanwhile, abandoned this language altogether.

There are two aspects to 'prioritisation': electoral and policy-based. Let's start with the former.

We live in a country with a range of views. While large parts of the population share a frustration at the 'political class', the things they want the political class to do vary. In UK politics during the 2010s there has been a Scottish nationalist movement demanding independence, a Bennite movement calling for undiluted socialism, a Brexiteer movement demanding full 'sovereignty', and a Europhile movement wishing to reverse Brexit – to name just a few. Each of these crusades speaks for a slice of the population, yet claims to speak for more.[13]

On top of this you have countless campaigns assuming the mantle of insurgent: a countryside lobby attacking an urban elite; trade unions attacking a business elite; climate-change sceptics attacking an environmentalist elite; green campaigners attacking a corporate elite; a 'taxpayer' lobby attacking a public-sector elite, and so on. And that's before we get into the everyday expectations of voters – for lower taxes, more nurses, less immigrants, lower inequality, greener communities, more compassion for refugees, cheaper petrol, free universities, a stronger army, more personal liberty, a lower welfare bill, and so on.[14]

The above demands are hard to reconcile. Yet each represents interests (and voters) who will be alienated if ignored. The fact that 'the powerful' must cater to these differing expectations undermines the Puppet Master myth. The sheer range of 'anti-establishment' voices, each with vehement, opposing goals, cancel each other out. What sort of unaccountable plutocracy, after all, must split the difference of so many contradictory perspectives to retain power?

To be clear, this does not mean the above priorities are equal, and that governments should merely reflect the mean average. For example, I think addressing climate change and inequality should be the top priorities. But it is still obvious to me that these things are being juggled with the priorities of voters who care more about other things.

Electorally speaking, then, the range of aspirations and ideals within our population rebukes the Puppet Master. The notion of a wicked, omnipotent elite can only exist, at least in a democracy, if we assume our own viewpoint represents everyone's.

Let's move to policy, the second aspect of 'prioritisation'. This describes the technical constraints on governments. These are most obvious where there is popular support for a course of action but nothing is done.[15] Underlying this are questions about the balances we wish to strike.

The table below sets out some examples. These see-saw oppositions are simplistic. But they reflect the fact that most choices come down to a tension between two things which deliver benefits. With many, the tension is between two ideals prized by the left.

One practical example is higher education. The proportion going to university has risen from 3 per cent in 1950 to nearly 50 per cent today.[16] This vast increase in the resources needed presents a choice: reduce the number of students or find the revenue to maintain current attendance rates.

Table 10.1.

Priority	Counter-priority
Enough **growth** that the country can invest in public services	Enough **equality** that society doesn't become hierarchical
Enough **competition** that people generate prosperity via enterprise, and feel stimulated	Enough **collectivism** that everyone shares this prosperity
Enough **liberty** that individual freedoms are protected	Enough **authority** that people cannot harm the collective to further their own interests or ideals

continued

Enough industry that jobs are created, and people can travel and live in comfort	Enough environmentalism that we don't destroy our planet
Enough universalism that taxpayers feel bought into the system	Enough targeted spending that those with the greatest need benefit most
Enough investment/Keynesianism that there is growth and expansion	Enough prudence that we don't spend more servicing debt than running services
Enough foreign intervention that we don't ignore suffering abroad	Enough pacifism that we don't create suffering or vacuums for despotism
Enough globalisation that we can be a diverse, outward-looking country	Enough protectionism that we can stop communities being washed away by change

The latter approach raises the question of revenue. Full state subsidy would be ideal if money was no object. But given that resources are finite, we must choose how highly we prioritise free universities.

This creates tensions between priorities. The first is between those who do not go to university and those who do. Is it fair for the former – who earn less over their lifetimes – to 100 per cent subsidise the latter? Or is an educated populace so valuable that we should ask those who do not go to fully fund those who do? Answering this depends, according to Rawlsian logic, on working out how much non-graduates benefit from the work of graduates. But it presents a clash of two things the left instinctively backs: support for less well-off people and free education.

Secondly, there is a tension between younger children and students. Given that most gaps open up well before the age of eighteen, scrapping fees should be way down the priority list from an equality perspective. Funding childcare, early years, primary schools, secondary schools or bringing back the Educational Maintenance Allowance (EMA) would all be of greater urgency (in roughly that order).[17] Otherwise you're prioritising middle-class people who would have gone to university anyway. (I would argue that free universal services are, in general, only progressive if the services in question are disproportionately likely to be used by the people most in need.) However, the alternative argument says that free higher education is part of the 'cradle to grave' ideal, and is more important than building or re-opening SureStart centres. Again, this presents a clash: between equal opportunities and universalism.

Thirdly, there is a conflict between research and teaching. Student fees partly go on things which do not directly benefit the student, like scientific research. This is an area where Britain is a world leader, and many believe our future lies in investing in this sector. But there could be lower fees if universities focused more on teaching. So, here too there is a conflict: between academia and affordable education.

Puppet Master thinking rejects these choices. It pretends free higher education is ideologically 'marketised' or perniciously withheld by 'the powerful'. Perhaps this would stack up if the Exchequer was so awash with cash that the need to prioritise disappeared – if we discovered new oil reserves or a way of taxing the 1 per cent at an unprecedented rate. But, for now, the need to prioritise remains.

Moreover, globalisation amplifies the oppositions in the table above. Where a balance could once be struck, many are becoming 'either or' choices. For instance, the quickest route to economic equality might be a 'socialism in one country' approach. Britain would probably become fairer but could also become poorer, with worse public services. Globalisation makes this choice – growth versus equality – much starker.

New Labour opted not to go down this route. They chose to tackle inequality incrementally, while participating in the world economy, tolerating the City and investing the tax proceeds in the poorest communities. Criticising this is fine, but what is the rival policy choice? An honest socialist might offer a genuine alternative, suggesting that we prioritise equality over prosperity and protectionism over globalisation; that we jettison wealth and diversity in return for more redistribution and stronger communities. I do not, on balance, agree with this route, but there would be integrity in championing it. But because Corbyn was a populist he pretended these balancing acts did not exist. His Puppet Master approach encourages the idea that oppositions like those in the table earlier are false choices, put forward by the establishment.

Former Labour speechwriter Philip Collins describes Obama's presidency as 'the discovery that power is not there'.[18] This mirrors a discovery made by many politicians. The adage tells us 'you can please all of the people some of the time or some of the people all of the time'. But modern leaders – even those as impressive as Obama – increasingly find themselves pleasing none of the people any of the time. They face polarised electorates and unprecedented global forces. Their intransigence comes from the difficulty of getting a broad enough, plausible enough compromise to satisfy those they serve – not from excessive power.

Arguments like this seem technocratic. Those who stress tough choices become the 'eat your greens' candidates. Yet past radicalism has relied on thinking in precisely these terms. Nye Bevan heralded the 'language of priorities', and the 1945 government maintained post-war rationing while building the welfare state. Among the most valid criticisms of New Labour, meanwhile, was that it was not honest enough about the trade-off between public spending and taxes – pretending there could be 'no losers'.

Yet since Corbyn became leader the tendency has been to move ever further from the language of priorities, taxing a little and spending a lot.[19] Left populists criticised as 'neoliberal', for instance, Chuka Umunna's idea that we should raise taxes to fund the NHS.[20]

The electoral success of austerity policies in 2010 and 2015 show, if nothing else, that the public are not necessarily opposed to the language of 'tough choices'. To deliver change, the left must understand the possibilities and limits of power, thinking through serious, alternative forms of prioritisation. The Puppet Master removes the ability to do this. It ushers us towards demagoguery and away from radicalism. And it creates a lack of answers, which means that, even in their present manifestation, the Tories remain the 'natural party of government'.[21]

11
The Case against the Puppet Master Continued (Society)

Let's continue to focus on the weaknesses of the Puppet Master, looking at the realities of social change.

SELF-PERPETUATION (THE MATTHEW EFFECT)

The third thing the Puppet Master fails to account for is the Matthew Effect. Otherwise known as 'accumulated advantage' or self-perpetuation, this describes the process where the rich get richer and the poor poorer. It is attributed to the Gospel of Matthew (25:29): 'For unto everyone that hath shall be given, and he shall have abundance, but from him that hath not shall be taken away even that which he hath.'

Self-perpetuation features in the small, everyday ways in which we exercise choice: buying an album by a band we are familiar with; hiring the better-qualified applicant for a job; choosing to live near friends; allowing ourselves a trivial act of nepotism. It applies to bigger things too: inheritance being passed down the generations, or the disproportionate purchasing power of larger companies. These things repeat themselves, replicating and amplifying inequalities that already exist – especially if multiplied many times over, as others make the same choices.[1]

This is the main problem with capitalism: all things being equal, things become less equal. The less planning or intervention there is, the more unfairness capitalism breeds. Over time, small differences become big ones; success breeds success and failure breeds failure. A place like London evolves, over a generation, into a mega-city – creating a gap with 'the rest' that feels insurmountable.[2] The people doing well find it easier to continue doing well, by making the same mundane, vaguely selfish choices we all make. Property and poverty are handed down; wealth and deprivation repeat themselves; sand shifts along the river-bank, sweeping into already deep pockets, exaggerating meanders, creating ox-bow lakes.[3]

Globalisation magnifies the scale of this. Existing advantages are given a transnational dimension, reducing the potential for regula-tion and increasing the size of audiences. A modern tech entrepreneur accumulates and hoards advantage quicker than innovators of the past. A corporation can choose where it bases itself and sell to more markets. A house in London gains value at unparalleled speed as the city becomes globally sought after.

These problems with capitalism are set against its ability to gener-ate wealth from which everyone can benefit and to raise living standards significantly. So, the goal for social democrats is to keep a degree of capitalism, but to intervene regularly enough that inequali-ties are stymied.

But the key point is that self-perpetuation is emphatically not a case of an ugly watch in a beautiful field. It's organic. Capitalism at its worst does not impose rules from above; it removes them.

What's strange about the Puppet Master diagnosis is that it delegitimises this sophisticated, structural critique of accumulated advantage and instead imagines capitalism as an authored process. Thus, many on the populist left miss the most powerful argument against the system they oppose – namely that it's chaotic, untame-able and amoral.

Of course, there is no question that a few wealthy people try and use the influence money brings to secure their position. Those who do best out of capitalism are usually more sympathetic to it. And one consequence of unfettered free markets is that they create monopo-lies and cartels. But these things are marginal compared to the locomotive power of the system itself. Indeed, even if a beneficiary of capitalism wishes to take on the role of Puppet Master and wield influence, they remain beholden to the diametrically opposed commercial need to 'give the people what they want'.

When we look at Piketty's inequality charts sloping gradually upwards – or at London's incremental rise at the expense of mill towns and seaside resorts – it seems clear that the chief problem is an economic free-for-all, not a hidden dictatorship.

For a more detailed example, let's return to the media – specifically Rupert Murdoch. In the eyes of left populists, Murdoch embodies the Puppet Master. He is seen as unaccountable, coercive, self-interested and right-wing. The left's preferred description of Murdoch is as a media 'baron' – a despot crushing his serfs.

I have already argued against the assumption that figures like Murdoch are the shapers of opinion, as the Puppet Master claims. And we have seen how papers like the *Sun*, rather than brainwashing the public, change their editorial lines to reflect and magnify existing concerns. But let's consider why Murdoch's power exists in the first place.

The daily readership of the *Sun* is over a million. This compares favourably to the *Morning Star*, Britain's only explicitly communist paper, which has 10,000 to 15,000 readers. While the *Morning Star* does not have the marketing budget of the *Sun*, it is available wherever the demand exists. The left-of-centre *Mirror*, meanwhile – which is probably a fairer comparison – still has only half the *Sun*'s readership.

No one is forced to buy the *Sun* or banned from buying other papers. Rather, the *Sun* is a consumer product in a poorly regulated sector – the result of supply-and-demand economics. It emerged in the 1960s to fill a gap in the market left open by the *Mirror*, and established dominance thanks to a clear voice and identity. The paper reflected and reinforced the perspective of a new social tribe – upwardly mobile, working class, self-employed, non-unionised, socially conservative.

The *Sun*'s success self-perpetuated, creating a virtuous circle. This at points led the paper (and Murdoch) to claim they could swing elections. But this was based on the commercial advantage they had accumulated. It was ultimately reliant, however obvious Murdoch's right-wing, pro-Brexit leaning was, on its readership. (*The Times*, for instance, also a Murdoch title, backed Remain, in recognition of its more pro-globalisation audience.) Once papers cease to reflect how readers feel, their power departs. This may now be happening with the *Sun*, as circulations dwindle for all papers and their core demographic shrinks.[4]

Attitudes to Murdoch ultimately show the misdiagnosis underlying the Puppet Master. Believers in the myth envisage the *Sun* as a mouthpiece for capitalist elites. In fact, the paper represents capitalism at its most reckless and volatile, driven only by consumers' immediate grievances. The law of accumulated advantage means it grows its brand, furthers its reach and reinforces the existing state of affairs.

As explanations for how markets work and why they're flawed, the idea of the Matthew Effect is at odds with the Puppet Master. The steady accumulation of profits, through the forces of supply and demand? The elevation of global celebrities, brands or media outlets? The opening up of wealth gaps in an unregulated economy, thanks to a million everyday choices and habits? These anarchic facets of capitalism are downplayed by those who reimagine it as an authored system.

COLLECTIVE RESPONSIBILITY

In 1966, five years before John Lennon sang 'Imagine', The Beatles released 'The Taxman' on their album *Revolver*. The lyrics, written by George Harrison, reflect his frustration at higher rates for the super-rich brought in by Harold Wilson's government. The song adopts the persona of a government tax collector, confiscating hard-earned money. It represents the state as punitive, untrustworthy and unaccountable – a Puppet Master, in effect

Revolver is supposed to epitomise 1960s counter-culture and non-materialistic, anti-establishment values. Sung by individuals who would consider themselves anything but conservative, it is an insight into the Puppet Master's fourth flaw: its capacity to under-mine collective responsibility by encouraging us to imagine we're the oppressed underdog. The fable destabilises notions of social contract and economic contribution, inviting believers to be angry at the plu-tocracy above rather than check their privilege.

This is partly about basic hypocrisy. Given that they oppose elit-ism so vocally, it is galling to see Diane Abbott or Shami Chakrabarti sending their children to private schools, or Len McCluskey borrow from his union to buy a £700,000 flat.

In reality, radicalism requires self-sacrifice – not just from elites but from everyone better off than average. Academics point out the 'bitter pill' that 'to raise significant revenues in a progressive fash-ion would require not just higher taxes on the super-rich, but also higher marginal income tax rates for middle and upper earners'.[5] Likewise, truly egalitarian policies require downward mobility as well as upward. In a socialist society, many of the children of the left-wing middle classes would end up in low-status jobs (albeit bet-ter paid, with better services, and more opportunity for their own children).

The Puppet Master myth pretends this isn't true. It passes the buck ever-upwards. The 40 per cent rail against the 10 per cent, who rail against the 1 per cent, who rail against the 0.1 per cent. As one columnist points out, being elite is 'something that happens to other people'.[6] Even George Harrison, a member of a band 'more famous than God', was able to imagine himself as the little guy, guarding his pennies from a mercenary overlord.

The collective responsibility flaw links to self-perpetuation. If we accept the self-perpetuation argument, we see inequality as the sum of a million tiny acts of myopia or self-interest – magnified and reinforced by a system which needs more intervention. For this to change, those with above-average privilege need to do less well; to accept collective responsibility. But if we *don't* accept the self-perpetuation argument, we fall for the idea that we are the downtrodden 99 per cent, ruled by a Puppet Master who has done this to us.

This delusion appeals to our meritocratic instincts. Few today like to think they were 'born with a silver spoon in their mouth', and those who have lived comfortable lives often pretend they have not. The Puppet Master, with its distinction between selfish, all-powerful 1 per centers and oneself – the self-made 99 per center – offers a way of reframing things.

You will often, for example, hear a progressive graduate who comes from the most privileged 20 per cent or 30 per cent of society bemoan the Oxbridge dominance of their industry. They are right to complain about this dominance, which is a disgrace. But less often do you see the same person reflect that they are blocking the way of the 80 per cent or 70 per cent who are far more deprived. Likewise, sending your child to private school probably feels more acceptable if you imagine you are the underdog – trying to give your offspring a fighting chance against a rigged system.

Again, we see the consequences of this with student fees. The two fifths of our population who attend university view themselves, generally, as closer to the left. Many were supportive of Corbyn's Labour with its anti-elite rhetoric. This group is also from the more privileged parts of society, relatively speaking. But often they do not view themselves as such.[7]

In the 2017 election, Labour courted students with its promise of free higher education. The undertones of the campaign invited middle-class students to believe they were among the many against the few, with tuition fees a Puppet Master imposition. This led to a manifesto which wasn't actually very egalitarian – taking from the richest decile, but giving straight back to the second- and third-richest deciles.[8] The Puppet Master myth encouraged society's 'haves' to believe they were 'have nots' – instead of considering where resources were really needed.

This pattern appears elsewhere. Studies find that Corbyn fans are little more economically redistributive than supporters of centre-left candidates. They do, however, *believe* they're more left-wing. And they are more drawn to anti-state, anti-establishment thinking.[9] The consequence is that privileged believers in the Puppet Master shake their fists at the power above, creating a sort of faux radicalism or left nimbyism. Those who receive inheritances can feel they are the little guy. Gentrifiers in London indulge expensive artisan tastes while railing against the 'social cleansing' of their area. Libertarianism takes the place of social justice.

This does not mean that if you have got a privileged background or expensive tastes you forfeit the right to want a fairer society – nor that you should be judged by an impossible, puritanical standard. That sanctimony is part of what this book is criticising. What it does mean, however, is that you should aspire to a more coherent and self-aware diagnosis than the Puppet Master allows. Blaming all-powerful elites cannot be your way around the realities of a radical agenda.

Would we really be willing to miss out on university to make way for a poorer person who deserved it more? Would we really forgo a foreign holiday so our income could be invested in international aid? These are the questions of socialism. They would, of course, be starkest when asked of the super-rich. But they are dilemmas for anyone with more to lose than to gain from a meaningful redistribution process. It does not make us immoral to feel compromised by these questions. But the problem with the Puppet Master narrative is that it distracts us from them altogether, diverting the blame elsewhere and creating a socialism which is low cost and guilt-free.

12
What is the Golden Era?

'Time travel is a discretionary art: a pleasure trip for some
and a horror story for others.'

– *Zadie Smith*

REVOLUTIONARY AND
EVOLUTIONARY OPTIMISM

The previous fable, the Puppet Master, is a pessimistic narrative
when it comes to human progress. As the metaphor of an ugly watch
in a beautiful field suggests, the myth is libertarian at core, portraying a world which could be – and was once – pure and free, but
which has been perverted by the inorganic machinery above (governments, big business, and so on). This is encapsulated by the notion
that global elites have hijacked the post-war consensus, imposing
'neoliberalism' and promulgating crassness and greed.[1]

This idea does much to explain the appeal of Corbyn. Alan Bennett,
for instance, criticised the Tories as 'totalitarian' in 2015, explaining
his attraction to Corbyn's politics on the basis that 'There has been so
little that has happened to England since the 1980s that I have felt
happy about . . . One has only had to stand still to become a radical.'[2]

Conversely, YouGov research finds that the relatively small group
who say that society is getting better are also the most likely to trust
institutions and to have a sense of democratic agency.[3]

Hence, the Puppet Master leads neatly into our third myth: the
Golden Era. This refers to narratives of decline and to the feeling

that the left is swimming against the tide of change. It describes a sense that things have been getting steadily worse; that only a U-turn can avert the dystopia ahead.

Golden Era believers may have sunny dispositions. The myth is not about a pessimistic temperament. Rather it is about a 'declinist' (rather than progress-based) version of history; a world steadily departing from the values we care about. The good times can only be achieved, according to Golden Era disciples, by stamping on the brake and reversing – not through embracing the things we like about the twenty-first century, and finding modern answers to those we do not.

There is a hopefulness of sorts in this. It suggests we will ultimately prevail over our oppressors. Hence many left populists claim to be optimists. But this optimism exists in spite of the feeling that things are moving in the wrong direction. It comes from a sense that the losing streak is about to end.

The chart I have drawn below visualises two types of optimism. The difference is between theories of change based on revolution and those based on evolution.

We can see this difference by looking back at a 2013 political spat between two comedians, Russell Brand and Robert Webb. Brand, a passionate believer in the Puppet Master, talked of his 'optimism' while simultaneously asserting that we were 'ambling towards oblivion' as a society unless something drastic was done.[4]

Webb, by contrast, asked Brand to consider 'What were the chances, in the course of human history, that you and I should be born into an advanced liberal democracy? . . . I recognise it as an unfathomable privilege.'[5] He acknowledged progress, despite knowing that it had been too slow, and fearing that advances were in danger. Brand's optimism was revolutionary, Webb's was evolutionary.

Attitudes to the 2018 Royal Wedding are another example. For some on the left, it was a bleak symbol of entrenched privilege, and of the media's willingness to endorse inequality. But others viewed it more optimistically. To them it was progressive to watch a mixed-race divorcee from an ordinary background marry into the Royal family – with the centrepieces of the ceremony being an African-American pastor and a gospel choir.[6] The difference between these

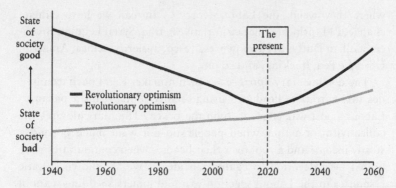

positions wasn't between contrasting values but between belief or otherwise in the Golden Era; between the view that the wedding of Harry and Meghan was definitive proof of decline, and the view that it signified a progress of sorts.

The right-wing press's subsequent treatment of the couple suggests that perhaps the left should have been more willing to see it as a positive development – to be embraced and protected.

THE SPIRIT OF '45

Christopher Shaw writes that 'the folk memories that underpin Labourite nostalgia are as enduring as the elite resonance of the stately home'.[7] Left populism thrives on the idea of a lost past, when the ideals of the left manifested themselves in an authentic, unspoilt way. The Golden Era supplies a version of history to support this.

The Golden Era existed, according to the myth's present incarnation, before the 1980s; before 'neoliberalism'; before Thatcherism and Blairism blurred class lines. It represents a glorious, uncomplicated past, an extended version of the famous 1976 summer (the 'hottest since records began'). Hose-pipe bans, cut grass, the tinkle of the ice-cream van; red rosettes and the creation of the NHS.

The world said to have replaced this Golden Era is dystopian by comparison. No Nye Bevan. No Keir Hardie. No mining villages where they weigh the Labour vote ... Instead we have climate change, PFI (priocate finance initiatives), Iraq, Syria, Lehman Brothers, Gillian Duffy, MPs' expenses, Tesco, austerity, selfies, Amazon, Uber, Le Pen, fracking, and so on.

The documentary *Spirit of '45* by filmmaker Ken Loach exemplifies this narrative. Produced using archive footage, it's a paean to Labour's post-war effort to 'win the peace'. The film eulogises the collectivism of a time when people did not want much beyond a steady income and a roof over their heads – when communities were united by a devotion to egalitarian ideals. We are shown ecstatic responses to the Labour election win and miners shedding tears of joy at the creation of the welfare state. Anyone sympathetic to Labour would struggle to not be moved.

Loach's idyll is brought to a halt, within the documentary, by the election of Thatcher. This ushers in the new, 'neoliberal' era, characterised by poverty, industrial decline and dog-eat-dog individualism. Hence, *Spirit of '45* acts as a romantic counterpoint to a right-wing modern world which is, Loach suggests, in its 'final throes'. [8]

Much of Loach's nostalgia – and that of other Golden Era believers – relates to class. Solidarity among working people is felt to have been destroyed by Thatcherism, and a longing for its return is a driver of the myth. Owen Jones describes his wistfulness for 'the brass bands and union banners', the 'vibrancy', and the 'sense of pride in a shared working-class existence' that the period before the 1980s for him represents. [9]

The contemporary zeitgeist is considered selfish, bigoted and greedy by comparison. George Monbiot, for example, mourns modern materialism, which he describes as 'a social affliction, visited upon us by government policy, corporate strategy, the collapse of communities and civic life, and our acquiescence in a system that is eating us from the inside out'. [10] He argues that we are failing to see what matters, or to live the good life.

Corbyn-supporting singer Lily Allen made a similar critique in her 2009 single 'The Fear'. She took aim at the soulless, money-obsessed twenty-first century, mourning the fact that people do not 'know what's right and what's real any more'.

In its more overtly political incarnation, the Golden Era suggests that Labour modernisers sold out on the party's original ideals. 'Unchallenged by craven Labour,' Monbiot wrote in 2014, 'Britain slides towards ever more selfishness.'[11] For many, this translated into support for Corbyn, a politician seen as having been 'on the right side of history' in resisting most changes since the 1970s[12] – and into disdain for Tony Blair, the only Labour leader 'who did not want to turn the clock back for a single second'.[13] The 2020 maiden speech of Labour MP Zarah Sultana summed up this idea, describing 'forty years of Thatcherism'.[14]

In policy terms, meanwhile, the Golden Era tends to identify ideal solutions from *before* things went wrong – rather than to address present reality. Golden Era believers seek to undo ancient mistakes, or to get past policies right at the second attempt.

For example, Corbyn and McDonnell's support for Irish Republicanism comes from the fact that Northern Ireland exists as a consequence of imperialism. The populist left have long championed a united Ireland, even after the Good Friday agreement.[15] If we could turn back the clock to before British colonisation, a united Ireland would clearly be the progressive goal. But seeing as the colonisers are long dead – and a significant minority in the country emphatically don't want a united Ireland – the goal must be the most peaceful possible compromise and the dismantling of borders and barriers between the two countries.

The Golden Era originates from philosophies which idealise the state of nature. Examples include the work of Rousseau, Plato's idea that our world is only a shadow of the original, or the biblical notion of Eden.

This raises another question: is the Golden Era a new narrative for the left, or has it always existed? By definition, you would think, the myth could not have been believed in the past . . .

This is true to a point. The Golden Era account of history has gained significant extra traction since the 2008 banking crisis. The term 'neoliberalism' – used to describe the forces that have perverted and polluted the Golden Era – burst into common usage only in the last five or ten years.

However, a spirit of retrospection has always existed on the left. Those inspired by Corbyn may be nostalgic for the 'authentically' Labour 1945–51 government[16] (some sport T-shirts asking, 'What would Clem do?'). Yet the far left of the time did not believe they were living through a Golden Era without disappointment or compromise. Labour's founding purpose was even felt by some to have been betrayed by Attlee, a man who supported the monarchy, sided with America in the Korean War, signed Britain up to NATO and made a virtue of his suburban pragmatism ('The people's flag is palest pink,' Attlee joked).[17] The *New Statesman* claimed in 1954 that Attlee's government had been 'the only event of its kind in history which contributed almost nothing new or imaginative'.[18] Ralph Miliband said the 1945–51 government merely wanted to 'improve the efficiency of a capitalist economy'.[19] Tony Benn remembered the Attlee government as having 'no real socialism in it'.[20] And there was frustration with the 'failure to redistribute wealth or break down rigid class barriers'.[21] Had he been in Parliament, it seems likely that Corbyn would have been the first to cry betrayal. Indeed, as recently as 2014 he criticised Attlee's 'neo-colonialism'.[22]

So, while contemporary left populists imagine the post-war years as the roar of unchallenged socialism, things at the time did not feel so halcyon. Even in the aftermath of a New Jerusalem being constructed, there were accusations that those who had built it were bean-counters and sell-outs, unfit to lace the boots of the giants who had come before.[23]

Indeed, if you look at British history, it's hard to find a time when left-wing values were satisfied in the way the Golden Era supposes. Closer inspection of previous Labour leaders – even those remembered as impeccable socialists – often reveals more expediency than we like to recall. Historian Tom Crewe points this out:

What authentic version of the Labour Party is Corbyn fighting for? Presumably one that existed before he entered the House of Commons in 1983, given that he was one of the top ten Labour rebels even in the 1983–87 Parliament. It is, I think, from the foundation myth of the Labour Party as a movement of idealists and working people finding solidarity in the struggle for their rights that he derives his chief inspiration. Corbyn's hero is Keir Hardie. Yet Hardie . . . successfully argued for the party to be called 'Labour' rather than 'Socialist' for fear of alienating potential supporters, and refused to back campaigns for the extension of the franchise because he was more anxious to secure practical reforms . . . There has never been a Labour Party that has not made compromises in the hope of improving its chances at electoral success.[24]

This brings the Golden Era into focus. As Crewe implies, the myth does not just stand for an economic reading that says 1945–79 was a socialist utopia. It represents a quest for something departed; a Labour Party spirit which was original and true; an age of real and meaningful struggle; and, consequentially, a benchmark against which modern life can never quite match up.[25]

In this light, the popularity of the Golden Era myth since 2008 can be viewed differently. In the same way as an adolescent going through a tough patch may idealise their childhood, the left breathes life into the Golden Era in times of uncertainty. Faced with a globalisation process to which we don't have answers, a narrative of decline has gained popularity.

DECLINE, ISOLATIONISM AND CHANGE

The worst consequence of the Golden Era is the failure to face the future. In particular, the myth stops the left from finding ways for progressive values and globalisation to coexist.

The Golden Era was a period before globalisation (at least in its contemporary form) had really begun. The decline which the myth mourns mainly stems from the harmful consequences of globalisation – the departure of jobs abroad, the rise of multinational corporations, and so on. Likewise, globalisation has rendered obsolete (for now, at least) many levers traditionally used by the left, such as command economics or domestic wealth taxes. Regaining power of these levers is difficult in the short term, without withdrawing from globalisation wholesale – which would probably involve making the country poorer and less culturally open.

Believers in the myth do not accept this. They are, therefore, amenable to resurrecting the Golden Era in its entirety, believing it to be a left-wing idyll from which we have catastrophically departed. They never engage fully with what a reversal means. At best, they behave as if simultaneous drifts to the left and to the right since the 1970s have happened completely independently of each other.

Labour's Brexit stance epitomised this. Corbyn is a Golden Era believer, and a life-long Eurosceptic as a result. The EU symbolises, for him, the advance of global capitalism. His precedent for this was Tony Benn's Alternative Economic Strategy in the 1970s, which proposed that the UK become a siege economy to hold back the changes afoot. Benn campaigned against Britain joining the Common Market in 1975 and continued, throughout his life, to oppose the EU and the economic integration of nations. Corbyn has followed suit throughout his parliamentary career, describing the EU as a 'European Empire' and a 'Frankenstein' project.[26]

As a result, Corbyn's endorsement of Remain in 2016 was expedient and half-hearted. He suggested triggering Article 50 immediately after the referendum, and continually hid from the issue from then on. He sacked pro-EU shadow ministers, abstained on many of the major votes, and refused for a long time to back a second referendum on the final deal, despite it being party policy. Labour's 2017 manifesto, meanwhile, involved withdrawal from the single market and the end of free movement.[27] Only in 2019, thanks to a looming No Deal and immense pressure from within Labour, did he temper his pro-Brexit instincts.

Yet throughout this, Corbyn's rhetoric stressed support for immigrants and refugees; for world peace, prosperity for all, social liberalism and the environment – causes which are advanced by the integration of countries.

We see this contradiction more explicitly among the 'Lexiteers' (left-wing Brexiteers) with whom Corbyn aligned before 2015. Dennis Skinner openly subscribed to isolationism, for instance, while taking for granted positive developments over the same period. Ken Loach allies Europe with 'neoliberalism', claiming it has 'caused hardship and poverty for millions of people'[28] – but remains committed to pro-migrant causes. Former Labour MP Kelvin Hopkins argues that:

> [a social democratic world] existed in the immediate post-War dec-ades, and it worked brilliantly, with full employment, burgeoning welfare states and the living standards of working-class people ris-ing at an unprecedented rate. We should all work to re-establish that world.[29]

The notion that the toothpaste will painlessly go back into the tube like this is one of the great Golden Era misconceptions. The idea is that we can extricate ourselves from globalisation while los-ing nothing by way of prosperity or diversity.

Indeed, the Brexit negotiations – which have been compared to the 'removal of an egg from an omelette'[30] – show the impossibility of returning to the good old days. Britain will, in all likelihood, have to embrace economic hardship and capitulate to anti-migrant feeling if we are to revert to pre-globalised socialism. And even if Brexit does give British socialists extra freedom to borrow and nationalise,[31] the economic hit will be such that we will just as likely find ourselves in a tax-cutting race-to-the-bottom, to keep investors and jobs.[32]

This is why the rejection of interconnectedness – exemplified by Brexit – has united the left and right tips of the political horseshoe. Nobody doubts that the castles on these hills are different: an inequality-free, protectionist Never-Neverland in the case of the for-mer; an immigrant-free, colonialist Narnia in the case of the latter. But, because both view history through a Golden Era lens, they for-get the things from the past that are at odds with their values. Ken Loach evokes the equality and solidarity of the 1950s – but not the dangerous working conditions, jingoism or snobbery. Nigel Farage recalls patriotism, paternalism and empire, forgetting the national-ised and unionised economy (which he'd surely object to). Both make the same backward-looking prescriptions, on the basis of wholly dif-ferent memories.

Golden Era myopia is exemplified by responses, on the left, to Blue Labour. The concept, created by academic Maurice Glasman, was an effort to devise a 'conservative socialism that places family, faith and work at the heart of a new politics of reciprocity, mutuality and solidarity'.[33] A Eurosceptic ideal for many,[34] Blue Labour harked back not just to 1945 (which Glasman considered to be the point when Labour first became bureaucratic and elitist) but to before that.[35]

Unlike left populists, Blue Labourites do not delude themselves: they simply feel that losing certain progressive aspects of an interconnected world is a price worth paying for more economic equality and a greater sense of community. I do not agree with this. But it's a respectable view, which doesn't rely on the Golden Era.

Yet Glasman's embrace of non-progressive aspects of the past meant the idea never really caught on in left-wing circles. Commentator Neal Lawson epitomised the general response: 'Two thirds of Blue Labour I get. One third I don't.'[36] Lawson valued the emphasis on community, and on curtailing financial globalisation, but was less enthused by 'flag, family and faith'.

The failure of Blue Labour also shows why left-wing Golden Eras are harder to resurrect than we imagine. Labour MP Bridget Phillipson sums this up:

Elegiac lyricism about a vanished world of large unionised workplaces full of men doing semi-skilled jobs, shared cultural experiences, shared religious affiliation, and tight community links does not amount to a plausible programme for government. That world has gone, it isn't coming back.

She adds:

let us not forget . . . that many of those jobs were hard and dangerous. The reality that my son will probably never work down a coalmine, and that my daughter will probably not leave school to work in a textile mill at fifteen is one I welcome, even as I worry about . . . what their future will hold.[37]

Once we examine the old days, we see that the left has achieved a lot for a group that has been, left populists claim, 'on the defensive and intellectual retreat' since the 1960s.[38] We get a picture of a past which was more collectivist, secure and fair in some ways, but which also had worse quality of life and more right-wing social policies. This does not just apply to the rights of minorities but to living standards in Labour's traditional heartlands. The pre-'neoliberal' Golden Era was the age of the lunatic asylum, *The Black and White Minstrel Show*, the typing pool and the Secondary Modern.

Indeed, the things we like from the Golden Era often connect to the things we do not. Workplace solidarity overlapped with tribal hostility to minorities in some quarters. Stronger communities were frequently tied up with a reliance on traditional gender roles. It is hard to fully resurrect one side in these equations without resurrecting the other.

This also applies to many of the areas where left populists seek to 'undo' errors. When it comes to industry, for instance, the actions of the Thatcher governments meant that, compared to many European nations, Britain's post-industrial shift was painful and unfair. But the solutions which left populists propose – 'tearing down the whole edifice of Thatcherism [and] healing Britain of the damage done',[39] or re-industrialising the north in an effort to return to that era (as Corbyn has suggested)[40] – ignore the fact that the situation before Thatcher was far from perfect.

Likewise, reversing fully the situation in the Middle East, by dissolving the state of Israel, might please some left populists. But it would also – even setting aside how bloody it would be – resurrect the issue which first created the situation, of a huge, historically persecuted and stateless diaspora.

DECLINE AND NIHILISM

There are other consequences of the Golden Era. Chief among these is the sense of crisis which the myth generates. It invites campaign strategies which are devoid of an optimistic vision, feeding despair and nihilism.[41]

Some left populists refute this. They believe that narratives of deterioration chase out complacency, create shared roots and help recruit for good causes.

To discuss this, we must first separate decline from nostalgia. There is a difference between feeling things were *better* in the past – the only answer being to go back – and feeling that things were *good* in the past, offering a shared experience to learn and take strength from.

According to research, the latter can 'enhance a sense of meaning', playing a 'pivotal existential function'. Some studies even suggest that nostalgia and optimism are linked.[42]

But a sense of decline – which is what the Golden Era myth really describes – does not have the same effect. Decline cannot be a building block for progress. It's true, to a point, that highlighting how bad things are acts as a wake-up call – if you focus on specific issues. People may respond in small ways, by recycling waste or donating money. However, a feeling of historical decline generally leads less to urgency and agency than to hopelessness and individualism. (This is an important thing to remember as the UK deals with the fallout from COVID-19 – particularly in the context of the bleak economic outlook once the immediate crisis has passed.)

Studies like Broken Windows Theory (published in 1982) emphasise that the more residents feel their area is falling into ruin, the more disrepair and antisocial behaviour spirals.[43] A self-fulfilling prophecy develops, where people have less stake in their neighbourhood, turning inwards and contributing to the decline. In the face of a bigger crisis – a society of unending broken windows – the effect is surely the same.

The aftermath of the First World War, for example, was a point when pessimism was widespread and understandable. The consequence was not a collective urge to make things better, but the disillusionment and attraction to extremes which contributed to the Second World War. The opening lines of D. H. Lawrence's 1928 novel *Lady Chatterley's Lover* sum this up:

> The cataclysm has happened, we are among the ruins, we start to build up new little habitats, to have new little hopes. It is rather hard work: there is now no smooth road into the future: but we go round, or scramble over the obstacles. We've got to live, no matter how many skies have fallen.[44]

For Lawrence, a lack of progress and purpose did not lead to a belief in a more egalitarian society. In the rest of *Lady Chatterley's Lover*, he presents the individual sphere as a refuge to hide in. His view, one critic points out, was that 'an industrialized, rationalized England was, by and large, a lost cause'.[45] Thus, Lawrence's polemic was one of libertarian individualism, with widespread education and social progress deemed impossible.[46] 'The only thing was not to care.'[47]

Lawrence was not alone. Many people in the inter-war years – especially artists and writers – slid into nihilism, individualism or even fascism (with its promise of a coherent social order) as a refuge from a world in decline.

The book *The Politics of Cultural Despair* by Fritz Richard Stern looks at the rise of Nazism in this light. He critiques several cultural theorists in inter-war Germany for indulging in the 'dangers and dilemmas of a particular type of cultural despair'. According to Stern, these theorists

> attacked, often incisively and justly, the deficiencies of German culture and the German spirit. But they were more than critics of Germany's cultural crisis; they were its symptoms and victims as well.[48]

Using Golden Era narratives, these critics emphasised an original German spirit which had been forgotten. In the process, they encouraged the mentality which opened the door to Hitler, with his promise to restore German greatness.

A modern parallel is the subset of Bernie Sanders's supporters who threatened to vote for Trump following Hillary Clinton's victory in the 2016 Democratic Primaries. We should not overstate this: just 22 per cent of Sanders supporters said they would vote for Trump, and it seems unlikely that even this number followed through.[49] However, for the minority who did, or who did not vote, the central idea was that Clinton represented 'continuity' of America's decline. She was portrayed as a 'more of the same' candidate (the same, of course, being Obama). And, whereas Clinton was seen as representing a 'further slide' towards 'global dynastic rule', as one put it,[50] Trump at least pledged to do as Sanders had promised, and put the brakes on – albeit in a far more reactionary way. (The 2020 Democratic Primaries seemed to have many of the same dynamics at play, with loathing for Joe Biden often appearing to exceed opposition to Trump.)

Indeed, research found that a gap in optimism – not a gap in policy – was the major distinction between Sanders and Clinton backers in 2016. The former were more likely to emphasise that inequality or life opportunities were getting worse, even though they were less likely to back policies that would remedy these things.[51] Hence, the Sanders–Clinton divisions were less 'leftists versus centrists' than 'declinists versus non-declinists'. On one side were those who felt there had been a slide into 'neoliberalism' since the Golden Era and wanted to see it stopped at all costs. On the other were those who believed – like Obama – that only by moving forward, through the globalisation process, could the 'arc of the moral universe' be made to 'bend towards justice'.[52]

Of course, you could point out that wanting 'change' is not the same as wanting 'reversal'. Obama himself won on a change agenda. Yet it is striking that the 'change' left populists propose almost always represents a form of Golden Era-style isolation. They often support protectionism or re-industrialisation, seem relaxed about cutting migration and oppose many international institutions.

Hence, the Golden Era is key to how we frame the debate. If we share left populists' sense of a 'neoliberal' decline having occurred, then even a vote for a politician like Trump starts to make sense, as a last hurl of the dice.

In the UK, Brexit is a symptom of the same thing. By believing in decline narratives, we have made them self-fulfilling. Britain looks like it is heading towards a poorer, less equal and more culturally insular future – thanks to the tales of crisis and apocalypse promoted by the Brexit right and the 'Lexit' left. Decline narratives beget decline.

This is exacerbated and enabled by the fact that, as we will discuss in more detail later, a sense of decline is endemic to prosperous nations. Brits and Americans, for example, are more pessimistic than citizens in countries with much lower living standards.[53]

Populists use Golden Era narratives to tap into this. Yet because they do not have answers, all they are able to propose are reckless, counterproductive tonics which make the situation worse.

The better approach is to face the future realistically and optimistically, providing a narrative for where the country goes from here. As the pollster behind the above research on prosperity and pessimism concludes:

> If they are to revive their fortunes, mainstream politicians [must] persuade voters of something . . . fundamental: that life today is not as bad as millions of voters feel, and that the future is not as bleak as they fear.

PROGRESS AS A DEFAULT?

The difference between declinists and non-declinists raises the question of how far we go in refuting the Golden Era. Do we reject any claim that anything is getting worse?

At the extreme end of the spectrum sits a group of pro-globalisation liberals who take a stance not a million miles from this. Sometimes known as the New Optimists, these include the likes of Stephen Pinker, author of *The Better Angels of Our Nature*. They use data-driven arguments to prove that things are moving in a progressive direction. Their role is iconoclastic, confronting Golden Era believers with good-news narratives which are statistically watertight but which often don't *feel* true.[54] The trends they chart include the decline of violence, poverty reduction, economic growth, falling inequality *between* countries, shrinking nuclear arsenals and the rising number of democracies. They make powerful and true arguments.

However, to reject Golden Era approaches doesn't require an unsceptical embrace of this swashbuckling belief in progress. To begin with, New Optimists can, in some cases, give the impression that advances are inevitable, rather than a result of human choices. Looking at the rise of an uber-reactionary like Trump, it's obvious that progress can all too easily be stopped. Indeed, the unexpected appearance of a global pandemic this year demonstrates that nothing can be taken for granted.

Furthermore, there are many issues which are moving in the wrong direction, where change is urgently needed: climate change, housing, the impacts of automation, deep inequality *within* countries, the rise of mega-cities at the expense of regions and towns, the largest refugee flows since the Second World War, and so on. It is possible to overdose on the New Optimism and assume that these things too will right themselves.[55]

So, rejecting Golden Era dogma doesn't mean embracing all-out progress narratives. It just means engaging empirically with the ways the world is changing. It means recognising that, while history has included better and worse periods for progressive values, there has never been an Arcadia in the way that left populists like Ken Loach imagine.

Ultimately, many New Optimists provide incontrovertible good news. They are correct to ask why left-wingers disregard or disbelieve the tidings they bring, and are justified in wondering if left populism is a state of mind that would exist come-what-may – feeding off dissatisfaction with the present, regardless of the facts.

Indeed, this is why the Golden Era is alarming. Because the myth makes decline the default, it doesn't allow for peace, prosperity, equality or enjoyment of the good times if they materialise – or if, as in some cases, they have already materialised. The notion of a society in right-wing decline – with the left forever swimming upstream – encourages a 'nothing to lose' mentality which ultimately jeopardises our achievements.

Anthony Crosland concluded *The Future of Socialism* by saying that Labour should place 'greater emphasis on private life, on freedom and dissent, on culture, beauty, leisure and even frivolity'.[56] The left needed an offer for people who wanted happy, fulfilling lives; those who had once struggled to stay afloat but who, by 1956, had achieved many economic basics.

His central point, underscored by the book's recurring question, 'Is this socialism?', was that progressives had to find a way to exist if they won. Crosland did not claim that this moment had arrived. But he thought it had moved closer, and that advances should be recognised so that new challenges could be addressed. What would Labour policies look like as the population grew more prosperous? How could socialism be more outward-looking and socially liberal? To be effective in a developed country, the left could not always start from a premise of deterioration and failure.

This remains a distinction between populists and pluralists within Labour. The latter are less likely, for instance, to say we should 'tear down' or 'smash' the system,[57] and are presented by populists as defenders of the status quo as a result. To the extent that this is true, it is the result of different perceptions about what the modern status quo is. Pluralists wish to defend advances in living standards. They want 'continuity' when it comes to the increasingly socially liberal attitudes of the population. They seek to uphold 'establishment' support for international human rights. They want 'business as usual' when it comes to the reduction of developing-world poverty. And they believe that an imperfect institution like the EU is better than what came before.

Hence, unlike Golden Era believers – who hold that progressive values have been on a losing streak for decades – pluralists face a tricky balancing act. They seek ways of consolidating the benefits of our interconnected world, while ensuring that these benefits are not overshadowed by the big drawbacks of globalisation. Accusations of timidity or lack of ingenuity here are justified. But accusations of conservatism – as though there is something right-wing in seeking to maintain left-of-centre achievements – are not.

13

The Appeal of the Golden Era

There are four 'quests' which guide people towards the Golden Era myth. Like the triggers for the Dark Knight and the Puppet Master, these are not particular to the populist left – although in some cases they are more pronounced.

THE QUEST FOR OLD CERTAINTIES

Our lives as children lacked self-consciousness and the freedom to make our own choices but were often happier. We had fewer experiences but fewer disappointments. We were not aware of the things beyond our grasp.

The quest for old certainties is the political equivalent of this. It refers to nostalgia for times when decision-making was less complex and society was simpler.

It is a quest which is getting more widespread. Polling in 2012 to mark the Queen's Jubilee found that, while 65 per cent of Brits said that living standards have improved since her coronation, only 30 per cent felt that the country had 'changed for the better'.[1] A significant proportion acknowledged advances in medicine, transport, technology and education, but still felt Britain was in worse shape than in 1952. The table below shows this (excluding 'neither' and 'don't know').

The answers of those over sixty – who have lived through the entire period – are an accentuation of the result. This group were

Table 13.1. Source: YouGov

	Agree (all ages)	Disagree (all ages)	Agree (over-60s)	Disagree (over-60s)
'The quality of life for the average person in Britain has changed for the better over the past 60 years'	65%	19%	72%	18%
'Britain has changed for the better over the past 60 years'	30%	43%	27%	55%

particularly appreciative of progress in their health and wealth, yet were disproportionately negative about the state of the nation. So, even within a group very much aware of advances made, the feeling persisted that something has been lost along the way.

This is partly because older people of every generation are more nostalgic.[2] But this is only half the story. Other research compares young people's optimism about the future with previous generations', and finds that contemporary young people are much more likely to say their parents' lives were superior.[3] In other words, British optimism is falling 'in real terms'. Why?

For many on the left, the answer would be that inequalities have undermined material improvements. There is no doubt that this is a big factor. A world with rising inequality is a world where the pressure of 'keeping up' is more pronounced, and where the opulent lifestyles of others are on vivid display.[4] As George Orwell wrote, 'The lady in the Rolls-Royce car is more damaging to morale than a fleet of Goering's bombing planes.'[5]

Yet a hankering for equality is only part of the quest for old certainties. Many economic inequalities, after all, have grown up alongside demographic change and a geopolitical reordering. Societies have become intermingled and liberal, and the distance that an individual travels from home in their lifetime has increased exponentially. Exposure and scrutiny have shone a light on things that never troubled us before.

So, greater equality is just one trapping of a 1950s society which was simpler in a range of ways. Peter Kellner sums this up when analysing the above polling:

> We know that we are better off, healthier, better educated and better informed than our grandparents. We travel further, live longer and enjoy more freedom. But we respect our politicians less. We regard our neighbourhoods as less safe and less friendly. We regret that Britain has been relegated from the premier division of world powers. Many of us think that globalisation, immigration and Europe have changed Britain for the worse. Inequality has grown.

This provides a near-perfect synopsis of the factors which drive the quest for old certainties: a desire for a world less confusing; for a society less technically, culturally and ethically complex; for communities which were more localised, informal and steady; for an economic structure without riches 'beyond our grasp'; and for a period when you knew where you stood on class, nationhood, sex and party politics.[6]

The quest for old certainties provides ammunition for right and left alike. For right populists, the old certainties are to do with rules, sovereignty and respect for elders. They relate to common sense on race and the work ethic, and to Britain knowing where we stood in the world.

For left populists, old certainties represent straightforward socialism. The challenges of the post-war years seem, from our present vantage point, simpler than modern hurdles. Besides which, it was easier for progressives to choose sides fifty years ago. Dilemmas that now split the left, like 'red versus green' and 'open versus closed', were less prominent.

Wrapped up in this is a contemporary preference for 'authenticity', which is a 'sub-quest' of the quest for old certainties. In a world which many fear has become a chrome dystopia, authenticity, carries increasing weight. This is most obvious among post-materialist groups, manifesting itself in distressed clothes, exposed brickwork, farmers' markets and other harmless forms of shabby chic. People are increasingly proud of their ability, as consumers, to know their lumpy but locally sourced apple from their pesticide-polished one.

This has fed the demand for a political discourse that 'reflect[s] the growing currency of authenticity' – including expectations that politicians should be personal and informal.[7] Increasingly, as 'consumers' of politics, we believe we can tell faux authenticity from the real thing.

Indeed, the great success of both left and right populists is in creating a stereotype of the modern, inauthentic politician, identifiable by their perma-tan, toothpaste smiles, sharp suits and reliance on spin.[8] These caricatures make the 'old certainties' of the Golden Era all the more appealing.

Looked at like this, we can understand the Golden Era appeal of a left-populist politician like Corbyn, compared by some to a 'craft ale'[9] – or of a right populist like Trump, who appears to 'resurrect the spirit of the authentic American entrepreneur'.[10] Each represents something which feels, to the wary politics consumer, less mass-produced. Each fulfils the desire for the straight-talking politician of yesteryear who knew the group for whom they spoke and called a spade a spade.

The sophisticated, uncertain modern world can take much of the credit for increases in quality of life. And however wistful some are for mining communities and the family butcher, most are glad that other 'old certainties' have retreated, be it corporal punishment or infant mortality.

Yet the quest for old certainties remains a powerful emotional driver. Whether through localism or through attempts to demystify democracy, we should take seriously the effects on human happiness of an ultra-complex world. If pluralists do not think about this, then the quest for old certainties will continue to create a licence for populists.

THE QUEST TO FEEL PROGRESS

The earlier in the economic development process a country is, the more optimistic its people feel. One survey, mentioned already, showed that among seven countries – India, Thailand, Indonesia, Brazil, Britain, Germany and the US – there was a correlation between high GDP and disagreement with the statement, 'The next generation will probably be safer, richer and healthier than the last.'[11] Affluence and pessimism are linked. (None of the countries polled is notably more equal than the UK, so equality doesn't explain the findings.)

The same goes for broader ideas of change. According to another poll across nations, Brits are among the least likely to say 'the world is getting better', and Chinese people are the most likely.[12]

This brings us to the quest to feel progress, which describes the need to believe that your society is going somewhere. This explains, in my view, why the average person in twenty-first-century China or India is less susceptible to decline narratives. Despite lower living standards, people in these countries see the promise of a freer, fairer, richer life for their children. They have a clearer direction of travel.

By contrast, developed countries have already gone through this. That is not to say that places like Britain are at the summit. But the near-vertical ascent in terms of development, which is currently being scaled in India and China, is over in the UK. We are on flatter terrain.

Hence, unlike during periods of explosive growth or social improvement, many Westerners no longer feel that their countries are progressing. They fear we have 'peaked' (especially as, in our ageing societies, many of those who lived through these periods are still alive and recall the sense of progress). This holds true even if the reason for the lack of progress is that many of the steepest climbs are behind us. There is less of a clear answer to the question 'where do we go from here?' As a result, memories of those steeper climbs – of the Golden Era, when there was a lofty end-point to clamber towards – become rosy.

So, the quest to feel progress is about the conviction that the best is yet to come. It fuels the Golden Era myth, because we recall the struggle towards a goal more strongly than its fulfilment. 'To travel hopefully is better than to arrive.'

Again, this has a particular manifestation on the left. For example, the reality is that we cannot create the NHS or the welfare state a second time. The challenge now is how to fund, expand and structure them. But the quest to feel progress means that we eulogise the era when we were struggling to build these institutions.

The aforementioned Ken Loach film *Spirit of '45* is a good example, with its suggestion that the immediate post-war period was a better age. This is despite the fact that, to state the obvious, it was only necessary to create an NHS because we did not at the time have one. Hence, Loach's film is a celebration of past struggle and of the spirit which made that struggle bearable.

Indeed, the question of 'where next?' for social democracy explains, in part, the resurgence of the Golden Era narrative. We are yet to develop an egalitarian narrative, backed up by policies, for where we're going. In the absence of this, it falls to populists like Corbyn, who at least offer change of some sort, to cater to it. Even if their solutions actually represent a step back, these populists provide a sense of movement and struggle. They offer momentum, if not progress (excusing the pun).

Ultimately, the quest to feel progress gets people on the left out of bed in the morning, whether they are populists or not. As the character of Jean puts it in *Labour of Love*, James Graham's play about the Labour Party, 'We're a movement. That's what we do. We *move*.' The challenge is how we fulfil the desire to keep advancing, at a point when some egalitarian advances have been made but while the best steps to address other, looming issues remain unclear.

THE QUEST FOR URGENCY

In *An Inspector Calls*, by socialist playwright J. B. Priestley, the capitalist patriarch Mr Birling explains to his family: 'I'm talking as a hard-headed, practical man of business. And I say there isn't a chance of war.' The play was written in 1945 but set in 1912, and the dramatic irony is obvious. Birling adds, 'The Titanic – she sails next week . . . Unsinkable, absolutely unsinkable.'[13]

Fears about this type of smugness drive the quest for urgency. This describes the suspicion that acknowledgers of progress undermine the case for change, and demean the suffering that continues to exist. It says that the Golden Era story keeps people on their toes, helping to avoid Birling-style 'business as usual'.

An example of this is the response to Steven Pinker's 2011 book *The Better Angels of Our Nature*. Using a range of datasets, Pinker charts the decline of almost every type of violence, from genocide to the smacking of children.

The reaction to this from many on the left was one of disbelief and anger. A *Guardian* reviewer – who admitted to not having finished the book – called it 'a comfort blanket for the smug' which trivialised the Iraq War.[14] Further to the left, *International Socialist Review* described *The Better Angels* as a 'snow job', designed to be well received in establishment circles.[15] The authors criticised Pinker for 'relativizing' suffering and reinforcing the 'apologetics for Western Imperial violence'. Some criticism focused on Pinker's methodology, particularly the decision to count the proportion killed by violence, not the overall number. Others said that the book ignored non-violent suffering or was complacent.

Pinker had a rebuff to these points. He convincingly defended his decision to focus on proportion, not overall number.[16] He explained why his book could not have charted the decline of 'all bad things'.[17] And he took seriously the major violence that persists – refusing, for example, to predict that the fall in violence would continue.[18]

The real question is why some left-wingers were so determined to disagree with Pinker. Indeed, the subtext of most criticism was that, true or not, *The Better Angels* should not have been written. His good news about violence was certainly less welcome than the bad news about inequality provided by Thomas Piketty in *Capital in the Twenty-first Century* – which was hailed as proof of something long suspected.

The reasons for this lie in the quest for urgency. As Pinker acknowledges, 'No one has ever recruited activists to a cause by announcing that things are getting better . . . Bearers of good news are often advised to keep their mouths shut.'[19]

The attitudes of many on the populist left very much reflect this. Following the 2015 election, for example, journalist Stephen Bush was asked online whether 'the purposes for which Labour was created have largely been achieved'. Bush's perfunctory response – 'arguably' – prompted furious accusations of complacency.[20]

Meanwhile, *The Future of Socialism* – a sophisticated analysis in 1956 of how much progress had been made on Labour's founding goals – is dismissed in the same way. 'Crosland's thesis might be summed up [as] "We've won,"' writes Owen Jones.[21]

Up to a point, this is fair enough. We can see the benefits of the quest for urgency in many campaigns for good causes. The public are encouraged to help end social or humanitarian problems, on the basis that these crises are getting worse. Charities, social marketers and interest groups have taken this approach, and newspapers, businesses and local authorities have followed suit.

Yet this has limitations. Not only can the quest for urgency lead, in a climate where everything is presented in this way, to the despair described in previous chapters, it can also stop us evaluating progress. While Golden Era believers are right to caution against the idea that there is a shelf of warm air lifting us ever upwards, the alternative view – that we need to deny achievements to sustain energy – is equally unhelpful.

THE QUEST FROM ROMANTIC DISSENT

'People of our generation aren't able to die for good causes any longer. We had all that done for us, in the thirties and the forties . . . There aren't any good, brave causes left.'[22] So complains Jimmy Porter, protagonist of the 1956 play *Look Back in Anger* – the original 'angry young man' text.

Jimmy knows previous decades were not a Golden Era. The war looms large in the memory, as does the poverty before it. By 1956 the fortunes of working-class men like Jimmy were improving, and he effectively concedes that his cohort has 'never had it so good' (as Harold Macmillan famously put it).

Yet Jimmy still rebels against his sanitised and risk-free historical moment. He regrets his interests being aligned with the political direction of the era. Herein we see the quest for romantic dissent, our fourth explanation of the Golden Era narrative. This is the desire to feel we are battling against the direction of travel – that we are a lone voice against a dystopian zeitgeist.

The quest for romantic dissent fuels the Golden Era, because the very idea of dissent is premised on a society moving in the wrong direction. The example of Jimmy Porter is useful because it shows that, even at a juncture with little basis for a decline narrative – a juncture in fact venerated by contemporary socialists – there were still people who wanted to believe in one.

I refer to 'romantic' dissent because underlying the quest is a desire for glory, or else an idealised and tragic vision of a past washed away by modernity. Sometimes, the quest is for something raw and true, lost because of technological or material gains.[23] Other times it is for a yesteryear which seems more heroic or real – closer, somehow, to what it is to be human.

For a modern example of the quest, let's look at Russell Brand's essay 'We No Longer Have the Luxury of Tradition'.[24] This was the centrepiece of a *New Statesman* edition which Brand edited in 2013.

> The formation of the NHS, holiday pay, sick pay, the weekend . . . were not achieved in the lifetime of the directionless London rioters. They are uninformed of the left's great legacy as it is dismantled around them. Our materialistic consumer culture relentlessly stimulates our desire. Our media ceaselessly engages our fear, our government triangulates and administrates, ensuring there are no obstacles to the agendas of these slow-thighed beasts, slouching towards Bethlehem.

Brand adds that, in recent decades, we have 'succumbed to an ideology that is 100 per cent corrupt', and predicts a 'struggle for survival if our species is to avoid expiry'.[25] He yearns for the 'service of the land', heralding 'Pagan' and 'Celtic' codes of 'protection and survival' and regretting that these worlds have been 'aborted and replaced with nihilistic narratives of individualism'. 'The Spiritual Revolution has come and we have only an instant to act,' Brand declares. While others 'burp and giggle', he's able to see that 'the survival of the planet' is at stake.

Brand's decision to quote W. B. Yeats's apocalyptic poem 'The Second Coming' ('slow-thighed beasts . . .') – to imply the march of elites towards world domination – is telling. Yeats, an aristocratic poet who led the Irish Romantic movement, epitomised the quest for romantic dissent. He loved heroic gestures and was drawn to mythologised recollections of Ireland's past, dreaming of the moment when that world would be violently restored.[26] He lamented that 'All the more intense forms of literature . . . lost their hold . . . as life grew safe.'[27] 'The Second Coming' epitomises the beauty which Yeats found in the prospect of disaster.

Brand writes that 'aesthetically, aside from the ideology, I beam at the spectacle of disruption'. Similarly, Yeats felt 'ecstasy at the contemplation of ruin',[28] wishing to make Ireland 'ready to plunge into the abyss'.[29] And, again like Brand, Yeats was financially insulated from the implications this would have for ordinary people – if done as an activity in itself, without a peaceful end-point in mind.[30]

Russell Brand isn't representative of all left populism. But his views show how people can construct narratives of decline so as to fulfil a personal need for meaning. Often, these narratives have an element of truth. But the quest for romantic dissent – for a sense of impending crisis, against which a few brave individuals must struggle – means the narratives are embraced unquestioningly and entirely.

The quest for romantic dissent is, after all, gratifying. The Golden Era lets us feel that we are visionaries or saviours – who can see through the 'sequin-covered vacuous heroes' (as Brand puts it) who others are coveting. This gratification is part of the reason that exciting countercultures exist. There will always be those who, by temperament, define themselves against the direction of travel – often asking the right questions in the process.

Indeed, the quest for romantic dissent is, like the other quests we have looked at, built into many humans. Even Dwight Eisenhower acknowledged that 'Life is certainly only worthwhile if it represents struggle for worthy causes ... I am quite certain that the human being could not continue to exist if he or she had perfect security.' In this light, we can maybe understand the 'connection' which someone like Russell Brand finds in 'the ripped-up paving stones and galloping police horses'.

Yet we must remember that many of those who lived through the Golden Eras which Brand conjures were struggling for the alleviation of poverty and war, or for the provision of basic rights, resources and safety – the very opposite, in other words, of revolution for its own sake.

14
The Case against the Golden Era
(Global Economy)

To reiterate, the argument against the Golden Era is not that society is always improving. Rather, the criticism comes when declinist assumptions trump evidence and analysis. So, although I personally believe the 'arc of the moral universe' does 'bend towards justice' in the long term, it can still bend in the wrong direction for long periods, or have strands that have yet to bend the right way. On climate change and wealth inequality, for example, I would say that believing things are headed in the wrong direction right now makes you a realist, not a proponent of the Golden Era.

So what, specifically, should we be suspicious about with the myth? Drilling down, there are three characteristics which mark out the pluralist, non-believer in the Golden Era from the populist believer.

The first is the acceptance that, even if the post-war era *was* emphatically superior, we cannot go back. Reversing the decisions made in the intervening years will not return us to the Golden Era. Nor will 1950s policies yield the same results in the 2010s. An industrial, unionised workforce won't re-materialize. Mistakes in foreign policy cannot be unmade, only compensated for. And 'socialism in one nation' will not be the same if we are the only country practising it, as it was when we were one of many.

The second is the willingness to celebrate progress. There are many areas where, from a progressive viewpoint, the 'lines are going up'.[1] Believers in the Golden Era tell us that these are anomalies or free-market window dressing. But we may still wonder, if falling global poverty and declining racism have occurred on the watch of a shift to the right, whether perhaps that shift either isn't happening or isn't all bad. Either way, we need to question our assumptions.

The third characteristic is the view that the things which have become more progressive are often linked to the things which have got less so. This is not to say that reductions in racism (falling hostility to interracial marriage, for example) owe a debt of gratitude to tax-avoiding multinationals. But it is to concede that it's hard to divorce the two entirely. They are both products of a more interconnected world.

This is probably the most important place of divergence between Golden Era disciples and Golden Era sceptics, and it relates to the first and second differences listed above. If you see advances and declines as in some sense linked, then you will acknowledge the difficulty of keeping only the parts of the modern world which you like; the difficulty of accelerating and reversing at the same time. If you are a believer in the Golden Era, on the other hand, then you will more likely think that positive changes would have happened anyway.[2] Progressive shifts will be seen as having slipped through the 'neoliberal' net. This encourages the idea that we can wind the clock back to the 1950s when it comes to ejecting all multinational companies, but retain present levels of diversity, internationalism and prosperity.

THE 'NEOLIBERALISM' STORY

The 'neoliberalism' narrative is the coronary artery of the Golden Era myth. It leaves pluralists perplexed, but is central to how left populists see the last seventy years. The basic idea is that, during the period between the post-war era and the present day, a left-wing Arcadia was dismantled. During that timeline the policy consensus – and with it the public mood – shifted in a reactionary direction on most fronts, and continues to do so. A tolerant, Keynesian Golden Era, built on community, freedom, fairness and equality, was torn down and privatised by elites. And a new epoch, based on greed, bigotry and dog-eat-dog competition was welcomed in. In the UK, every government since 1979 is seen as having been complicit in this.

The definition of 'neoliberalism' is imprecise.[3] It is impossible to find a version of 'neoliberalism' which applies accurately to all the governments included under the umbrella but which does not apply to at least some of those held up as alternatives – be they modern Scandinavia or 1950s Britain.

To put this to the test, eight definitions of 'neoliberalism' are over-laid on my diagram below. Governments from different countries and eras (chosen fairly randomly) are drawn in. The various perimeters show which countries/governments fall into each definition of the 'neoliberal consensus', and which do not.

First, there is the definition of *true neoliberalism*, in which the government does not intervene in any way, except to provide an army and a police force and to facilitate trading. We clearly do not inhabit this sort of society, and have not since before the First World War.[4]

Secondly, there is what we might call *neoliberalism as neoconservatism*: an ultra-conservative form of modern government exemplified by Thatcher and Reagan. These 1980s governments did not practise *true neoliberalism* (or anything close, as far as the size of the state is concerned), but they certainly moved their countries radically to the right.

Thirdly, while *neoconservatism* and *true neoliberalism* are separate, you could group them together as *neoliberalism as small state ideology*. 'Neoliberalism' here is an umbrella ideology, key advocates being Hayek, Friedman or the Mont Pelerin set. Users of this definition might concede that 1850s and 1980s levels of government intervention were pretty different. But they would say the end goals were not.

None of the above could be applied to New Labour, which was not a small state ideology.[5] Labour's focus on investment, equality and employment was a clear break from neoconservatism. So, why is New Labour included in the 'neoliberal consensus'? There is a fourth definition that might answer this: *neoliberalism as the middle way*. After all, the term 'neoliberalism' at one point described a form of US liberalism which avoided the pitfalls of both free markets and full state planning.[6] Britain's embrace of 'the third way' fits this

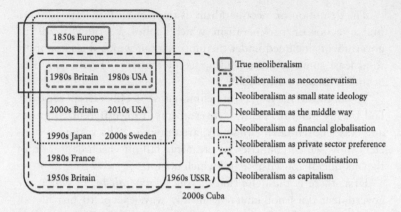

definition, with its effort to deliver social liberalism and economic justice within a global market economy.

Neoliberalism as the middle way seems to partially capture what people mean, given that the term is frequently aimed at 'Blairites'. However, according to this definition, 'neoliberalism' is an *alternative* to – not a continuity of – neoconservatism (which is unbothered by social justice or public services). Thatcher was not, by this definition, 'neoliberal'.

Fifthly – if we are looking for a classification that includes New Labour *and* Thatcherism – the answer might be *neoliberalism as financial globalisation*. The real change since 1980, after all, is the fluidity of capital. This has led to de-industrialisation, deregulation and tax cuts to attract investment, and to bigger inequalities between regions and individuals.

However, these challenges apply to nearly all developed countries – from Kohl's Germany to Obama's USA, from Scandi-socialism to Italian Berlusconism. By this definition, 'neoliberalism' is not an ideology but a set of conditions in which modern governments operate.[7] Some embrace it; others pull up the drawbridge; most do something in between.

Critics of 'neoliberalism' rarely cast their net this wide. And they usually mean something more ideological. So, a sixth definition might be *neoliberalism as private sector preference*. Commentator Abi Wilkinson, for example, acknowledged that 1997 saw a break from neoconservatism, but said that New Labour still qualified as 'neoliberal' thanks to a 'belief that [the] private sector does things better'.[8]

There is truth in this. Though the proportion spent by the state grew significantly, Blair and Brown both seemed agnostic about public ownership and accepted the balance of nationalisation and privatisation which they inherited, seeking partnership between the two. They encouraged schemes like PFI, the test being service quality and free access for all. There was arguably enough sympathy towards the private sector that New Labour could be grouped with Thatcherism – as distinct from the post-war decades. However, *neoliberalism as private sector preference* again scoops up several highly egalitarian nations. Japan (a country based on 'collective capitalism') and Sweden (a social market economy) both rely on the private sector to run services, in some places more than the UK. They have low inequality despite a tendency towards private provision.

A seventh definition could be *neoliberalism as commoditisation*. Marketisation, managerialism and return-on-investment are seen as symptoms of a society that knows the cost of everything and the value of nothing.[9] Yet here too it is hard to see where neoliberalism starts and ends. After the war, food and resources were rationed and Nye Bevan 'stuffed with gold' the British Medical Association to get it to buy into the idea of the NHS. The USSR also commodified society, using planners, not markets.

I don't see that there is currently less value for human life now than during these times. Indeed, the UK government's response to COVID-19 – which saw a Cabinet of Tories stage a mass intervention in the economy to protect lives – must surely give us pause for thought here. Does twenty-first-century society really venerate markets and disregard human life, in a way that we did not in the past? The only thing that has really changed, in my view, is our ability to measure outcomes. You would have to go back a long way to find an era when resources, outputs and endeavour were not measured for value.

Lastly, the definition might just be *neoliberalism as capitalism*. According to this, the Attlee and Wilson premierships were also 'neoliberal', featuring private wealth, home ownership and consumerism. Likewise, every European social democratic country since 1945. If 'neoliberalism' just means non-communist, then there has been no 'sea change' moment when Britain became 'neoliberal'.

Often, 'neoliberalism' is used to mean any and all of the definitions above. Abi Wilkinson provides this potted definition: 'A programme of privatisation, deregulation and financial liberalisation, guided by an overarching individualistic ideology which tells us competition is the only workable basis for organising human activity and the logic of the private sector should be applied universally.'

Since the Second World War, almost no nation has fulfilled this in its entirety, and few have eschewed all aspects. Most European countries favour 'the logic of the private sector' when it comes to food, but not when it comes to health. Obama did not sign up to an 'overarching individualistic ideology', but Trump certainly does. Trump, meanwhile, opposes 'financial liberalisation' between countries in a way that Obama did not.

Of course, it may be that 'neoliberalism' is not a label that an economy is or is not, or an ideology that a government subscribes to or does not. Perhaps it is something that you are closer to or further away from. However, if there are degrees of 'neoliberalism', then it's striking how few commentators discuss it in this way. You rarely hear, for example, that Britain moved from being 30 per cent neoliberal in 1970 to 70 per cent neoliberal in 1990, retreating back to around 50 per cent neoliberal by 2010. Nor do people discuss exactly what degree of 'neoliberalism' is desirable (presuming the answer is not a Trotskyite 0 per cent).

Moreover, economic definitions like the eight above are frequently conflated with non-economic problems: failure to do more on climate change,[10] hostility to immigration, 'Western imperialism', snobbery, Brexit, civil liberties infringements, and so on. These are all included in the 'neoliberal consensus' at points – even though many were more acute in the post-war years.

*

As a result, the 'neoliberalism' narrative serves three negative functions. First, it makes a Dark Knight of anyone who cooperates, even slightly, with international capitalism. Secondly, it creates a Puppet Master conspiracy theory out of the shift from a series of national economies to a single global one.[11] And thirdly, it diminishes all progress since the pre-'neoliberal' Golden Era.

The 'neoliberalism' story offers a meta-narrative for all that's wrong with contemporary society. If we are to challenge it, we must explore the more complex account of the past seventy years.

So, rather than unpacking the Golden Era's flaws, as we did for the Dark Knight and the Puppet Master, we will instead chart seven alternative readings of post-war history, over the course of this chapter and Chapters Fifteen and Sixteen. These are, in each case, simplified and condensed. But they show how left-wing and right-wing shifts are tied to one another, and demonstrate that progress has been, at worst, mixed.

The first reading is *isolation to interconnectedness*, which explores the declining power of nation states. The second, *local scale, national scale, global scale*, explores the impact of globalisation. The third, *Attlee, Thatcher, Blair, Brexit*, looks at how 'Overton' consensuses have risen and fallen. The fourth and fifth, *equal rights, equal opportunities, fair outcomes* and *direct challenges to indirect challenges*, map the changing essence of the problems the left faces. The sixth, *groupish, individualist, post-materialist*, looks at public attitudes and cultural values. The seventh, *innocence to awareness*, describes the role of information, education and the media.

I. ISOLATION TO
INTERCONNECTEDNESS

One question never pondered by left populists is why, if we have drifted so far towards conservatism, many on the right believe Golden Era narratives of their own. *Mail* columnist Peter Hitchens, for example, claims that David Cameron ended up having 'more in common with the Socialist Workers' Party' than with conventional Tories.[12] This isn't uncommon among right populists. In America, Trump's slogan was 'Make America Great Again', and his supporters suggested that RINOs (Republicans in Name Only) had surrendered the party's original purpose.

This feeling on the right encompasses a sense of decline about the rise of human rights, the preoccupation with the environment, the loss of Britain's (or America's) place in the world and 'overcompensation' on race and gender. It extends to economics, too. Right populists say that we have moved towards an over-generous welfare system, an over-sized state, an over-willingness to 'blame society', excessive international aid and regulations that suffocate enterprise. We only need to look at the Tea Party's obsession with their country's 'socialised' healthcare to see this.

If the right has won so comprehensively, then why aren't they more triumphant? And if they have lost, then why aren't we on the left happier? Both Golden Era narratives cannot be correct.

The reality is that – rather than a shift to left or right – a move from isolationism towards interconnectedness has changed the parameters. The mobility of big business, for example, has meant that governments increasingly placate large multinationals. Left populists see this as proof of a rightward shift sweeping all before it. But, on the other side of the ledger, the shift towards internationalism has meant acquiescence to human rights rules and global emissions targets. Right populists treat these as wholesale capitulations.[13]

The table below sets out the key oppositions. And the visualisations that follow show how left and right have had their wings clipped by the *isolation to interconnectedness* shift. The horseshoes in each diagram represent the political spectrum at different points, with the dark and light perimeter lines showing the limitations that an interconnected world has imposed on left and right respectively. Some of the shifts are technical, while others relate to social norms changing, thanks to contact with other cultures.

Table 14.1.

Rightwards drift	Leftwards drift
Globalisation	Internationalism
Economic liberalism	Social liberalism
Free trade	Free movement
Big business	Mass migration
Inequality within countries	Equality between countries
Lower taxes on global rich	Higher focus on global poor

The first, Diagram 1, shows the political horseshoe at a relatively early stage – as it might have been several decades ago.

In essence, progressive and conservative governments alike have had their room for manoeuvre altered by a world where borders matter less. Populists on both sides are reluctant to think through the challenges of an interconnected world, instead arguing that their opponents have been 100 per cent triumphant.

Indeed, there is little acceptance, among populists, that there is any give and take at all between left interconnectedness and right interconnectedness. Most believe you can choose one without the other. Left populists argue that government policies can be socially liberal but economically protectionist; internationalist but anti-globalisation.[14]

If they are forced to choose, isolation is often the populist back-up. As a result, left populists end up taking insular stances, or inadvertently collaborating with the hard right. The cooperation with Enoch Powell in the 1975 European referendum was an early instance of this. Labour's pre-Brexit opposition to freedom of movement is a modern example.[15]

The reality is that it's hard to contribute to peace in Syria, or to build a consensus on climate change, while refusing to trade with other countries. Likewise, it's difficult to travel widely as a population – or to accept more migrants and refugees – if you have a siege economy. And it's almost impossible to square the fall in prosperity that protectionism would bring with Britain remaining a

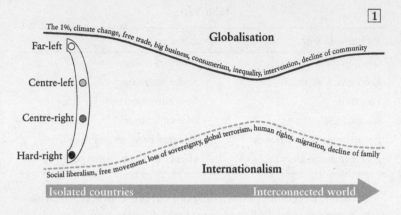

country that foreigners want to visit or live in.[16] Similarly, multi-lateral solutions to inequality (a Robin Hood Tax, for example) won't get far if you withdraw at the same time from multilateral platforms like NATO.

The same goes for the spread of social reforms (on capital punishment, abortion or LGBT rights). These occur much faster in a world where progressive steps are visible to and replicable by other nations. They are less likely if there is no integration between countries. This is part of the reason why internationalism and social liberalism go hand in hand.

Humanitarian intervention is another example. The left's foreign policy outlook is premised on an age with no 'international community', when countries were self-contained, self-interested entities. But what should the policy be in a world where colonial arguments have been largely beaten – where our instinct is to help, not plunder? What should we do – as an interconnected nation whose destiny is bound up with those of other nations – when we see foreign crises on our TV screens? The answer clearly cannot be either blanket intervention or blanket non-intervention. Yet left populists find it easier to sit back on assumptions from the isolationist era, by blaming 'Western imperialism', than to think through these questions.

This is not to say an uncritical embrace is the only way of adapting to the *isolation to interconnectedness* transition. There are different

ways of striking the balance between internationalism and globalisation. But it is hard to imagine a country rejecting every tenet of the
latter while remaining a beacon of one-world tolerance.[17]

Diagrams 2–5, below, show the implications of the *isolation to
interconnectedness* shift over time. Diagram 5 shows the conventional spectrum turned on its head, with 'open versus closed' replacing
'right versus left'.[18] We saw this in France's 2017 Presidential run-off,
where the mainstream left and the mainstream right were swept
aside. The final ballot was between an all-out internationalist globalist (Macron) and an all-out nationalist protectionist (Le Pen).[19]

In the UK we spent most of the 2015–20 period closer to a Diagram 3 or 4 scenario, largely because both main parties were under
isolationist leadership. Anti-immigrant, pro-sovereignty Brexiteers
set the Conservative agenda. Anti-interventionist 'Lexiteers' set
Labour's. The attempted Change UK breakaway and the 2019 Lib
Dem surge both represented, in different ways, efforts to break this
deadlock and build movements supportive of interconnectedness.

Indeed, during the last few years both of Britain's main parties
have been constantly on the verge of splitting, the fault lines being
between isolationism and interconnectedness.[20] Populists are in the
isolationist camp and pluralists are in the interconnectedness one –
with the latter telling the former that they cannot choose only the
aspects of interconnectedness that they like. Brexit has tended to be
the battleground for this, but the tensions run deeper.[21]

It should be said that the issue is not just that rejecting globalisation means rejecting aspects of internationalism (or vice versa, if you
are on the right). It is also that a successful economy is almost impossible without accepting the shift towards an interconnected world.

The centre right, for instance, has historically advocated mild
nationalism and social conservatism, alongside market-based economic pragmatism. But Brexit renders these things irreconcilable.

Meanwhile, the centre-left ideal is to combine a strong economy
with radical redistribution – growing the pie but splitting it as you do.
Yet *isolation to interconnectedness* means that this social democratic
formula – always reliant on a balancing act[22] – has come to feel like a
zero-sum choice: a strong economy *or* an equal one. In a globalised

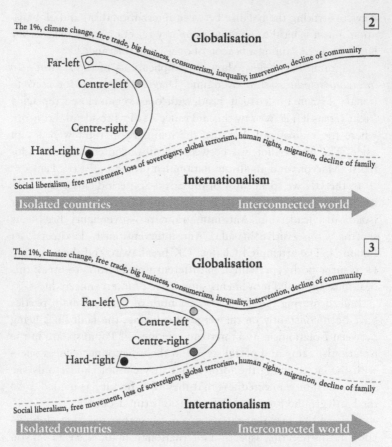

context, the pursuit of growth often means bigger and bigger concessions, to attract companies which are indifferent to borders.

This creates accusations of a race to the bottom. If we look at the steady reductions in UK corporation tax, we can understand why many fear that the pursuit of investment brings diminishing returns.[23] Indeed, corporation tax has fallen dramatically in almost every OECD country, largely thanks to the *isolation to interconnectedness* transition.

Labour is thus torn between growers of the pie (who point out the

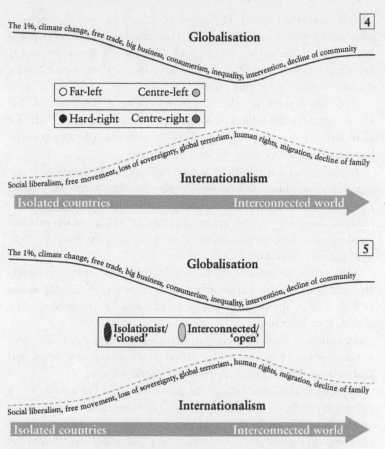

hardship of recession and the investment in the poorest that even modest growth can bring) and splitters of the pie (who point out that equality is the abiding goal of the left). In short, would we prefer a nation with affluent CEOs whose taxes pay for new schools, or one with fewer CEOs and fewer new schools?[24] Corbyn supporters should be honest that their politics will harm prosperity. His opponents should concede that theirs mean that inequality can only be tackled gradually.

In truth, there is a desperate need for interconnected responses to an interconnected world. If Europe could act as one, then wealth inequalities could be addressed.[25] Yet the problem is that the populist left – even if correct in some of its diagnoses – has consistently favoured the solutions of an isolationist age, without being honest with itself about what this means.

Arguments about whether 'open versus closed' has replaced 'left versus right' have rumbled on for years.[26] It is often pointed out, for example, that young people tend to be economically and socially liberal, compared to older, 'closed' generations.[27]

Indeed, some left populists accept parts of the *isolation to inter-connectedness* shift, but find ways of shoehorning it into the Golden Era narrative. Progressives who work with the *isolation to inter-connectedness* shift are caricatured as pro-globalisation liberals and rootless jet-setters, more concerned with boardroom diversity than with genuine equality.

Hence, despite there being a complex trade-off between progressive and conservative parts of *isolation to interconnectedness*, the shift is seen by the populist left as a right-wing phenomenon and a sign that we have lost.

In reality, although interconnectedness has narrowed the room for manoeuvre, there are still big differences between how centre-left and centre-right parties deal with interconnectedness.

Moreover, the narrowing of the parameters is a bottleneck, not a permanent state of affairs. It has mainly happened because we're at a halfway point in the *isolation to interconnectedness* shift – experiencing the downsides of developments, like fluid capital, without yet being interconnected enough to solve them supra-nationally. The left needs to help build more transparent and democratic international structures, so that we can push to the next stage.

As the final visualisation, Diagram 6, anticipates, if and when this happens, clear blue water will open out between the internationalist left and the globalist right. Core values will reassert themselves and real debates – like the rate at which an EU-wide corporation tax should be set – will take hold. Meanwhile, isolationist populists of left and right will increasingly overlap.

Hence, while support for a coalition of internationalists and

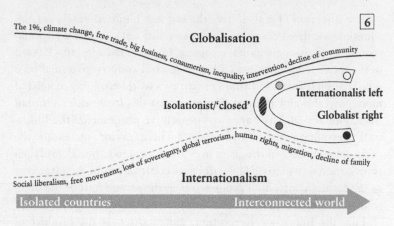

globalists may be an appealing short-term tactic, it is not a sustainable platform. There are few policies that could fulfil, in the long term, the ideals of both the pluralist left and the pluralist right.

Those Labour supporters described as 'centrists' by the left are effectively those who believe that embracing and shaping the *isolation to interconnectedness* shift is the only option.[28] They see internationalism as the route to egalitarianism,[29] and favour a fully interconnected world, where you can tackle wealth inequality in a joined-up way. By contrast, the far left tend to see egalitarianism as the route to internationalism, and are suspicious of 'world government' for Puppet Master reasons. They would advocate creating a truly egalitarian country in splendid isolation (which you can then replicate elsewhere).

II. LOCAL SCALE, NATIONAL SCALE, GLOBAL SCALE

The next transition is *local scale, national scale, global scale*. This looks in more detail at the intersections between technological change, economic scale and the tools required to regulate capitalism and reduce inequality.

The direction of travel, over the last few hundred years, is from countless localised economies, to a series of self-contained national economies, to a single global economy. In recent decades, this has led to the move from Britain as a late-industrial country governed by a set of national levers to Britain as part of a world economy in need of more powerful global levers. Underpinning this *local scale, national scale, global scale* shift are two consecutive phenomena: the Industrial Revolution and globalisation. These events increased the geographical range of the economy – from local to national, and then from national to global. The latter now confronts us in the same way as the former confronted progressives in the second half of the nineteenth century and the first part of the twentieth century.

Like the Industrial Revolution, globalisation is the product of new technologies: mass production in the case of the former; the internet, the media and the electronic mobility of businesses and capital in the case of the latter.

Like the Industrial Revolution, globalisation brings both prosperity and inequality. There are legitimate claims to 'lift everyone', but a small group claims much of the spoils.[30]

Like the Industrial Revolution, globalisation creates economic migrations. There was a shift from local to national in the case of the former (cities such as Liverpool and Sheffield became national economic hubs). And there has been a move from national to international in the case of the latter (e.g. the rise of London as a global metropolis).

Like the Industrial Revolution, globalisation widens audiences. The former created celebrities with national fan bases and products with UK-wide reach. The latter created global celebrity culture and let brands gain international recognition.

Like the Industrial Revolution, globalisation demands that policy levers increase in scope. The role of national government served this function in the case of industrialisation (national income tax was meaningfully introduced only in the early twentieth century). The present need to supra-nationally tax big business and the super-rich is the equivalent example for globalisation.

Like the Industrial Revolution, globalisation leaves the left bereft of answers. In the case of the former, this was manifested in the decline of the Whig/Liberal Party (and earlier, in the 'Luddite' tendency). In the case of globalisation, it raises existential questions about Labour's purpose.

But ultimately, like the Industrial Revolution, globalisation isn't going anywhere. The genie is out of the bottle. Just as industrialisation was ultimately shaped into something progressive (something, indeed, which Golden Era believers now hanker for),[31] globalisation will be managed only if we accept and engage with it.

Part of the reason that the post-war consensus feels like a Golden Era is because it came at a point where many of the inequities created by industrialisation had relented. The levers of national government were still powerful, and the political left controlled them in many countries. The inequality and poverty that mass production brought had been significantly tamed. In this regard it was an 'exceptional' period, as Piketty and others note.

It was ended by a set of technological and communications advances which meant that individuals, industries and wealth became mobile. National governments' power to take the necessary economic steps was reduced.

This relates to what Branko Milanović, a former World Bank economist, calls 'Kuznets Waves'. The term 'Kuznets Wave' is an adaptation of the economist Simon Kuznets's famous up-and-down 'Kuznets Curve'. This summed up the belief, dominant in the second half of the twentieth century, that inequality would first rise and then fall, as a country developed.

Kuznets's theory has been undermined by the work of Piketty, among others, who showed that inequality is on the rise across the developed world. But Milanović's adaptation of the Kuznets Curve theory is important. It suggests that Kuznets was not so much wrong as that he was thinking of development in terms of a single event (an industrial revolution within one country). But, according to Milanović, a new Kuznets Curve is created each time there is a technological shift: 'my reformulation of the Kuznets Curve into Kuznets Waves comes in because I consider the current increase [in inequality], in the last 25 or 30 years, to reflect essentially the second technological revolution, and globalization'.[32] In short, there have been two seismic shifts.[33]

The diagram below represents, in an ultra-simplified way, a schema for what this looks like. It depicts two Kuznets Waves of rising and then falling equality, each triggered by technology expanding the horizons of capitalism.

Within Kuznets Wave 1, there was a lag time between the new technology having this effect and the required levers – national levers, in this case – being used to address the socio-economic consequences. We are currently in a similar lag time with Kuznets Wave 2, and must hope that the necessary global levers will be grasped in the same way. With this in mind, I have optimistically extended the timeline to an imagined future where Kuznets Wave 2 begins to fall.

What this suggests is that, having spent a century conquering one Everest of inequality, progressives now find ourselves walking up a second mountain, in the form of globalisation. In the post-war years – the Golden Era – we were merely coming down the side of the first wave.

Almost every other developed country is in the same ascent when it comes to inequality – with varying steepness. And this explains why a return to the post-war settlement is not viable. Applying national levers when everyone else is working on a global scale will

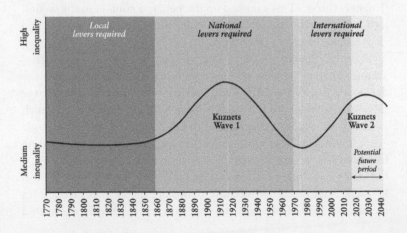

not help, any more than the levers of the early-nineteenth-century market-town economy would have protected you against the inequalities caused by mass production. The only approach is to work at the level at which the economy works. This is part of the reason why the 'Lexit' justification for leaving the EU is so frustrating.

Anthony Crosland wrote in 1956 that:

> The most obvious fulfilment of our socialist ideals lies in altering not the structure of society in our own country, but the balance of wealth and privilege between advanced and backwards countries . . . Socialists must always remember that inter-national now surpasses inter-class injustices and inequalities.[34]

Written as the country descended the slopes of Kuznets Wave 1, this sentiment was very much of its time. It highlights a difference between Kuznets Waves 1 and 2. The ascent of Wave 1 in my diagram resulted in inequalities *within* countries as well as inequalities *between* countries. Richer nations pulled away from poorer nations, and the richer people within those rich nations pulled away from the poorer people.[35]

The descent of Kuznets Wave 1 resulted in decreasing inequality within countries, but did less for inequality between countries – as Crosland's quote effectively acknowledges. The poorest people in the rich countries caught up with the richest people in those same countries during the post-war years. But, in a very broad sense, poorer countries remained poor and richer countries remained rich.

The last four decades have seen the opposite happen. Poorer nations have caught up in the wake of globalisation (a process known as 'convergence'). But the richest people have, in almost all countries, become steadily richer than the poorest people.

The diagram below imposes a schematic dotted line for inequality *between* countries on to the previous visualisation, to distinguish this from the Kuznets Waves of inequality *within* countries. In simple terms, the direction of travel is from inequality between countries to inequality within countries.[36]

The reason for the recent rise in inequality *within* countries is the

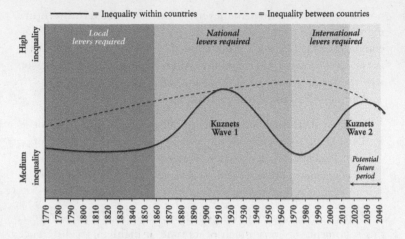

declining importance of borders. The shapes of national economies have often been stretched to breaking point by this. At the top of the economy, individuals can keep wealth offshore or migrate to different parts of the world for higher salaries.[37] And companies can base themselves in lower-tax countries or else can wield extra bargaining power about where they are based.[38]

Meanwhile, the reason for the fall in inequality *between* countries is also the declining importance of borders: the arrival of relocated industries in developing countries, the end of colonial rule, and the mobility of workforces. For instance, the economies of Asian countries have grown through trade, and because manufacturers have moved there. Migrants from Poland have moved to places like the UK – earning money and sending it home. And developed countries now provide aid to poorer countries which they once took resources from.

In effect, the lines are crossing over, meaning that the assumptions of 2020 are close to the opposite of those made by Crosland in 1956. The 'structure of society in our own country' is now getting more unequal, whereas the 'balance of wealth and privilege between advanced and backwards countries' is at least moving in the right direction.

The shift from inequality *between* countries to inequality *within* them has ramifications for how people think about 'deserving' versus 'undeserving' poverty. This might explain why, back in times of lower inequality within countries and higher inequality between them, the public were more progressive when it came to support for the welfare state – and less progressive on race and nationhood. The plane of struggle was between all the inhabitants of our country – who would equally enjoy the spoils – and all those of another.

Younger generations, by contrast, often see themselves against a global backdrop. Attitudes to immigration are increasingly based on economic competition, not nationality, and people are less likely to give the benefit of the doubt to fellow nationals using the welfare state.[39]

The response to the 2011 London riots is a case in point. Much of the anger online – which tended to come from younger or better-networked observers – was aimed at the entitlement of UK citizens who, comparatively speaking, were not needy or deserving. In fact, many drew contrasts between poorer individuals in the UK and those in other countries: 'Don't blame poverty [for the riots]. Africa knows poverty,' wrote one.[40]

This signifies a shift away from the attitudes you would expect in a world of competing national economies – and towards the types you would expect in a single global one.[41]

The *local scale, national scale, global scale* transition is a catalyst for urbanisation. It concentrates activity on to our economic hubs – with the UK, for example, becoming more reliant on London. If people travel and trade no further than the county where they live, it stands to reason that a market town is the commercial centre. If they travel and trade across the nation, bigger conurbations become the hubs.[42] And if they travel and trade internationally, then the focus will shift to 'mega-cities'.[43]

Hence, the 'agglomeration' process – the economic term for things amassing together – gradually shifts the focus towards a handful of vast centres. Each of these acts as a global regional hub for a certain industry. London, for example, is effectively Europe's financial centre. Smaller cities and towns have struggled by comparison.

Reliance on these centres as the 'goose that lays the golden egg' means that they, like the high earners and big companies they're home to, are more answerable to the global market than to national rules.[44]

The diagram below shows what this looks like in Britain. It is simplistic and schematic, once again, and is intended only to show the direction of travel. (In the UK, London has always loomed above the rest.)

A good example, away from the UK, is the contrasting fortunes of Chicago and Detroit, two geographically close American cities. Chicago was once the US meat-packing hub and Detroit was the car-manufacturing centre. These industries left in the second half of the twentieth century.[45] But the rise in global finance, and the need for a hub in the Mid-West, meant that Chicago remained a leading world city. Detroit, on the other hand, became an emblem of post-industrial decline and population exodus. An area with two industrial cities became able to support only one global centre.

Again, this plays out in social attitudes – giving rise, in the UK, to the 'London versus the Rest' values divide. This has been much discussed since the Brexit vote.

At earlier stages of the *local scale, national scale, global scale* transition, cultural capital and social attitudes would have been more intermingled, with each town having a cross-section of values. But the move of younger and university-educated people to global hubs has meant a division into cosmopolitan areas with unprecedentedly high cultural capital and other areas with very different perspectives. People in the former are more likely to have travelled internationally (through work, or through having disposable income for holidays). They are more likely to subscribe to ideas of 'universal justice'.[46] They are more likely to have left their home towns.[47] They are more likely to be digitally networked.[48]

David Goodhart's book *Road to Somewhere* describes this as the difference between 'Anywheres' and 'Somewheres'.[49] Anywheres are 'citizens of nowhere' – as Theresa May fatefully put it. Somewheres view issues via a more localised prism and see politics in terms of the national interest.

Many other commentators have made similar prognoses about the post-Brexit divide. But the Somewheres and Anywheres definition is

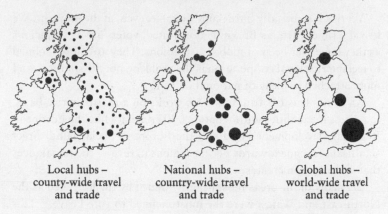

Local hubs –
county-wide travel
and trade

National hubs –
country-wide travel
and trade

Global hubs –
world-wide travel
and trade

especially important, thanks to the role it attributes to place. In effect, Goodhart's model identifies global outlooks in settlements that operate at a global economic scale and national outlooks in places that don't.

It is hard to see how we can heal the polarisations at play without healing the regional economic disparities. Hence the importance of reducing the Kuznets Wave 2 of inequality within countries.

As we have said, efforts to address this must be done using global levers; otherwise they risk returning us to a state of protectionist competition. The answer, Thomas Piketty points out, must be 'egalitarian-internationalism'.[50] This would involve surrendering a significant degree of sovereignty so as to champion an idea like the global wealth levy proposed by Piketty (or even a transnational minimum wage).

This will involve accepting the legitimacy of globalisation – including aspects the left is uncomfortable with, such as free trade and multilateral nuclear policies. But the potential benefits of permitting an element of 'world government' on issues like taxing wealth are immense. Similarly, there is the possibility of a more Keynesian approach to regional investment, giving areas economic engines of their own instead of the present 'big city as breadwinner' model.[51] (Similarly, issues like migration and climate change also need transnational solutions.)

Yet this is politically hard – unthinkable, even, at the moment. We live at a time when, as Brexit demonstrated, voters are as suspicious as they have ever been of global institutions. They are more inclined to feel international cooperation is the problem, not the solution, and more attached to ideas of national culture.

An example is EU funding. This works on a redistributive basis, to redress inequalities within nations. EU schemes like the European Regional Development Fund and the European Social Fund direct significant revenue towards poorer regions to reverse the imbalances that globalisation creates.

Yet many of the areas most heavily funded by the EU, such as the North-east and Wales, were the most inclined to vote Leave.[52] This was partly, I would argue, because the EU's global levers aren't strong enough to instil a beating economic heart into communities: the EU still looks like part of the problem, rather than an insufficient part of the solution. But it was also because the EU became a proxy for cultural issues about patriotism and political correctness.

In a nutshell, then, the British left's challenge is to persuade the public that global levers can solve deep unfairness and regional inequality – and that we don't lose anything of our true essence as a country by grasping them.

The answer, in my view, is to embrace internationalism on most policy fronts, putting ourselves at the heart of world institutions, extending their democratic remit and developing egalitarian policies at a transnational level. We would have to be pro-migration, pro-Paris Accord, pro-EU, pro-NATO, pro-Tobin Tax, pro-trade, pro-refugee, and so on. We would need to champion EU-wide policies on tax avoidance, the breaking-up of monopolies, the international regulation of the financial sector and the adoption of transnational agreements about how many refugees each country takes. We would need to welcome anything that delivered greater cooperation between nations – and even consider ideas like the Transatlantic Trade and Investment Partnership (TTIP).

At the same time, we would need to be comfortable enough with British culture to reassure the public that solving problems internationally wouldn't require us to surrender identity or traditions. We would need to abandon squeamishness about the Union Jack and respect for the armed forces. We would need to support the Royal Wedding or a good-natured international football rivalry. And we would have to jettison completely the aspects of left-wing identity politics which verge on farce.[53]

This would win us the right to make progressive arguments on immigration or Europe. It would let us get to the root of challenges such as wealth inequality, climate change and the dominance of London – while providing security for those who worry that this means diminishing everything that Britain stands for. It would be a chance to create a modern equivalent to the politics of Clement Attlee which promoted a 'world state' as a solution to war and want while reclaiming patriotism from the right.[54]

Those who see this as a capitulation are working on a false basis. Instead of being a form of 'neoliberal' rule, most aspects of world government would temper free markets. As incoming EU rules against 'off-shore' tax arrangements show, cooperation between countries can protect against the extremes of capitalism.[55]

Meanwhile, rather than being on the same continuum, patriotism is a buttress against nationalism. The distinction is like the gap between confidence and arrogance. The more you have a genuine sense of who you are, the less you mask insecurities by bragging or bullying.

The populist left would accept little of this – hence why they're poorly placed to address the changes that have taken place. Corbyn himself is a perfect example. He was unilateralist, anti-NATO, protectionist, Eurosceptic and opposed to intervention of all kinds and international cooperation of most (it is hard to imagine him hammering out an emissions deal with China). He saw transnational organisations as vehicles for imperialism. Yet, culturally, he indulged in anti-patriotic gestures – refusing, for instance, to sing the national anthem or bow to the Queen. He saw patriotism and national security as Trojan Horses for racism and jingoism, and was easily badged as un-British as a result. In other words, he was close to the opposite of where Labour needs to be if it wishes to address the *local scale, national scale, global scale* transformation.

15
The Case against the
Golden Era Continued (Politics)

We will now look at three further shifts, which more explicitly relate
to party politics and public opinion.

III. ATTLEE, THATCHER,
BLAIR AND BREXIT

A surprising argument made by some Corbyn backers is that he isn't
actually that left-wing: it is the mainstream that has moved. One
letter to the *Guardian*, for instance, claimed that Corbyn was a
mild social democrat, who only looks radical because 'the Overton
Window . . . has shifted very considerably to the right in the past 30
years'.[1]

Framing Corbyn as a moderate centre-leftist, bypassed by the
rush to 'neoliberalism', is far-fetched. He was among Labour's most
outspoken critics even in the 1970s, and his 'anti-imperialist', Marxist leanings put him in a different tradition from the historic Labour
mainstream.[2] Nevertheless, the *Guardian* letter-writer's argument is
common on the populist left. So, let's explore changes in the political
consensus since 1945. We will call this narrative *Attlee, Thatcher,
Blair, Brexit*. And we will, like the letter writer, use the 'Overton
Window' to look at how the mainstream has moved.

The Overton Window is a niche creation of the US libertarian
right. It has been borrowed by the populist left in recent years. It
described policies that are politically mainstream and publicly sayable. Things outside the window are viewed as extreme, fringe ideas.

THE CASE AGAINST THE GOLDEN ERA CONTINUED (POLITICS)

The Overton Window 'is not static', and the case made by left populists is that it has been hauled steadily rightwards.[3] Those who believe this ignore the technical constraints on policy-makers and instead say that ideologues have manipulated the window for reasons of greed. This leads the concept to come with Puppet Master baggage. However, rather than dismissing it, let's engage seriously with how the mainstream has moved.

Below are a series of diagrams suggesting where the Overton Window sat at various stages. We could argue all day about the degrees of change or the chronological brackets chosen. But the diagrams are an effort to assess broad directions of travel.

The shifts mapped are partly circumstantial. How much credit can the Attlee government take for higher taxes on the rich, which they inherited from the war era? Likewise, how much credit can Blair take for increases in social liberalism, which were happening anyway? But, in a way, this is the point. Whether or not you accept that there are phenomena beyond the power of politicians, you need to do so equally – for governments of the past as well as for those of the present.

The horizontal axis in each of the following diagrams is the economic spectrum, and the vertical axis is the social/internationalist one. The traditional political scale, meanwhile, runs diagonally from liberal left to reactionary right. The dark grey rectangle in each diagram shows the Overton Window for that period, and the light grey rectangle shows the previous Overton Window (except in the first diagram, which does not have one).

The diagram below represents Consensus 1, the period before and during the Second World War. The war is an anomaly, so we dwell less on the period 1939–45 than on the period running up to it.

This was an era with low living standards, slum dwellings, poorly regulated heavy industry and high inequality (although the latter was inadvertently reduced by the toll of war). It was also an era before civil rights and before many social changes we now take for granted. Ingrained snobbery and jingoism were the order of the day, and beliefs about the ethnic and social supremacy of certain groups were widespread.

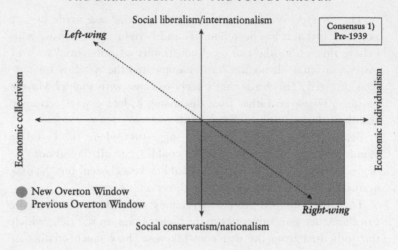

Winston Churchill was able to promote colonialism, stating, in 1937, that 'I do not admit . . . that a great wrong has been done to the Red Indians of America, or the black people of Australia . . . by the fact that a stronger race, a higher-grade race . . . has come in and taken its place.'[4] We lived in a right-wing country, economically and socially.

The subsequent 1945–64 period saw the rise of what is now known as the post-war consensus, built by Clement Attlee's great reforming government (see Consensus 2). The diagram illustrates the leftward direction the Overton Window moved in economically, with the British people rejecting the previous consensus.

The shift towards economic collectivism was the most pronounced we have seen – with massive new investment in health, welfare and housing, as well as the nationalisation of key industries. Hierarchical aspects remained – grammar schools and low access to higher education, for example – as many of the new interventions were based on providing a safety net for the first time. But, at the level of economic collectivism, this remains a period where the Overton Window moved unprecedentedly to the left, initiated by Labour but supported by subsequent Tory governments.

The story is more mixed when it comes to social and internationalist

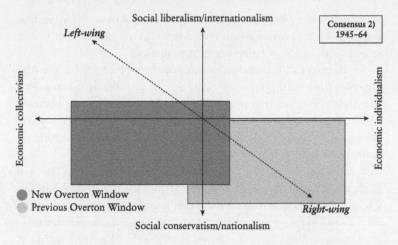

advances. The era was defined in part by decolonisation, which was a priority for the Labour government. India was granted independence and the number of countries under British rule fell.

With that said, the UK still tried to keep parts of its empire, as developments in Suez in the 1950s showed. By 1960, when Harold Macmillan gave his 'winds of change' speech committing in full to self-determination, Britain still had an empire and occupied swathes of Africa – a situation with which most Brits were perfectly satisfied. So, it would be hard to argue that the 1945–64 consensus departed from colonial assumptions – certainly compared to modern expectations. Foreign policy based on nationalist expansion remained within the Overton Window, even if it was moving out of it.

Back home, this was an era of 'No blacks, no dogs, no Irish'. Migrant communities were subject to persecution which – however appalled we are by Nigel Farage's rhetoric – are hard to imagine today.

Former Education Secretary Alan Johnson recalls in his memoir, *This Boy*, the murder of an Antiguan carpenter in 1959, incited by Oswald Mosley's Blackshirts.[5] Johnson writes of the febrile atmosphere in the impoverished district of London in which he grew up, where racist street beatings were common. The Notting Hill Race

Riots had taken place just a year before, and Johnson describes how the lack of legal provision, combined with the attitudes of the police, stopped the attackers being brought to justice.

So, the 1945 shift in the economic consensus had not come with a great shift in social policies or attitudes. Britain remained conservative and nationalist, reflected in the legal frameworks and policies in place. Ideas of genuine equality on many fronts – e.g. the removal of capital punishment or the legalisation of abortion – were outside the mainstream.

Consensus 3, below, shows the next period, 1965–78. This saw changes on social liberalism and internationalism. Whereas Anthony Crosland's proposals to strip back the 'socially imposed restrictions on the individual's private life and liberty' were at the peripheries of the Overton Window in 1956, by 1978 they had moved within it. Censorship, divorce laws, 'penalties for sexual abnormality', abortion laws and hanging[6] were reduced or removed, and protections for minorities were enshrined in law. This was also the period of the sexual revolution and civil rights movements, although wider social attitudes took longer to catch up on these fronts.

But the 1965–78 consensus also marked a shift away from economic collectivism, which was deemed to be functioning badly. Opposition to trade unions became 'sayable' as a result of the three-day week, concern about pay restraint and the Winter of Discontent. Likewise, there were anxieties about the creation of a 'brain drain', thanks to early financial globalisation. And British Rail services were rationalised for the first time, on the basis of economic need.

This was set against shifts to the left, like the opening of new universities and the end of grammar schools in most of the UK. But there was still a movement away from nationalisation and unionisation as defaults.

Consensus 4 describes the Thatcher–Major years. There is a marked swing towards economic individualism, with big elements of the post-war consensus pulled apart and chronically underfunded. The country saw privatisations, tax cuts, a decline in public investment, the selling-off of council houses, the 'smashing' of the unions,

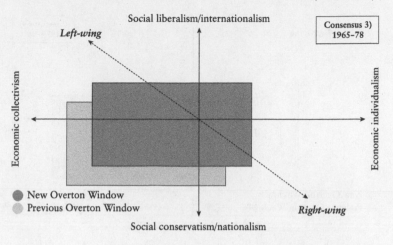

the deregulation of the City, and so on. This was especially pronounced before 1990.

Many of these things were happening elsewhere in the developed world, thanks to globalisation. But the right-wing emphasis of the Thatcher governments meant that, compared to European equivalents, changes had painful long-term consequences.

It also meant that Labour abandoned the positions which were most at odds with the new consensus. Anti-globalisation and anti-capitalist stances became unsayable.

Meanwhile, there was a southward shift too, with a resurgence in divisive policies on immigration and cohesion and the introduction of Section 28. The story is more complex in other places, such as with Europe, in the case of Major. But 1979–96 consensus did not, it would be fair to say, focus on promoting equalities or extending rights.

Internationally, approaches to Northern Ireland and South Africa reflected, in different ways, a reluctance to fully repudiate colonialism. And the Falklands War remains the last episode of true flag-waving jingoism in the UK.

Let's move to Consensus 5 (p. 000), 1997–2010. The spectrum below charts this. To begin with – as the northward direction of the

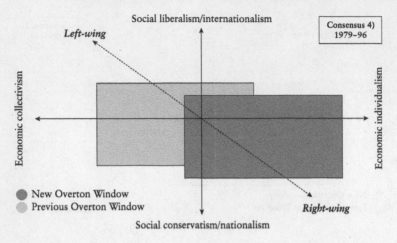

Overton Window suggests – there was a clear post-1997 shift towards social liberalism. Government policy broke from the past on rights for LGBT groups, women, racial and religious minorities, children and even animals.[7] This move was enshrined in the Equalities Act and the Human Rights Act, and reflected changing social attitudes.[8]

Internationally, there were commitments to tackle climate change multilaterally, to give the regions more self-determination, to cancel Third World debt and to treble aid.[9] These initiatives represent a move towards international cooperation. The Africa Commission, the Good Friday Agreement and Britain's determination to be at the heart of Europe would not have happened under the prior administrations. Until Brexit, it seemed that any government would need to endorse this new consensus.

Let's move to economic collectivism and social justice. This is the area where the Golden Era narrative is most pronounced, and where the accusation of a post-1979 watershed moment is most acute: 'Ever since the late 1970s, the dominant philosophy has been one of rugged, unabashed individualism.'[10]

It would be stupid to claim that 1997 saw the Overton Window return to 1945–64 levels of collectivism. Tony Blair's rewriting of Clause 4 and agnosticism on public ownership reflected a refusal to

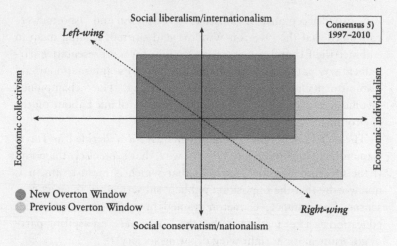

Social liberalism/internationalism

Left-wing

Consensus 5)
1997–2010

Economic collectivism

Economic individualism

● New Overton Window
○ Previous Overton Window

Right-wing

Social conservatism/nationalism

go against the inherited consensus. So too did the failure to regulate the City to the necessary levels. Compromises here were partly made because some collectivist methods were considered ineffective in delivering progressive goals. But they also stemmed from a feeling that the centre ground had shifted rightwards and that certain policies would be viewed as dampening aspiration if Labour even whispered their name.

Yet there was also a break from Consensus 4. Rather than being a continuity of 'rugged, unabashed individualism', the period saw a larger state and a new emphasis on social justice.[11] Thatcher's attitudes to poverty and inequality were firmly rejected in favour of full employment, equal opportunities and public investment.[12] A popular appetite for better services drove this. Setting aside public ownership, on which Labour changed little, there is a long list of policies backing this up: EMA (education maintenance allowance), the minimum wage, the halving of pensioner and child poverty, the New Deal, and so on.[13] Few of these were mainstream during the previous consensus – under which the Prime Minister could claim there was 'no such thing as society', and her Employment Secretary could tell people to get on their bikes to find work.

Moreover, if we remind ourselves of 2005–10 Tory policies, we see a broad acceptance of Consensus 5. Cameron and Osborne were convinced that the Overton Window had shifted, leading them to embrace the EU and gay marriage, to aim for a representative parliamentary party, and to maintain Labour's international aid commitments and levels of public spending. They championed income equality and the NHS and tried to outflank Labour on the environment.[14]

These 'hug a hoodie' commitments are now derided as David Cameron paying lip service. Yet, in a way, that is precisely the point. If the Overton Window describes that which is mainstream, it is noteworthy that the opposition publicly subscribed to the new consensus. For instance, Cameron framed his rejection of grammar education as a key test of whether the Tories were 'an aspiring party of government' or a 'right-wing debating society'.[15]

The above will ring hollow in the light of austerity and Brexit. The national debt provided an opening for the Overton Window to be moved back to the right economically.[16] The coalition portrayed as social luxuries policies like SureStart and Building Schools for the Future. They cut tax, welfare spending and public-sector jobs.

In reflection of this, Consensus 6 shows the shift in the Overton Window after 2010. It depicts a move towards levels of economic individualism akin to the Major years (although not the Thatcher years).

With this said, parts of the social justice agenda remained. It is hard to imagine the Tories symbolically ringfencing health and education, for example, were it not for the changes since they had last held office. Likewise, on many other policies put forward after 2010. Conservative support for the minimum wage – opposed by them in 1998 – was part of the reason that Cameron and Osborne's record on inequality remains better than it could be.

Meanwhile, there is also a move south in the diagram, marking the resurgence of Euroscepticism and the 'tens of thousands' immigration target. This is offset somewhat by the retention of the socially liberal aspects of Consensus 5, such as civil partnerships.

Some of the things above were thanks to the Lib Dems'

moderating influence, and many are cosmetic. The living wage was undermined by welfare cuts, for example. But they show that, despite Cameron having won permission to cut spending, 'pull yourself up by your bootstraps' Thatcherism had been pushed outside the Overton Window. To be allowed to lead a coalition government, the Conservatives needed to adopt the language of social liberalism and equal opportunities. And, to a certain extent, they had to mean it.

The next consensus would be the post-Brexit one. It's unclear what it looks like at the time of writing, so I have not charted it. However, it's likely that the Overton Window will shift significantly southwards, as we become more culturally insular and socially conservative.[17] Brexit will, most likely, lead to straitened times, intensifying anti-immigrant tensions. It could mean fewer Britons travelling internationally, and fewer tourists and migrants wanting to come here. With a bona fide right populist at the helm, in the form of Boris Johnson, this seems especially likely. Priti Patel's immigration crackdown in February 2020 is a sign of things to come.

The UK's post-Brexit position on the economic gamut is less clear. It is possible to imagine a collectivist departure from the EU, in which Britain shares more equally the resources left once wealth departs.[18] However, there will be a countervailing pressure, once this bites, to keep investors, jobs and better-off taxpayers on UK soil, by deregulating and cutting tax.

The COVID-19 pandemic is, of course, a huge unknown here, overshadowing even Brexit. The crisis has demonstrated, for example, the need to value key workers, create social support structures and fund the NHS. And the government's unprecedented intervention in the economy could change the context fundamentally. On the other hand, the social repercussions from COVID-19 will create immense pressure on jobs and resources, potentially entrenching inequalities and leading to another period of austerity. All of these things make the position of the Overton Window in five or ten years' time even harder to predict.

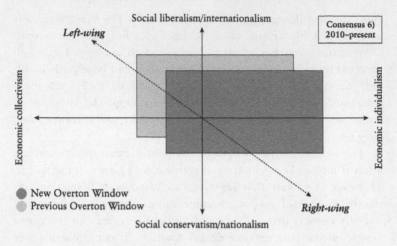

The impression you would get, listening to many Golden Era believers, is that Britain has moved from the top-left quadrant of our diagram to the bottom-right quadrant over the past seven decades; from fairness and community to greed and bigotry. Yet the reality is a muddled and piecemeal series of changes.

The diagram below, which has all of the Overton Windows we have looked at overlaid, demonstrates this. It shows the consensus inching in a more progressive direction each time Labour is in power. The shifts have been helped and hindered by external factors. But there was never a pure, historic moment when the Overton Window sat unashamedly in the top-left corner. As one academic points out:

> Labour's enduring successes in 1945–51, 1964–1970, 1974–1979 and 1997–2010 were great liberal reforms and extensions of social justice, from the National Health Service to the minimum wage. They did not bring a mythical socialist future any closer. Labour advanced despite, not because of, its original socialism.[19]

To simplify the messy overlay, we might say there have been four really major changes since 1945. To begin with, the Overton Window moved close to the economically collectivist pole (marked '1.Attlee' below). It remained more or less there until Thatcher's

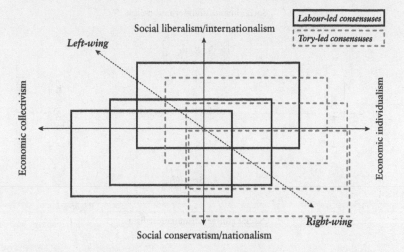

governments pushed it towards the economically individualist pole ('2.Thatcher'). From the 1990s onwards it moved towards the internationalist poll of our spectrum, and about halfway back towards economic collectivism ('3.Blair'). And it is now likely to move due south ('4.Brexit').

This is pretty crude. But it nevertheless has a greater ring of truth – if we want a meta-narrative – than the shift from progressive to reactionary described by some left populists.

The myopia of the Golden Era stops any acknowledgement of this. George Monbiot, for instance, claims that Labour 'always look like their opponents, [but] with a five-year lag'.[20] Rather than noting the progress made – however insufficient – when Labour governs, left populists take the least charitable view that they possibly can of outgoing Labour prime ministers. The allegation is always that they accepted the inherited consensus and changed nothing.

A good example of this myopia is Margaret Thatcher's suggestion that New Labour was her 'greatest achievement'. This is routinely repeated by the populist left as evidence that 1997–2010 Labour was continuity Toryism. However, Cameron's claim to be the 'heir to Blair' – which represented an acknowledgement that the Conservatives would need to focus on public investment and social

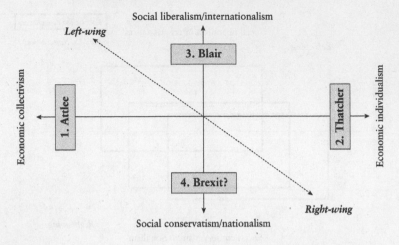

justice to win again – is often treated as further proof that Labour became 'Tory lite'.[21] In reality, the latter quote signifies the opposite. If you are to take Thatcher's comment seriously, as evidence that Brown and Blair had to embrace parts of her legacy, then you must take Cameron's seriously too, as proof that Labour also redrew the Overton Window.[22]

The biggest problem with this myopia is that it is self-fulfilling. The myth of 'original socialism' means that each time power is lost the populist left decides the outgoing administration achieved nothing compared to its red-blooded forefathers.[23] The search begins for someone who can take us back to our roots. This helps Conservative attacks to stick, and means the public hears little positive about Labour in government.

Moreover, the search for 'original socialism' is a search for something that was never there. It is time-consuming and lets Tory governments set the narrative. Would Britain really be crippled by austerity and on the cusp of a Boris Johnson-led Brexit, for example, if Labour had regrouped in 2010, championed their record, learned from their mistakes and climbed back into the saddle as an alternative government?

Beneath this is a deeper truth, which is that consensuses are seldom shaped from opposition. There is no 'Duncan Smith consensus' and no 'Foot consensus' among our diagrams. Parties almost always need to start inside the Overton Window, before they are trusted to move it.[24]

This acknowledgement is a central difference between left pluralism and left populism. The former's theory of change is based on meeting people where they are and shifting the mainstream; the latter's is based on taking stances from beyond the window, which drag the mainstream leftwards.

The latter approach is flawed, even in the case of Corbyn. Labour's better than expected 2017 performance may be seen as proof by some that a radical opposition can make the running. Yet this was enabled by major concessions to the mainstream view of the day – on Trident, welfare, Brexit and immigration. It came against a Tory leader who had inadvertently placed herself outside the mainstream. And it was still unsuccessful. The year 2019, meanwhile, saw Labour propose ideas that lacked credibility and take positions that were at odds with the public mood – the result being a thumping defeat. The hard right of the Tory Party now set the agenda for the next consensus.

During the period since Labour lost power in 2010, the Overton Window has unquestionably moved rightwards – certainly compared to its direction of travel in the decade immediately before. This should give pause for thought to those on the so-called left of the party, who set the running during this period.

IV. EQUAL RIGHTS, EQUAL OPPORTUNITIES, FAIR OUTCOMES

As we have said, John Rawls mapped out two principles, the second containing two parts, for how a society might be devised from the original position:

1. The first principle is that **basic liberties and rights should be distributed absolutely evenly.** As you would not, behind the veil

of ignorance, know your gender, your sexuality, your race, your class, and so on, you would design a society where you were not prevented by things beyond your control from voting, from avoiding arbitrary imprisonment, from being free to move around or go to school or own property, and so on.

2. The second principle is that **'primary goods' should be distributed evenly.** Primary goods include income and wealth, property, access to information, education, opportunity to fulfil your potential, social efficacy. This means that, not knowing what your own genetic endowments will be (e.g. whether you would be born clever, stupid, artistic, entrepreneurial, strong, weak, and so on), you would design the society in such a way that:

A) There is absolute **equality of opportunity** to fulfil yourself when it comes to life chances.

B) There are **fair outcomes.** Inequalities of outcome should only exist if they benefit the weakest at least as much as the strongest. This emphasis on fair outcomes was referred to by Rawls as the 'difference principle' – an acknowledgement that there are some natural differences between people.

The first principle was, Rawls believed, of higher priority than the second, and the first part of the second was of higher priority than the last part. If you did not know which individual you would be born as, you would first ensure there were no barriers actively stopping you from fulfilling yourself. Secondly, you would ensure that your potential was not held back by circumstance. And thirdly, you would ensure that, were you born less capable, you would not be deprived of the prosperity generated by those with more talent. *Equal rights, equal opportunities, fair outcomes.*

This ordering seems correct. Equal rights surely come first, in that you would first ensure society was *in principle* non-bigoted. Prioritising equality of opportunity – the more complex effort to ensure that society is *in effect* non-bigoted – would not make sense. What would be the point of pumping resources into university access schemes, for instance, if certain minority groups were legally barred from higher education?

Likewise, it makes sense that fair outcomes are a lower priority than equal opportunities. To use a false dichotomy for a moment, which of the following would we choose from behind the veil of ignorance: a society where TV executives earned ten times the wage of pot-washers but where background held little sway over who did what? Or a society where TV executives earned twice as much as pot-washers but where people from deprived backgrounds received little formal education and inevitably became pot-washers, while people from privileged backgrounds without exception became TV executives? We would consider both scenarios an affront. But a society of fair outcomes would probably lose its appeal if it was also a society of rigid pre-destiny.

In short, fair outcomes lose their relevance without equal opportunities. And both are impossible without equal rights.

These sequential building blocks form our next narrative: *equal rights, equal opportunities, fair outcomes*. This looks at how the UK has done in fulfilling Rawls's three consecutive principles.

We will start with equal rights. A hundred or so years ago, we were a long way from fulfilling Rawls's principles. Women could not vote. There was almost no emphasis on education for the working classes. Economic inequality was immense.

By 1945 progress had been made, with universal suffrage achieved. But the basic freedoms of people in poorer social classes were not acknowledged in practice – less still those of minority groups. There had been no civil rights process. Homosexuality was illegal. Access to decent education and healthcare were denied. Discriminatory attitudes to children, women and the elderly were upheld in policy. And the prism of empire meant that even social liberals of the day saw equal rights largely in relation to those on British shores.

After the Second World War, this changed. Reforms meant that basic entitlements like the right to healthcare and security were extended to the population as a whole, with the creation of the NHS and the welfare state. These may not immediately strike us as rights-based reforms. But they were about providing a safety net so that your social class and physical capabilities did not stop you doing basic things.

These were followed, in the 1960s and 1970s, by social legislation following the civil rights movement. This included the Race Relations Act, the Equal Pay Act, the Married Woman's Property Act, the Sex Discrimination Act, the Sexual Offences Act and the lowering of the voting age. In the 1990s and 2000s, there followed the Disability Discrimination Act, the Equality Act, civil partnerships and gay marriage, the lowering of the age of consent for homosexual sex, and the Racial and Religious Hatred Act. These solidified and codified steps already made and enshrined in law the increasingly liberal attitudes of the population.

Purely from a rights point of view, there is little that anyone in the UK is restricted from doing on the basis of faith, disability, ethnicity, class, gender or sexuality. The assumptions underpinning this have been absorbed into our national culture and political discourse. (Transgender rights are arguably an exception to this, and are a source of controversy which I will not go into here.)

A very small example of this in action is the House of Lords. If we look at the make-up of the House of Lords over time, we firstly see the 1958 Life Peerages Act, which introduced non-hereditary peers, and then, in 1999, the removal of almost all remaining inherited titles.[25] It has meant that figures such as Alan Sugar, Doreen Lawrence, Robert Winston and Andrew Lloyd Webber sit in the chamber – people who, whatever we think of them, have achievements beyond inherited rights.

A disproportionate number of appointed peers are still from elite backgrounds. And either way, we need a fully elected and representative second chamber. But the move from a House of Lords hamstrung by unequal rights to one hampered by unequal opportunities is significant.

On the first of Rawls's principles, we can call a tentative victory. Equal liberties and rights do, by and large, exist in the UK, as an aspiration of government and of the general public. Anyone who argued that a pensioner should not have a roof over their head because they can no longer work – or that a religious group should not be allowed to vote – would be out of step. There is no electable politician advocating racial segregation on buses or the withdrawal of the franchise for women. Problems clearly remain, and we should avoid complacency. But there have been big steps.

What, though, of equal opportunities? To clarify, this means absolute equality of life chances – so that where you're born has no bearing on where you end up. This is a highly egalitarian goal and is more radical than what is conventionally meant when politicians talk about equal opportunities, as we will see in a moment. (NB: I use 'social mobility', 'life chances' and 'meritocracy' as shorthand for 'equality of opportunity' in this chapter. We will mainly look at education.)

It seems, at first glance, that we have moved in the wrong direction here. Upward social mobility has stagnated, and we have spent the years since 2010 with a Cabinet dominated by Etonians. Virtually every prestigious sector, leadership position and university is disproportionately populated by those who went to private school.[26] However, that is not to say that the *commitment* to equality of opportunities has also lessened or that equal opportunities have moved out of the Overton Window.

Again, if we look at Britain a century ago we see a society with scant commitment to equal opportunities. Conservative Prime Minister Arthur Balfour warned peers voting on the 1911 Parliament Act that unless they behaved pragmatically they risked equalising life chances: 'You object to your tailor being made a peer, [but] you vote in such a way that your hatter and barber will be ennobled also!'[27] At that point, the school-leaving age was twelve. It rose to fourteen in 1918, but university remained the preserve of a private-school elite. In the First World War the influence of the class structure on the military resulted in the phenomenon of 'lions led by donkeys'.

In subsequent decades, politicians renounced this, as universal suffrage moved basic education for all into the political consensus. Yet the view remained that intelligence was 'fixed'.[28] Exceptionally bright schoolboys were 'lifted up' through scholarships. But little allowance was made for differences in opportunity, with intellect deemed to either shine through or not.

The tripartite grammar-school model, introduced in 1944, was a stab at creating a pathway for clever working-class children. In reality, it harmed the chances of the vast majority, thanks to its reductive view of what equal opportunities mean. Even amidst the radicalism of the post-war years the focus, perhaps with good reason, was on providing basic healthcare, shelter and social security (which we term 'rights' for the purposes of this chapter).

In the 1960s, a more sophisticated notion of equal opportunities came into vogue. Labour had long championed this, and the shift was assured in 1963, with the Tories acknowledging the need to seek out the potential in all children.[29] Grammar schools were phased out in most places. Meanwhile, the election of Ted Heath meant that the Conservatives were led, for the first time, by a meritocrat, not an aristocrat.

The 1980s were the strangest evolution in this process. Low investment in schools meant facilities fell into poor condition, driving middle-class parents into the private sector. And rising inequality curbed social mobility. The emphasis was on self-reliance, and while Thatcher signed up to the equal rights agenda (i.e. the idea that talented black or working-class children shouldn't be held back by random barriers), she did not subscribe to equal opportunities.

Yet at the same time the Tory rhetoric changed. Thatcher's success came through distancing the Conservatives from their establishment associations, and she argued in 1984 that 'it's not . . . where you come from, or who your parents are that matters. It's what you are and what you can do.' Working-class Tories like John Major increasingly used the language of social mobility.

Many of the 1997–2010 governments' achievements lay in putting a meaningful emphasis on equal opportunities.[30] However, the tensions this created show the challenges attached. In 2003, for example, the government angered private schools by setting up a commission compelling universities to accept more state applicants. The resulting blowback showed how the issue fell on the fault line between equal rights and equal opportunities. Private schools argued, from a rights perspective, against the 'discriminatory' and 'arbitrary' rejection of 'well-qualified candidates'. The government, on the other hand, championed equal opportunities, with Margaret Hodge calling for 'fair access for every individual to develop their full potential'.[31] The episode underscored the difficulty of creating genuinely *equal* opportunities, with the affirmative action required to level the playing field still highly contentious.

The emphasis on equal opportunities continued after 2010, rhetorically, at least.[32] And although the Conservatives' record is not great, a commitment to equal opportunities is now politically mainstream. Thatcher's sink-or-swim version of social mobility – where nothing would actively stop you progressing but nothing would help you either – is unsayable. Even in the most recent Tory leadership contest, all the candidates championed (in their language, if not in their policies) life chances for the poorest.

All of the above is complicated, however, by the fact that equality of opportunity now appears *less* good than in the mid-twentieth century. The post-war era saw high upward mobility, manifested in working-class baby boomers going into professional careers (and, in subsequent years, into higher education). This seems to undermine the argument that Rawls's second principle has, from a low base in 1945, become a steadily bigger part of the consensus.

Yet if we look at what has happened in detail, we see that the high post-Second World War social mobility was incidental and illusory in many places. As the economy changed, and skilled or professional jobs opened up, there was indeed a big rise in upward mobility. But this was not the consequence of more equal life chances in the 1940s, 1950s and 1960s. Under-investment and the grammar-school system meant that education levels remained unequal. Rather, it was the result of a one-off economic restructure increasing the need for white-collar workers. There was a dramatic uplift in skilled careers and higher education uptake, but this is not to be confused with a dismantling of the social hierarchy.[33] There was little focus on downward mobility (which is a prerequisite for genuine social mobility);[34] little evidence of those 'born to rule' ending up in factories or typing pools. There has never been a UK government that has cut the cord, in a long-term sense, between where people start out and where they end up.

With this said, the more equal a society is to start with, the more mobile it will be.[35] A high-mobility, low-equality society may be technically possible. But real equality of opportunity would probably involve resetting the clock to zero each generation, which would limit how big the gap in outcomes could become. This is proof that it is easier to achieve equal opportunities in environments – like those in the 1950s – that are more economically equal. But it is not proof that the class-bound society of the 1950s was an exemplar for this.

Overall, then, whereas equal rights have seen massive progress, the equal opportunities transformation is unfulfilled in practice (despite moving, decade on decade, into the mainstream consensus). Contemporary efforts to improve opportunities – such as big increases in the numbers in higher education – have done little to *equalise* life chances, even though they have lifted attainment and quality of life. 'Equal' opportunities have often come, in practice, to mean merely 'good' opportunities. This puts us at an uneasy juncture, where we have adopted the attitudes of a mobile and fluid society, while remaining a long way off achieving it in practice.

Turning this into truly equal life chances is the next step. And, while it remains politically difficult – reliant as it is on better off but less able children doing worse – it is not impossible. Shortening the economic ladder is an important first step, which can make the climb from the bottom rung easier, and the fall from the top one less painful.

This leads to Rawls's third step: fair outcomes. This is the issue, more than any other, where things are felt to have gone wrong. The UK's Gini-coefficient (the most common metric for measuring inequality) was relatively low until the end of the 1970s, but increased rapidly in the 1980s.[36] It broadly flatlined under Major, Blair and Brown. But it has never returned to pre-1979 levels, with Labour's more redistributive policies neutered by the difficulty of taxing the richest 1 per cent, and by the fear that doing so was electorally toxic. We are a wealthier society than a few generations back – and more of the social basics are provided. But we are also less equal. Not only are differences in outcome far too large, but there is little evidence of the richest being those whose talents benefit the whole (as Rawls stipulated that they should). Piketty's *Capital in the Twenty-first*

Century charts the rise in inequality in virtually every developed nation during the post-war period, demonstrating levels which no right-thinking person could describe as 'fair'. In Britain this is particularly acute.

Unchecked, inequality has the capacity to put other achievements in the shade. The threat posed by a society where gaps in outcomes are too large to be bridged – where people on the other side of those gaps are living lives too different to allow mutual understanding – is immense. We are already seeing this with shocks like Brexit, which are partly due to big economic differences between regions.

So, fair outcomes is, surely, an issue where the zeitgeist has surged to the right? We were a happy, equal society in the post-war years? The public demanded a low Gini-coefficient? Governments regularly checked and turned down the wealth-inequality thermostat?

As with equal opportunities, however, the reality is more complicated. Looking at the period since the Second World War, it seems that the notion of inequality in its contemporary sense – i.e. purely as a barometer of the *gap* between rich and poor – is relatively new to the political mainstream. Only since the 2008 crisis has it properly moved into the public consciousness. This is demonstrated by the new-found popularity of books like *The Spirit Level*, and by the willingness of politicians and commentators to talk about the issue.

This may seem apocryphal, given how much more equal the post-war era was. So, to be clear, I am obviously not saying outcomes have got fairer – just that political energy and public concern have not, up until the last few years, been directed at tackling inequality for its own sake.

Labour governments have always invested in the poorest, fighting inequality by default. The welfare state and the NHS represented a collective effort to prevent deprivation. These institutions meant there was only so far an individual could fall, and were followed by steps to improve education standards and employee protections. They created a floor, which was lifted and reinforced by subsequent governments.

And, although 'scrounger' arguments are made by right-wingers, who say the floor has risen too high, the need for a limit to how deprived people can become is something most support.

Yet a ceiling on inequality has never been a driving motivation in the same way. There is little consensus about how rich is too rich. As social policy professor Howard Glennerster points out, Beveridge's Social Plan (which formed the basis for many of the Attlee government's reforms), proposed that

> those who were not able to be employed in retirement, sickness or other legitimate reasons should receive a basic minimum income. The whole population should have access to free schooling, health care and a decent standard of housing. These would provide a floor on which individual endeavour could build and be rewarded. It would bring minimum security for all but not equality.[37]

For sure, the top rate of tax was higher in the years when this was being rolled out. Yet the continuation of these high tax rates, inherited from the war governments, was justified to fund the reinforcement of the safety net. Redistribution was a means to an end – the way of lifting the floor. It wasn't a de facto public good and its impact on equality was a byproduct of its central aim.

In 1979, of course, Margaret Thatcher put forward a new argument, claiming that you could make the poor richer by making the rich richer.[38] Rather than requiring the lowering of the ceiling, the floor could be lifted by removing the ceiling. She deployed the argument of 'the tide that lifts all boats' and persuaded many skilled working-class voters to back her.

Of course, the 1980s governments failed, in most ways, to 'lift all boats'. Even though the country became more prosperous – and some working-class voters benefited – there was chronic underfunding of services and the public realm, neglect for many regions and industries, and rising poverty, unemployment and homelessness.

The 1997–2010 Labour governments did elevate the floor, by contrast. They resumed previous Labour administrations' focus on reinforcing and lifting the safety net. The dramatic increases in employment, pay, spending on services and social security are well known. However, unlike past Labour governments, they did so in a climate where this was not sufficient to reduce inequality. In a post-globalisation context, the ceiling climbed faster than the floor could follow.[39]

The Blair–Brown governments deserve criticism for this. Yet we should be clear, in waging this criticism, that they would have been making this argument at a time when they were able to invest heavily *without* raising the taxes of the top 1 per cent (which they feared would send a damaging electoral signal, without adding much revenue to the Exchequer). In short, New Labour would have needed to be the first government to set out the case for taxing the rich for its own sake. They ducked this challenge, partly thanks to the difficulty of a transnational 1 per cent, and partly for reasons of electoral timidity.

The general public also tend to see lifting the floor as the priority, with the lowering of the ceiling only one way of doing this. Opinion research shows a widespread feeling that the income gap is too large, but much lower support for redistribution. In 2012, for example, the proportion agreeing with the former diagnosis was 82 per cent, but the proportion agreeing with the latter prescription was only 41 per cent.[40] So, there is more support for tackling inequality when it is discussed in the abstract than there is when solutions involving higher taxes are put forward (even among those unaffected by the higher taxes).

Other research suggests that it is deprivation at the bottom – not opulence at the top or inequality in the abstract – that drives concern about the gap between rich and poor. Support for redistribution dropped steadily throughout New Labour's first decade in government, for example – even though the 1 per cent grew marginally richer. Falling poverty and homelessness, investment in services and the public realm, and high employment and growth meant there was less desire to tax the super-rich. By contrast, in the late 1980s – when there was a similarly high Gini-coefficient but services were deteriorating and poverty worsening – the demand for taxes on the rich was higher.[41] The clamour for redistribution comes when people feel hardship at the bottom and see that there is surplus at the top to deal with it.[42]

Psychologically, this stacks up.[43] Studies explicitly testing the 'veil of ignorance' suggest that humans would, in fact, choose a state of affairs with less equality than Rawls himself believed was fair – on the proviso that there is a significant 'floor constraint' on poverty.[44]

All of this may seem like splitting hairs. Yet there is an important distinction between the view that taxing the rich is desirable to improve schools and hospitals and the view that it is desirable regardless. The former is a tax-and-spend approach, which the Tories dismantled in the 1980s. But the latter has never really been part of the mainstream.[45] Only in the last decade, in the face of anger about an undeserving rich after the crash, has it become so. The High Pay Commission, for instance, was created only in 2010. And Section One of the Equalities Act, which legally committed public bodies to reduce inequalities, was passed in the same year.[46]

Of course, all of the above reflects the fact that the problem has got worse, at least as much as it reveals a progressive shift in the discourse. In the 1950s there was not a super-rich to object to. And the last time there was inequality on a scale comparable to today's – in the early twentieth century – poverty at the bottom was so appalling that the need to alleviate it was, in itself, an argument for redistribution. It does not seem that there has ever been a situation like the one running up to 2008, where society was unprecedentedly affluent in material terms but where outcomes were so unfair as to be an issue regardless.

As Thomas Piketty points out, past reductions in inequality have mostly been the result of wars and crashes. These levelled economic differences and created – at immense human cost – favourable conditions for progressives to lift and reinforce the floor.[47] Given that inequality is liable to grow if left to its own devices – especially in globalised, low-growth societies – we have now, for the first time, to find peaceful and sustainable policies for creating fair outcomes, without relying on moments of violent destruction to do it for us.

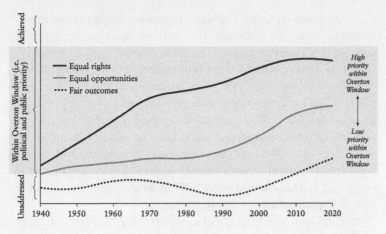

This is a key point missed by those, including Corbyn himself, who claim that the Corbyn project was vindicated by the subsequent response to the COVID-19 crisis.[48] Labour must find a way to invest more in services and to reduce inequality *without* depending on a global shutdown and the bottom potentially falling out of society. Of course, faced with the end of life as they know it, even the most right-wing politician will usually intervene to keep the country on life support (and a period of hardship will often follow, once the immediate threat has passed). The challenge – which is far from easy – is to explain how you can arrive at a sustainable form of socialism without a major economic disaster being either the prior cause or the ultimate consequence.

Above is a visual recap of the *equal rights, equal opportunities, fair outcomes* transition. It offers a speculative look at how Rawls's principles have moved into the mainstream. The grey 'Overton Stripe' represents the political and public consensus. The higher the line for each issue goes, the more it can be seen to have moved within the mainstream. Issues above the stripe are those which all politicians accept as non-negotiable. Issues below it are 'fringe' concerns, vying for consideration.

As we have said, the gradually increasing emphasis on Rawls's principles is set against the reality that, in practice, opportunities and outcomes haven't become any more equal.

Yet the latter point does not fully undermine the former. Rather, it proves that, on these two issues, successes in the past have been partly down to factors other than political and public appetite. The post-Second World War increase in upward mobility was due to a one-off economic restructure; the 1940s equalising of outcomes was down to an economic crash and then a war. Progressive governments were able to capitalise on all these changes. But none came as the result of a settlement that was vastly more ideologically committed to equal opportunities or fair outcomes.

A world with equal rights, equal opportunities and fair outcomes – not just for temporary periods when circumstances align but as a result of concerted policy choices – remains the progressive ideal. By looking at the unfinished evolution through Rawls's principles, we can start to see a way towards it.

V. DIRECT CHALLENGES TO INDIRECT CHALLENGES

The paradox described immediately above shows two things, moving in different directions: intention to solve problems and ability to solve them. Political discourse and public opinion are becoming more egalitarian on many issues, but the economic structure is becoming a harder place in which to enact this. *Equal rights, equal opportunities, fair outcomes* is thus part of a broader transition, from challenges which are the consequence of direct factors to those which are the product of indirect ones. Many of the most overt barriers have been overcome, and left-wingers are increasingly confronted by issues which stem from macro-economic, structural problems, alongside some of the cyclical and habitual tendencies in human nature. These often get worse without anyone causing active harm.

Table 15.1.

Direct challenges	Indirect challenges
Regressive	Non-progressive
Immoral	Amoral
Authored	Authorless
Causal	Systemic
Simple	Sophisticated
Oppression	Inaction
'Something hindering' Primary	'Nothing helping'/ 'Not enough helping' Secondary
Unfairness as the cause/aim	Unfairness as a symptom/by-product

The *direct challenges to indirect challenges* shift describes this move: from problems occurring for clear reasons through to them happening for more intangible ones. The table above sets out a series of 'before and after' transitions.

Ethnicity is a useful case study here. It is an issue where unacceptable unfairness continues to exist, but where the root of the unfairness has changed, to some degree, from *direct challenges to indirect challenges*.

In 1949, for example, diplomatic fallout occurred when a white British woman attempted to marry a black African chieftain in London.[49] Direct, widespread opposition was aimed at something which would now be unremarkable and celebrated. There was nothing indirect about the racism at play.

Meanwhile, the 'colour bar' existed across large parts of the economy, and BME groups were deliberately outlawed from many walks of life. The 1963 Bristol Bus Boycott was one of the most famous attempts to fight this, and the Race Relations Act of 1965 tackled the problem in law. Even so, direct forms of prejudice were widespread for some time after, both in public attitudes and within institutions like the police.

These were the consequence of policies which were overtly (or sometimes covertly) racist: public attitudes which were prejudiced, reinforced by rules and customs which permitted this to play out in how society was organised.

Recent decades have seen a slow stripping away of these discriminatory practices, as we saw earlier when looking at equal rights. Yet this is undermined by the fact that there has been far less progress on racial equality than most hoped for. In 2010, for instance, BME groups were still two and a half times as heavily represented in the prison system as they should be,[50] and remain significantly under-represented at the top of society.[51] Given that most forcible barriers have been taken down, progress – although happening – is unbelievably slow. The Black Lives Matter protests during 2020 have drawn attention to this.

Why, if there have been genuine strides forward, do these issues persist? The left-populist response would be that 1940s-style racism is alive and well; that bigotry and discrimination are merely disguised and sanitised by the establishment.[52]

There is a little truth in this. The government's disgraceful 'hostile environment' policy, culminating in the Windrush scandal, is a good example. Yet this does not stack up, overall. Discrimination is less permissible in law and in practice than at any point in British history – with levels of prejudice much lower than a few decades ago.[53] There are fewer direct barriers – be it in employment or the justice system – and there are frequent government efforts to target funding at young BME men, develop inclusion strategies or tackle 'male, pale and stale' trends at the top.

There are still many instances of genuine racism, of course, and these cannot be played down or understated. But the reasons for racial inequality are shifting incrementally from direct to indirect ones.

BME groups began as migrants or refugees in most cases and usually started out in the least well-off sectors, pay brackets and neighbourhoods. The more economically unequal and socially immobile the society, the harder it is for these cycles to break. A growing gap between rich and poor therefore causes a growing gap between BME communities and white residents. In Britain this meant that the reduction of direct barriers – in the 1960s and

1970s – was followed almost immediately by the increase in indirect socio-economic ones in the 1980s.

This has implications for attainment and employment, with concentrations of those who are less well-off – among whom BME groups are more common – going to certain schools and living in certain areas. Away from education, there is an absence of 'weak ties' (that is, informal networks which provide mentorship and forge introductions) and a greater likelihood of social problems.

This range of indirect factors means the average BME teen faces a steeper journey than the average white teen. Hence, progress towards racial equality is glacially slow. But the reasons for this are less and less that someone has behaved in a directly racist way or overtly blocked equality. The problem is not even, in many cases, one of inaction so much as insufficient action. Conscious or unconscious discrimination remains a factor, no doubt. But the central problem goes some way beyond this.

With other factors, like social class, it's the same story. Whatever we think about pernicious terms like 'chav', direct snobbery – against a regional accent or a non-elite school – has generally reduced a lot.[54] Yet a host of intangibles – private education, the rising number of postgraduate degrees, the impenetrable London housing market, unpaid internships, and so on – mean that advances are exceptionally slow.

Another example is 'social cleansing', the phrase used by the populist left to describe gentrification in London.[55] Severe as gentrification is, its causes are largely indirect: a case of the yawning economic gap, between the capital and everywhere else, creating massive demand for London living. Yet the term 'social cleansing' implies a process of direct persecution by class and colour.

The consequences of the chasm between 'London and the Rest' are, for me, among the most important issues Britain faces. But they are qualitatively different, in character as well as in effect, from the deliberate forms of extermination, deportation and genocide with which the term 'cleansing' associates them.

Failure to acknowledge the *direct challenges to indirect challenges* shift contributes to the deep non-sequiturs that now exist between right and left.

The right uses the fact that inequalities remain, despite direct barriers having been removed, as evidence that fecklessness is at fault. They point to 'political correctness gone mad' when they see, for instance, poorer students paid a maintenance allowance to stay in school.

The left counter that direct prejudice is alive and well – thinly camouflaged or hiding in plain sight. All present challenges – even complex issues, like climate change and public health – are regarded as the product of direct blockades.[56]

We saw this at play in the respective responses to the 2011 riots. On the one hand, the right-wing commentariat pointed out, there was nothing compelling urban youngsters to riot. There were no rights they were fighting for; no arbitrary barriers; nothing holding them back. In fact, there were many policies to mitigate their deprivation.[57] The left-wing commentariat argued the opposite. The riots were an act of protest against oppression by elite politicians and the police; a backlash against enforced poverty, wilful ghettoisation and deliberate subjugation.[58]

In truth, there aren't the direct oppressive barriers there once were. But the fact that rioters came disproportionately from certain backgrounds – and that these backgrounds were, generally, much more deprived – shows us that structural inequalities were still, indirectly, a defining factor.

Even in cases where there *are* obvious culprits, like Channel 4's 2014 decision to air the TV programme *Benefits Street*, the *direct challenges to indirect challenges* hypothesis holds up. *Benefits Street* was heavily criticised by the left for pushing a right-wing agenda. Yet its real aim was not to make an ideological point but to spark controversy and win ratings.[59] There is no doubt that *Benefits Street* was divisive. But this is a side-effect of its commercial agenda – not the result of direct propaganda. If Channel 4 thought there would have been easy titillation in an exposé of tax avoidance, then they would have made that instead.

A show like *Benefits Street* therefore feels distinct from the challenges of five or six decades ago, when there was a common view that the ruling class knew how to run things and a suspicion of 'the great unwashed'. The overt chauvinism of that era has retreated, replaced – be it in the case of Channel 4 producers or of London property developers – by market pressure and the path of least resistance.

This gets to the heart of what the *direct challenges to indirect challenges* shift is really about: namely, the move from the left's opponents being directly supportive of a tiered society to their being supportive of policies which create injustices as a byproduct. It is the difference between traditional conservatism, which favoured maintaining hierarchies for the sake of stability, and Thatcherism, which preached instead a form of pure individualism. These phenomena are qualitatively different.

Many will, again, see this as hair-splitting, and say that there is little moral difference between causing direct harm and causing indirect harm. Putting the 'bottom line' above fairness and wellbeing is surely just as bad as deliberate prejudice?

To respond to this charge, let's imagine two companies.

Company A looks to hire applicants who have been to elite schools. Their director prefers employees who are male, well-spoken and white and who come from 'good stock'. He would prefer that those without this lineage did not work for him. As a result, Company A hires upper- and middle-class applicants with 2:2 degrees over working-class applicants with Firsts.

Company B, in contrast, looks for applicants with Firsts; the more prestigious the university and the higher the mark the better. As a result, those they hire are disproportionately from privileged backgrounds (thanks to all of the systemic factors which mean that middle-class children are more likely to go to university). Company B's director has no issue with working-class applicants, but there simply aren't many who have degrees that are as good. He is not going to jeopardise his business by gambling on those with worse qualifications.

Neither Company A nor Company B, caricatured as they are, are ethical businesses. An egalitarian company would go out of its way to have a representative workforce and would do better for it. But I do think that the move from a Company A-dominated economy to a Company B-dominated one represents an advance of sorts.

Whether you agree with me or not about this, the important thing is acknowledging the shift in context, from *direct challenges to indirect challenges*. The pretence that we live in a system dominated by a Company A ethos breaks down potential dialogue between left and right and distracts from the true problems of a Company B-dominated economy.[60]

16

The Case against the Golden Era
Continued (Psychology)

Lastly, let's look at some of the transitions in values, attitudes and expectations that have taken place since 1945.

VI. GROUPISH, INDIVIDUALIST, POST-MATERIALIST

The shifts we have looked at all relate, at least in part, to changes in the public's values. There is now less tolerance of prejudice, but a greater focus on personal autonomy. There is less discrimination and deference, but a stronger emphasis on self-sufficiency. Many arbitrary barriers have been dismantled, but have often brought down with them 'arbitrary' support structures, like class identification and community.

The tendency is to see these changes as impositions by 'the powerful'.[1] This is the narrative set out by left-libertarian filmmaker Adam Curtis, for example, in the documentary *Century of the Self*. Curtis describes a shift from a society driven by material-resource needs to one powered by abstract appeals to self-image. 'Elites' engineered this using Freudian psychology, according to the film, to placate the masses.

Setting aside its conspiracist tone, there is truth in the change which *Century of the Self* portrays. But what if you accept the transition, but think that an evolution in the public's attitudes has driven political decision-making – not the other way around?

Guardian columnist George Monbiot explores this, using what he calls 'the values ratchet'. He sees the UK as having moved from 'intrinsic' to 'extrinsic' values. Intrinsic values are, in Monbiot's view, wholly positive: 'self-acceptance ... tolerance, appreciation, cooperation and empathy' and 'a powerful desire to help others'. Extrinsic values are the opposite: 'lower empathy, a stronger attraction towards power, hierarchy and inequality, greater prejudice towards outsiders, and less concern for global justice and the natural world'.

The 'values ratchet', Monbiot says, is the process where reactionary, extrinsic values come to govern policy, thanks to politicians failing to challenge them. This means that our politics becomes more right-wing with each year that passes. It was through indulging the extrinsic values promoted by Thatcher, Monbiot argues, that Labour lost its way.[2]

This analysis initially feels compelling. The accusation is that politicians have abetted the public's worst instincts, not shaped them. This is more sophisticated than Puppet Master explanations.

Yet a glance at the decades before Thatcher shows that so-called intrinsic values weren't the order of the day. Political deference, xenophobia, snobbery, jingoism, the death penalty, domestic violence? These phenomena were offset by virtues which are less prevalent now, like pride in community and an ethos of self-sacrifice for the whole. But they were not the product of self-reflective, altruistic or universalist value systems.

The problem with Monbiot's assessment is that it assumes values are a zero-sum proposition. Instead of saying different values overlie or build up, depending on life experiences, the extrinsic versus intrinsic analysis describes a tug of war between the compassionate and selfish instincts in each person. 'These clusters exist in opposition to each other: as one set of values strengthens, the other weakens,' Monbiot writes.[3]

An alternative approach, already mentioned in Chapter Seven, is the British Values Survey. To recap, this divides the different human values into three layers, with one of the three being the central driver for any individual at a given time. These are:

1. *Groupish values* – defined by fear of threats to resources, and driven by belonging, conformity, authority, safety, and so on
2. *Individualist values* – characterised by aspirational, optimistic, status-driven and competitive motivations
3. *Post-materialist values* – built around social liberalism, universalism, internationalism, inner fulfilment and ethics

This framework argues that values develop based on needs. It rejects the division into compassionate and selfish values. Rather, it says that people are at different social and psychological life stages. Instead of a see-saw, the relationship between values here is more of a tissue effect; a build-up of different layers, partially dependent on culture and economics but also driven by personal experiences and natural differences.

The general rule is that, over the generations, groupish values are gradually replaced as the core, driving motivation by more individualist values, once rising prosperity makes the need to stick together less acute. These, in turn, are usurped by post-materialist values, once status concerns retreat. *Groupish, individualist, post-materialist.*[4]

The table below shows how this has evolved in Britain. In 1973, when values analysis was first carried out, over half the population had groupish values. Now it's a quarter. Levels of individualism have grown, as groupish values have gradually been replaced by individualistic ones. And post-materialist values have increased too, as people move 'through' the individualistic cluster.[5]

These figures run counter to Monbiot's view that we have seen a meta-shift from compassionate to selfish values. And they are a rebuff to the 'values ratchet' idea – which claims that by indulging certain values we enlarge them. In fact, it implies the opposite, suggesting that only once populations fulfil groupish and individualist needs do people (and generations) move towards the inner-directed and ethical values which Monbiot champions.

So if, like Monbiot, your ideal is a society of post-materialists, then helping other groups to fulfil their values needs is the way to get there. As we have seen with Brexit and Trump, attacking other value systems as immoral often entrenches and enflames the divides.

Table 16.1.

percentage of the population with predominantly ...	1973	2000	2005	2011	2016
... groupish values	56	35	24	39	25
... individualistic values	25	30	38	23	37
... post-materialist values	19	36	38	37	38

From a truly pluralist perspective, this is beside the point. The progressive aim should not be to indulge others, so as to coax them to post-materialism. Instead, assuming that we think it is government's role to meet the requirements of those it represents ('From each according to his ability, to each according to his need'), the goal is to help people fulfil themselves in whatever ways they want – as long as this does not harm others.

Monbiot's analysis epitomises a wider Golden Era misdiagnosis, which is to assume that Labour's electoral bedrock in the 1940s or 1950s was built on environmentally aware, ethical and altruistic impulses. In reality, the left's coalition was comprised of groupish motivations far more than post-materialist ones. Both sets of values eschew individualistic materialism. But groupish value systems do so on the essentially pre-materialist basis that they want to protect the resources and identity of their tribe – whereas post-materialists reject individualism in favour of an egalitarian, universal and holistic philosophy.

This demonstrates why globalisation has driven a wedge into the traditional Labour coalition. It has exposed, for instance, differences between the patriotic instincts of groupish voters in former heartlands and the internationalist impulses of urbane post-materialists.

Hence, the British Values Survey reveals a different dynamic to Monbiot's analysis. For sure, past societies were less individualist or consumerist. But this was because resources were scarce and people clubbed together. This manifested itself in tight-knit areas with traditionalist attitudes looking out for each other and scanning the horizon for threats. Collective identities were more powerful – with unionised industries and stronger communities. But this also led to attitudes which Monbiot would be unlikely to celebrate – like groupishness on gender, educational background, sexuality or nationhood.[6] In policy terms, Labour governments of the day invested both in social security (in the shape of the NHS) and national security (in the form of Britain's nuclear deterrent).

The misunderstanding here explains the left's romantic view of the Golden Era. And it is part of the reason why Labour often fails to understand changes in the population. What actually happened in the 1980s, for instance, was not that selfishness trumped compassion but that the balance shifted from groupish to individualistic values. The population became less willing to see themselves as needing collective protection. And Labour's coalition of groupish and (to a lesser extent) post-materialist values was unable to hold in the face of a swelling population of individualists.

Likewise, the view that younger generations' support for Corbyn shows that they're finally backing old-school socialism. The reality is that millennials are unprecedentedly liberal. Younger cohorts 'weaned in the age of choice' put stronger emphasis on personal autonomy and have less collectivist attitudes to welfare or unionisation[7] – while also being far more tolerant and pro-social. They are moving away, in key respects, from the racial, sexual – or class-based – groupishness that characterised the populace five or six decades ago.[8] A 2014 report found that

> Generation Y is more likely than other cohorts to believe the role of state should be more focused on providing opportunities and less on managing the risks individuals face. [It is] more concerned with personal independence and opportunity than compulsory systems of risk pooling and redistribution. However, younger people are no less likely to think that specific groups, such as the elderly, the disabled and low-income working families need to be supported.[9]

Within this, we can discern both socially liberal variants of individualistic value systems (often among BME groups and less well-off young people),[10] and ethical post-materialist value systems (especially among graduates). It is this that explains the surprise appeal of Corbyn. Rather than rediscovering the 'compassionate' values that existed pre-Thatcher, Corbyn at the peak of his powers lent voice to a younger cohort with unprecedentedly post-materialist and liberal ideals.[11] The process was not one of a pendulum swinging back.

One way of looking at the *groupish, individualist, post-materialist* shift is via the 'Angry Young Men' novels of the post-war years. John Braine's 1957 book *Room at the Top* is particularly interesting. Written two decades before the rise of Thatcherism – and set in the late 1940s – it contains early indicators of what was to come. The novel tells the story of Joe Lampton, an ambitious working-class man who moves from run-down Dufton to the affluent town of Warley to work in local government. Joe, who has returned from the Second World War to a more prosperous society, is adequately provided for. He has moved beyond the deprivation his working-class parents experienced. He has a job for life, and a white-collar one at that, thanks to the upward mobility of the time.

Yet individualistic Joe, exposed in Warley to levels of wealth beyond his town-hall existence, wants more. He sets out to escape his parents' groupish existence. Early on in the book, upon seeing a Warley man driving a sports car, he has an epiphany. Mulling over the social wire-work which both protects him from poverty and limits his prospects, Joe concludes:

> I made my choice then and there: I was going to enjoy all the luxuries that young men enjoyed. I was going to collect that legacy. It was as clear and compelling as that vocation which doctors and missionaries are supposed to experience, though in my case, of course, the call ordered me to do good to myself not others.[12]

Returning to Dufton the subsequent Christmas, Joe goes to his former local pub and suddenly finds that 'It was too small, too dingy, too working-class; four months in Warley had given me a taste for ... the authentic country pub.'[13] He remembers his parents, meanwhile, as frustratingly happy with their low status: his father is a 'Labour man' who would always look after 'his own' rather than himself.[14]

As the story unfolds Joe must choose between two women: Alice, for whom he would have to provide, and Susan, the spoilt daughter of Warley's richest businessman. Joe ultimately forms a Faustian pact, choosing money over love on the basis that 'People could be happy in those little houses with their tiny gardens ... They could be happy on my present income – even on a lot less. But it wasn't for me.' He decides he must 'force the town into granting the ultimate intimacy, the power and privilege and luxury that emanated from The Top'.[15]

Joe is a forerunner to the value changes in subsequent decades. His individualistic attitudes had moved beyond the group allegiances that had got the country through the war. And his decisions in the book anticipate the next thirty years of social history: the selling-off of public utilities; the aversion to tax increases, and so on.

While Joe is unattractive to egalitarian sensibilities, the approach he takes begins to look understandable – laudable, even, in places – when seen from his first-person perspective. As he views it, he's breaking from clannish orthodoxy and overcoming hierarchy. He may be egotistical – selfish, even – compared to his parents. But he is also meritocratic and self-aware. He doesn't identify as part of any tribe, and the primary battle is between him as an individual and the collectivist, stratified society that he feels holds him back.

Other Angry Young Men texts are similar. Alan Sillitoe's 1958 novel *Saturday Night and Sunday Morning* depicts Arthur, a young working-class man who also hates the groupish tendencies around him. This is directed at everything from his unionised workplace to institutions like the family, the Church and the military. He takes for granted advances since the war, and boasts 'I don't believe in share and share alike.'[16]

The Angry Young Men authors were products of a more educated, secure and prosperous era, but one which often remained class-bound and provincial. They would have hated the call to 'Rise with your class, not out of it,' and were unhappy with societies built on groupish needs. This explains why, despite starting life as firebrands and radicals, many moved rightwards over time.[17]

If the Angry Young Men books are portentous, they are not the end of the story. The rise in individualism has been followed by a rise in post-materialism, meaning a growing preoccupation with inner fulfilment, equality and the things that money can't buy.

We see this if we look at the 'gap year' phenomenon, which lets people find 'deeper' fulfilment, rather than joining the career ladder. Likewise, enthusiasm for fair trade and ethical production, and for cycling or backpacking.[18] Likewise, increasing numbers of young people volunteering, or trying to find work with charities, think tanks and social enterprises. Likewise, the popularity of yoga or alternative music festivals; of international cuisines or veganism. Likewise, the commercial pressure on big companies to have Corporate Social Responsibility departments. And, again likewise, the growing propensity for the liberal middle classes to vote 'against their interests'.[19]

Looking again to fiction, Hanif Kureishi's state-of-the-nation novel *The Buddha of Suburbia* is a good illustration. Written in 1990 but set in the late 1970s (thirty years after *Room at the Top* was set), the novel shows post-materialism in its adolescence. Many of the characters in *The Buddha of Suburbia* – including the protagonist, Karim – are straining to move beyond status-conscious conformity.

Karim's father reinvents himself as a spiritual guru and the surrounding cast seeks meaning and connection in a variety of ways. Most are culturally liberal, with many attracted to forms of socialism. They have fulfilled their more individualistic needs and crave inner fulfilment – be it political, spiritual or sexual. Eva, the middle-class woman at the heart of the book (who builds Karim's father's reputation as a guru) embodies the new post-materialism. She seeks exoticism, experimentation, self-actualisation and freedom of expression. She would be entirely at home at an event like the World Transformed – Momentum's countercultural accompaniment to the Labour Conference.

The post-materialism described in *The Buddha of Suburbia*

always existed in subcultures: the bohemianism of the Bloomsbury Set; George Orwell's decision to spend a year alongside the poor in Paris and London; the campus radicalism of the 1960s. Indeed, it is visible among a couple of the characters in *Room at the Top*. But post-materialist motivations are now, in 2020, evident in far larger proportions of the population.

Kureishi's novel shows this trend when it was still fairly new. And, while it is easy to ridicule as a hypocrite and a faddist a character like Eva, the post-materialism she embodies has also brought a range of progressive attitudes when it comes to internationalism, equality and sustainability.

Regardless of the merits of groupish, individualist and post-materialist value systems, the factors driving the transformations from one to the next are usually positive. The move from groupish-ness to individualism, for example, was the result of people having more disposable income, travelling further, seeing more things (and wanting those things for themselves), consuming more media and technology, becoming less deferential, and so on.[20]

This had a dark side, leading to Thatcherite policies which made the playing field less level (and, in fact, less competitive and merito-cratic). It led to communities being abandoned and to people being grossly over-rewarded. Yet individualism is also an inescapable part of the *groupish, individualist, post-materialist* transition, a gate-way to the values which someone like Monbiot lauds. If people identify as individuals rather than groups, they are usually less will-ing to judge others by the groups they come from.[21] Hence, the rise in individualism has inadvertently assisted the rise in tolerance and self-efficacy.[22]

The shift in emphasis towards post-materialism is also the prod-uct of positive change. Citizens in affluent countries are much more likely to have post-materialist values – thanks to the luxury of not having to worry as much about resource and status needs.[23] Pre-occupations like freedom of speech, preservation of natural beauty, universal morality, sexual liberation, human rights and the primacy of ideas over money have all become more dominant in developed nations – their salience nearly doubling between 1970 and 2000.[24]

Even the 2016 rise in authoritarianism – seen by some as proof that we are getting more conservative – arguably came as a backlash against the pace at which post-materialist and individualistic value systems have taken hold. The feeling that mainstream progressive parties no longer speak for a single class bloc – or that conventional conservatives no longer speak for a single national tribe – helps right populists to mobilise groupish values.

This reflects a wider difficulty for politicians: that of appealing to an electorate split by values and of keeping groupishness in the tent. The possibility of alienating one values set by over-appealing to another was less of a factor several decades ago, when there wasn't the current three-way split.[25] The risk, if the *groupish, individualist, post-materialist* shift isn't inclusive, is that we descend fully into our own version of the US 'culture wars'.

Talking about 'value sets' might seem like psychobabble – especially for those who view issues through the prism of class. The problem, they would say, is simple: from the mid-1980s on (and from 1994 in earnest) Labour triangulated away from those it was created to represent. Billy Bragg, for example, is critical of what he sees as New Labour's indifference to the working classes. And many claim that Labour's problem, pre-Corbyn, was that the party had abandoned its base.[26]

On the flip side, sceptics point out that Corbyn appealed most strongly to 'middle-class graduates' and 'wealthy city-dwellers', and highlight the way in which he alienated working-class voters from Labour as never before – the culmination of this being the 2019 election.[27] His supporters are derided for their 'croissant eating' habits.[28]

So, how does the *groupish, individualist, post-materialist* shift intersect with social class? To answer this, it is important to distinguish between class as a form of identification (e.g. self-describing as working class) and class as a form of work (e.g. having a manual job). Once we do this, we see three major changes since the Second World War, each of which relates to the *groupish, individualist, post-materialist* transition.

First, the proportion of the population doing manual and industrial jobs has decreased – from over two thirds in 1968 to less than half today.[29] This has impacted on values, and particularly on the proportion with groupish values – which, as we have seen, fell steadily over the same period.

Many in the 1940s and 1950s would have needed to club together by class and community, to protect living standards and guard against threats. But this has changed as home ownership has risen, the economy has deindustrialised and groupishness has become less of an economic necessity in parts of the country. As a result, larger proportions now have individualist or post-materialist value systems.

Secondly, class as a form of identification has become less straightforward, with more middle-class people identifying as working class, and vice versa. YouGov polling in 2014 showed that one in three adults now 'gets their class wrong'.[30] Of course, there have always been ambiguities and anomalies – the working-class Tories who Disraeli described as 'angels in the marble', for example. But these would have been rarer five or six decades ago. This is partly thanks to socio-economic complexities, which have made it harder to work out which class you fit into. But I believe it is also due to several major changes in values:

- The rise of individualist values often means higher levels of social aspiration among working-class voters. This is especially true among C2 voters, and helps explains why some of those in working-class jobs might identify as middle class.
- Meanwhile, the rise in egalitarian, post-materialist values among the middle classes means that they are less likely to feel proud of their high social status, and more likely to identify with other class groups.
- Lastly, there is an individualist tendency among those who are now in middle-class jobs but who self-define by their humble beginnings. These people are less politically left-wing and are – we might guess – proud of their working-class roots because they have had the aptitude to leave them behind.[31]

So, through working-class individualists, middle-class postmaterialists and middle-class individualists, class identification has become more complex.

Thirdly, there has been a decline in the correlation between voting and class. The aforementioned YouGov research finds that people are more likely to vote by the class with which they self-identify than with the class to which – in employment terms – they actually belong. Whereas political scientist Peter Pulzer famously said, in 1967, that 'Class is the basis of British politics – all else is embellishment and detail,' the link is now more tenuous.[32]

This is partly thanks to a wider range of factors feeding into people's politics – with faith, ethnicity, age, and so on, meaning more complex forms of identification.[33] But it is also the consequence of declining partisanship, with more people voting on an issue-by-issue basis, or weighing up the pros and cons of each party.

Again, this links to values, with the electorate more inclined to see themselves as individual entities and to vote in the ways that this implies. Whereas those with groupish values are politically tribal, those with individualistic values are more likely to be swing voters, choosing their parties on the basis of personal pragmatism.[34] And those with post-materialist values are more likely to pride themselves on being flexible and independent thinkers.

In short, the more individualists and post-materialists there are, the less politicians can rely on mobilising large blocs of support. Through this we can understand why politicians of both left and right have – in their keenness to appeal to a range of voters – pitched themselves in the centre ground, provoking accusations of 'retail policies' and 'triangulation'.

Overall, then, to recap, we have seen three intersections between class and values. First, a rise in individualistic and post-materialist values, as resources have become less scarce and the population has become less reliant on certain types of work. Secondly, class identifications blurring, as people's concept of their class becomes more value driven and less employment driven. And thirdly, the decline of class-based voting, as the collectivised voting patterns of those with groupish values have become less dominant.

Class is just one area where the *groupish, individualist, post-materialist* transition is in evidence. But there are many other issues where a shift has taken place: the declining role of nationalism, organised religion and the trade union movement are other examples.[35] And, like all of the shifts discussed, *groupish, individualist, post-materialist* is not a wholly positive or wholly negative story. It's simply a change that has occurred which has given to the left in some places and taken away in others. What it does provide, however, is a rebuff to the romantic aspects of the Golden Era – which suggest that the societies of yesteryear shunned opulence on moral grounds, knew how to live 'the good life' and cared more about the things that really mattered.

VII. INNOCENCE TO AWARENESS

The final shift, *innocence to awareness*, describes the move from a society which is blissfully ignorant to one whose innocence is lost. Across a whole set of areas, the scales have fallen from our eyes, meaning that we are much more conscious of what is going on beyond our own lives. This represents something close to a 'coming of age' for society, and a range of factors have contributed to it. These include:

- The rise of social media and the internet – allowing information and opinions to spread[36]
- Big increases in communications and news access, with hundreds of television channels, twenty-four-hour coverage, more probing newspapers, and so on
- Improvements in education, meaning higher expectations and a greater desire to analyse and cross-examine
- The rise of travel, nationally and internationally – exemplified by wider numbers of people moving away for university, and by increased contact with those who've come to the UK from abroad

From a progressive viewpoint, the consequences of the *innocence to awareness* shift are, again, both positive and negative. For example, we might turn on the television or look at our social media feed and – in a way that we would not have done in the past – watch a video about the refugee crisis. As a result, we might donate to a charity – or even decide to volunteer in the Calais Jungle.[37] But we may, equally, watch a video about the lifestyles of the super-rich in Monaco. And, as a result, we might feel inadequate; that we need more for ourselves.

A good example of *innocence to awareness* is trust for politicians, which has halved in the last thirty years, according to some estimates.[38] People are more likely to say that politicians are detached from real people; more likely to think they are corrupt, lazy or sleazy. The populist left promotes the idea of a Golden Era, when all parliamentarians were plain-speaking community spokespeople. They imply that these authentic representatives have been replaced by power-hungry suits, parachuted in.

This has been triggered by the repeated exposure of poor conduct by some MPs: 'cash for questions' in 1994, the expenses scandal of 2009, the sexual harassment accusations of 2017, and so on.

Much of this has been brought to the surface thanks to the factors described in the bulletpoints above. Peter Mandelson's 'guacamole' gaffe happened in front of journalists. Emily Thornberry's derision of a St George's flag is something she'd have kept to herself in the days before social media. Tory MP Anne Marie Morris's extraordinary use of the N-word was covertly recorded.

The crucial point is that it is the level of exposure and public awareness that has changed, not the behaviour of public servants. If we rewound three decades – or six, for that matter – we would not find a group of politicians behaving with more financial, sexual or democratic integrity. People are people, and among any given 650 MPs there are likely to be a few very nasty pieces of work and a number of others who are weak or lazy. The difference is that, in the deferential and opaque climate of the 1950s or 1960s, they more often got away with it.

Today, politicians and the decisions they make are scrutinised more than ever before – in the media, on the internet and via parliamentary committees, as well as via freedom-of-information requests, judicial reviews, think-tank analyses, and so on. MPs are secretly recorded and have historic social media posts unearthed. They are asked to provide bank statements and tax returns, and have their voting records available at the click of a button. They are examined on *Question Time* by a public which is less deferential and better informed.

These changes mean that twenty-first-century politicians will be more inclined to think twice about behaving corruptly or pushing a decision through undemocratically. They are less likely to get away with abuse or absenteeism.

Rising standards about constituency ties are symptomatic of this. The view that MPs should live in the seats they represent is a fairly modern phenomenon. Likewise, the belief that they should send their children to state schools, run weekly surgeries and be involved in the daily life of the area. These expectations emerged only as levels of scrutiny became more acute. As late as the 1970s and 1980s it was commonplace for parliamentarians to visit their constituencies every three to six months. So, while frustration with self-serving MPs or candidates parachuted in is valid, it is only thanks to higher stand-ards and greater transparency that we notice these things in the first place.

Academics point out two aspects of the human psyche that feed falling political trust. First, our negativity bias means we prioritise bad things we hear over good ones, leading to a steady accumulation of cynicism. And, secondly, our confirmation bias leads us to dis-count information that contradicts our existing view, meaning that once cynicism is embedded, it's hard to shake.[39]

There has been a steady trickle of bad news about politicians and institutions – Profumo, the Lavender List, Jeffrey Archer, 'cash for influence', cash for honours, the Panama Papers, the poor response to Grenfell, and so on – which the media publicises because they are predisposed to report bad things over good. And this means that, while each episode makes future abuses of power a little less likely, it leads us to feel the opposite: that things are getting worse.

This is the *innocence to awareness* transition in a nutshell. It is the phenomenon whereby we have seen progress in knowledge, understanding and capacity to tackle problems. Yet this makes it feel as if something has been lost.

Indeed, it arguably means that we miss some of the genuine problems that the shift has created. We seldom level the charge, for example, that MPs are rabbits in the headlights of public opinion, or that they do not present us with the hard choices. Yet these accusations are true – or, at least, truer – than the 'Westminster bubble' criticism more commonly made.

We can see this in other areas of public life – both when it comes to left-wingers' sense of moral decay, and to right-wingers'. On countless issues, fears have been enflamed by new awareness.[40] Bad news is increasingly accessible – even if there is less of it. The Metropolitan Police are probably less racist, but we are more likely to hear about it when they are.[41] There may be less child abuse, but it is more widely reported (both to police and by the press). We are far greener in our behaviour, but are also conscious, as never before, of how large the climate-change problem is. Crime has halved since the mid-1980s, but most people think it has risen.[42]

Indeed, rising awareness of problems is often, paradoxically, the catalyst for positive change. As Steven Pinker points out,

> the illusion of ever-present violence springs from one of the forces that drove violence down in the first place. The decline of violent behaviour has been paralleled by a decline in attitudes that tolerate or glorify violence, and often the attitudes are in the lead. By the standards of the mass atrocities of human history, the lethal injection of a murderer in Texas, or an occasional hate crime in which a member of an ethnic minority is intimidated by hooligans, is pretty mild stuff. But from a contemporary vantage point, we see them as signs of how low our behaviour can sink, not of how high our standards have risen.[43]

Similarly, Amartya Sen gives the example of Kerala, the region of India which has the best life expectancy but where the population has the worst view of its own health, according to self-assessment surveys. The Indian states with the lowest life expectancies, Sen reports, are those where people see themselves as healthiest.[44]

The *innocence to awareness* transition is not just a trite way of saying that things are getting better but we only hear the bad news.

I see it more as a magnification than a progression. Like our other change narratives, it has to do with a set of expanded horizons, creating both positive and negative consequences. As I have said, heightened awareness and increased cultural consumption might make us learn about the developing world or understand the feelings of an LGBT person who cannot get married. But it can also make us jealous of the rich and famous, or mean that we hear about the Rochdale sexual grooming gang and form dangerous generalisations.

Conceptually, *innocence to awareness* is one of the most sophisticated transitions. It connects positive changes, like the decline of political deference, with negative ones like the rise of online 'trolling'. The transition is also, to an even greater extent than the other narratives, irreversible.

The next step is not obvious. The current situation is one where people have lost respect for decision-makers, gaining stronger feelings of agency and a deeper consciousness of the wider world. But there is still, when the questions get too hard, a reliance on gut instincts and a desire to see issues through simplistic and self-serving prisms.

The answer will probably come only through genuine local engagement, and through political approaches that treat people as adults.

17
Strengths, Weaknesses and Admissions

Let's look at the criticisms that could be aimed at my argument. Until this point I have avoided overly emotional language. However, I'll adopt a more personal and biographical tone now, because this chapter relies on questioning and defending my own motivations.

BACKGROUND

The process of writing *The Dark Knight and the Puppet Master* began shortly after the election of Corbyn as Labour Leader. This was four months after the 2015 election, in which I'd worked as press officer to the Labour candidate in South Thanet – Farage's target seat. Despite having done this (and having worked as a press officer for Labour before), I was not and am not ambitious to work in politics.

For most of my life up until 2015, I was what you might call an unreflective Labour supporter: I backed the party unequivocally and was a member; I never went to meetings (partly thanks to moving around a lot); I leafleted and canvassed at general (but not local) elections; if there was a debate, I'd take Labour's side. I also volunteered on the David Miliband campaign and as a community organiser on the 2012 Obama campaign. I had a general conviction that the left was my team.

My family were Labour activists and my dad had been a frontbench Labour politician in the 2000s. So, my automatic support for

Labour dates back to recollections of canvassing on estates in Hackney when I was four or five, and of the very different mornings after the 1992 and 1997 elections.

As I grew up and went to secondary school in Norwich, the shine of this began to rub off, thanks to the Iraq War and the many other failings, real and imagined, of the last Labour government. Yet even if I didn't agree with some of their policies in government, there was a strong pride for me in being part of the Labour 'movement' – a pride which is felt by Labour members of all leanings.

A counterbalance to this, however, was growing up in a family in the political spotlight. I came to hate the simplistic approach of some protesters and to feel a disdain for the comedian or musician who got an easy clap on *Question Time*. Having had an insight into the workings of a politician's life, this sort of lazy populism was a luxury unavailable to me.

For me, the election of Corbyn embodied the above state of mind. I was in fact surprised by the visceral hostility Corbyn triggered in me. A lot of my friends voted Green at the 2015 election, but were suddenly enthused by him, and I ended up having several heated debates with people who, a few months before, I'd assumed saw things in roughly the same way as I did.

I was temping in the comms team at a London council at the time, and then doing a winter door-knocking project for a charity. I remember constantly checking my phone during the leadership campaign and in the aftermath of Corbyn's victory, reading and re-reading articles and tweets by Corbyn supporters, like picking at a scab.

I left the Labour Party in June 2017, two days after Corbyn's better-than-expected performance at the General Election. This may seem like a strange time to quit, but for me the issue had never really been about electability. It was about a populist style of politics which I felt was divisive and dishonest. The election underscored this – with Corbyn posing as the principled candidate, while triangulating on Europe, immigration and welfare.

I subsequently rejoined the party in the aftermath of the 2019 election defeat. Despite having long believed that Corbyn was electorally toxic, I must admit that I was surprised by how emphatic the defeat was. It was tragic to see the types of seats that Labour lost. The party is now on life support unless it changes dramatically.

The above may be particular to my own experience. But I have the impression that other Labour 'moderates', many of whom have been far more active campaigners than I ever was, feel the same way. Corbyn's essential pitch – and even more so that of his supporters – was that all Labour failings up until 2015 were due to a lack of principle. Hearing this from Corbyn, a man who had contributed so little to changing the UK for the better – and watching it repeated by supporters of his who'd never so much as delivered a Labour leaflet – was galling.

I was aware, in all this, that my feelings weren't fully rational or coherent. It was the stirring of an identity I'd never quite been aware of and, perhaps, of an anger at all the times that you end up, as the child of a politician, being mischaracterised. The accusation of being a Tory, levelled on social media at Liz Kendall backers, was to me personal, precisely because I so stridently felt I wasn't. It was the feeling of being ejected from an in-group which I'd taken for granted.

Indeed, my own hypocrisy was exposed here. I'd spent much of my life with a low-level, Dark Knight belief of my own; an assumption that I was on the side of the angels.

Yet while the strength of my feeling was partly a response to being out-grouped, I still felt that my basic argument was right. I had a deep uneasiness about Corbyn from Day One, which had nothing to do with how left-wing he was. His populist approach, for me, put him in a different category to well-meaning leftists like Ed Miliband or Michael Foot.

This book was my effort to turn the feelings of that summer into something coherent. I'm sure I've failed at points to look past my own perspective. But I've tried, on all questions, to unpack my views as rationally as I can.

POTENTIAL CRITICISMS AND WEAKNESSES

Let's go through some potential criticisms of the arguments made in this book.

The first might be that the three myths are 'straw men': that I am, in fact, the one guilty of creating myths. Does my critique itself create divisive caricatures? Do I 'Dark Knight' the far left?

I've provided examples throughout to back up my points. And I've differentiated between approaches common to all of politics and those which are more pronounced on the populist left. Admittedly, quite a lot of the evidence has leaned on a small group of commentators – Owen Jones, Paul Mason, Ken Loach, George Monbiot, and so on – who are the most successful exporters of the myths. But I don't, to reiterate, think everyone sympathetic to Corbyn is a left populist – although I think there is a powerful correlation between strength of support for Corbyn and level of attraction to the myths.

In short, I don't believe I've applied double standards or made Corbynism an exception to my pluralism. I've tried throughout not to be pejorative about the intentions or moral character of the populist left, and have not used phrases like 'Corbynista' or 'virtue signalling'. Left populists don't act in bad faith but on a false premise. All of those on my wing of politics need to remember this.

To the extent to which the book reinforces stereotypes, the far left may want to think about why these stereotypes are so pervasive. For example, the idea of left splitting – through its tendency to out-group allies – isn't a right-wing caricature. It's happened throughout history.

Indeed, there are unquestionably those on the fringes of contemporary left politics who have an unapologetic and open belief in the myths, with unpleasant results. For example, a man was pictured at a Corbyn rally wearing an 'Eradicate the right-wing Blairite vermin' T-shirt.[1] Cases like this may not be as representative as newspapers claim, but they're not fabricated. They typify a significant minority within the Corbyn-supporting left, and the question remains of why people like this are drawn to Corbyn's politics. Equivalent T-shirts aren't worn at meetings of the Fabians or Progress – however impotent people in these groups may have felt during the past five years. If pro-Corbyn politicians and journalists wish to suggest that the three myths are a figment of the centre-left imagination, then they must ask why those who evidently do believe in the myths endorse their politics.

Influential left populists in fact shoulder much of the responsibility here. The conduct of high-profile Corbyn outriders creates the mythology and mood music which attracts those with an extremist bent. Once you've written an article saying that 'Blairites' are self-serving to their core, then caveating that abuse shouldn't be directed at them becomes little more than a disclaimer. You're taking the risk that someone with less inhibition than you will decide these people need to be 'eradicated'. Indeed, left populists who disown extremism – however sincerely – find themselves in a false position. Their approach isn't a million miles from the dog-whistle politics of the right-wing press – who attack the character of refugees and exaggerate the scale of immigration, then wash their hands of the matter when far-right fundamentalists take them at their word.

Another potential argument against this book is that it's an apologia for the establishment: a set of fifth-column 'smears' intended to protect the status quo. Why else, some ask, would I take aim at my own side?

This is riven with Puppet Master assumptions, and the arguments against it have already been made. The book is written in good faith, by someone who'd consider themselves a socialist. I obviously can't unpick myself from my upbringing, any more than anyone can. But – as someone whose family had their phone hacked by the tabloids while I was glowing up – I can say that I'm not, to the best of my knowledge, an 'outrider', supplying narratives to my 'friends in the media'.

This links to a more serious point, which is why have I focused so much energy on a critique of the left, not the right? The answer is that I see populist approaches as the heralds of an intolerant and authoritarian politics. The populist mindset is regressive in its effects, if not its intentions, and is wholly at odds with socialism as I understand it. Thus, I regard left populism as little better than right populism. I aim my criticism at the populist left because I'm on the left – in the same way that, as a Norwich City fan, I'd see it as my duty to challenge unpleasant behaviour by fellow Norwich supporters, before criticising fans of other clubs.

With this said, there is a deeper question, which is why does less effort go into understanding left populism than goes into understanding right populism. Energy is rightly spent engaging with 'left behind' voters and reading books like J. D. Vance's *Hillbilly Elegy*. Yet it's more fashionable, on the centre left, to be disdainful rather than curious about those drawn to Corbyn.

Although I've tried hard not to be dismissive or condemnatory, I admit that I instinctively fall into this trap. This is strange, given that my values are far closer to the populist left. I believe there are five core reasons.

The first is, for me, personal. Coming from a centre-left family in the public eye, my primary negative experiences – being sworn at in the street or taken to task for government policy by a teacher – came from the left, on Iraq or civil liberties. This didn't often happen. But the fact that it did disabused me of the idea that left-wingers are any more personally decent – and made me react against those who believe that they are. Although subjective, this is worth acknowledging.

A second, related explanation is that left populists often initiate hostilities. Historically, the left-pluralist approach has been to hug close the populist left, if only through electoral pragmatism. But the left-populist tactic has been the opposite.[2] The caricature of the poor-hating or blood-thirsty Blairite was being circulated long before most people had heard of Corbyn. And, as a result of years spent blaming every centre-left fudge on jingoism or greed, he was given little by way of a grace period when his own time came.

In short, the far left tends to kick off the accusations of bad faith; to make them more forcefully than the centre left; to be more likely to see toleration as capitulation and to view the goals of their opponents as interchangeable. The centre-left accusation, for example, is that the *consequences* of far-left and far-right politics are often the same (sometimes known as Horseshoe Theory); the far-left accusation is usually that the *intentions* of the social democratic left and the Conservative right are the same. This amounts to little more than a squabble about 'who started it' – and does not exonerate the ultra-factionalism of some Labour moderates working for the party. But it's worth being honest about.

A third reason is proximity. The closeness, at the level of values, means that I'm more impatient with left populists' failings. Right-wing agitator James Delingpole, for instance, is merely an oddity with whom I disagree, whereas a left-wing provocateur like Matt Zarb-Cousin is acting under the same banner as I am. The populist left is like a sibling who looks and talks like you and lives in the same house but who constantly snubs or embarrasses you. It's harder to sympathise than with someone else's sibling.

Moreover, when left populists are held up as idols, proximity creates the feeling of a false prophet being worshipped. The claim that Corbyn has saved left-wing values has a sort of 'prodigal son' effect for the centre left – given that we believe we have been trying to advance progressive goals for a long period, with some success. Left populists perhaps feel the same way about left pluralists, so this isn't a criticism which can be easily disentangled from personal perspective. But it's there.

A fourth factor is class. The populist takeover of Labour has accelerated the gentrification of the party, with the public suggesting Labour has moved from 'bingo to quinoa' under Corbyn.[3] We're more cut adrift than ever from working-class communities, as the 2019 election showed. For many within mainstream Labour, this is a source of real anguish. It creates contempt for Corbyn's conspicuously middle-class and post-materialist base, who – although they didn't create the problem – have exacerbated it.[4] I must confess that despite being a) middle class, and b) a self-described values pluralist, I get a 'nails down a blackboard' sensation when I hear about privileged post-materialists engaging in interpretive dance in support of Corbyn at the World Transformed festival.

This is a weak argument, I know, based on a Dark Knight form of inverted snobbery. True pluralists need to embrace all values and to look for support across class groupings. Labour in 1997–2010, after all, appealed beyond the base, to upper-working-class and lower-middle-class voters who wanted aspiration or security from their politicians. Post-materialist values must be treated in the same way.

The fifth reason for my antipathy is that I genuinely blame the populist myths for the failures of egalitarian politics. Why, I wonder, is so much of the left's time spent arguing with itself? Why must we coax along those who prefer fighting to winning? Why is it that, for prospective Labour leaders, there is so much political capital to be found in accusing predecessors of betrayal? Our advances have been far slower than those in countries with a more rational political left, like Sweden. Had the pluralist mindset been the default across the British left in the last few decades, I believe we would be a more equal country. Indeed, if pluralist left-wingers get back into power any time soon, then they'll spend the next few years unpicking or making peace with Brexit – a highly reactionary development, which the populist left has, thanks to their belief in the myths, been an accomplice to.

No doubt, the populist left feel the same. They believe that, through our willingness to compromise or take incremental steps, we on the pluralist left have been the ones who hampered progress. Personally, I don't think this stacks up. But, as with all the points above, it's a matter of perspective.

One other potential criticism, this time from the centre left, is that my case is ineffective in its goal of defeating left populism. Some might say that my arguments don't seek to persuade the populist left or to meet them where they are;[5] others that I've failed to engage with the policy questions about the future of social democracy, choosing instead to dwell on the premise of the debate.

Both of these criticisms are true, in as far as they go. It's no doubt antagonistic to suggest that left populists' politics are founded on delusions. And certainly, the only way to really beat left populism is by having an alternative policy vision.

In response to the first point, however, I'd simply say that we have run out of options. We need to focus on the myths themselves before we can have a serious debate about anything else.

Much the same applies to the policy point. A discussion of policy is impossible while the populist myths distort the debate. Even the sort of loose proposals that someone like me might sketch out – Rawlsian fairness, egalitarian internationalism, support for global institutions, progressive patriotism, a focus on wealth, not income, a multilateral approach to inequality, reform of the trade union movement, hypothecation of the tax system, high immigration combined with ID cards, and so on – are shut down by the myths. To get to alternative policies, left pluralists need first to tackle the narratives which block debate.

TRUE FLAWS

There is one criticism I'd concede more willingly: the world as seen by pluralists is duller. There is no black-hearted nemesis; no far-sighted wizard behind the curtain; no lost Arcadia. Each issue is more procedural, more understated, less Technicolor. Most people are fairly good, most decisions are fairly hard, most eras are imperfect. Eradicating the myths means asking the political equivalent of the question posed by literary critics: 'What happens after the book?'

I mean this seriously. The three myths are built on a sense of just conflict. Without them, society offers less by way of friction and jeopardy. The Rawlsian goal is a world which is as tolerant, democratic, equal and fair as a neutral participant would ask for it to be. It's a society where the obstacles posed by the myths have been overcome. The possibility of this society one day existing asks us to ponder how happy it would make us on the left.

This question runs deep, to the essence of human nature. The liberal philosopher Bertrand Russell put the matter as follows, in the first of his 1948 Reith Lectures:

> [There are] unanswerable arguments in favour of world-wide cooperation, but the old instincts that have come down to us from our tribal ancestors rise up in indignation, feeling that life would lose its savour if there were no one to hate, and . . . that struggle is the law

of life, and that in a world where we all loved one another there would be nothing to live for.

Russell goes on:

When war comes the bank clerk may escape and become a commando, and then at last he feels that he is living as nature intended him to live . . .

[Humans] have all kinds of shocking impulses and also creative impulses which society forbids us to indulge . . . Anyone who hopes that in time it may be possible to abolish war should give serious thought to the problem of satisfying harmlessly the instincts that we inherit.[6]

A sustainable socialist society is similarly existentially challenging. So, perhaps embracing the myths guarantees a sense of meaning, purpose and struggle; an outlet for the instincts Russell describes. I myself have been happier at points in my life when I believed in the myths. Indeed, I almost envy the sense of clarity that left populists have. I wonder, even, if the Dark Knight, the Puppet Master and the Golden Era are essential to idealism and human fulfilment. To ditch them is to try to attain perspective. It's to accept that things are more mundane than we thought – that ghosts, or God, or Father Christmas don't exist. And it's to try to live a meaningful life all the same – without the intrigue, jeopardy and anticipation that the myths provide.

I can't answer these big questions. But I suspect that, if the world gradually gets safer – and if values continue to move beyond material concerns about resources – I won't be the last to ask them. This is part of the reason why developing 'grand narratives' to replace the myths is so important.

These might seem like maudlin points to be making so near the end of a book which has been about socialism and society, not about the meaning of life. But I do so because we on the left must get our relationship with idealism right.

18
Conclusions

CHARACTERISTICS COMMON TO THE THREE MYTHS

The Dark Knight, the Puppet Master and the Golden Era share several traits. This is why, despite being distinct, they often end up as bedfellows. And it is why belief or non-belief in them remains the key distinction between far and centre left. Those who believe opponents are immoral, that problems occur by design and that the world is getting more right-wing tend to be the same people as each other. Likewise, those who believe opponents are merely wrong, that chaos trumps conspiracy and that the world is getting better (at least as much as it is getting worse).

The Corbyn project's biggest controversies came when the myths converged. The anti-Semitism crisis stemmed from a mix of Dark Knight attitudes to the Middle East and a Puppet Master attraction to conspiracy theories. Corbyn's effective facilitation of Brexit fused a Puppet Master suspicion of 'global elites' with a Golden Era fondness for socialism in one country.

So, what are the myths' common characteristics?

To begin with, a genuine belief in the myths stems from – and leads to – a lack of solutions. The Dark Knight stops us from engaging with opposing arguments; the Puppet Master suggests that problems go unsolved because it serves elites better to ignore them; the Golden Era seeks refuge in the answers of the past.

The myths compensate for this lack of solutions with a deep, potentially dangerous sense of urgency. Believed in together, they allow counterproductive or extreme measures to make sense. Indeed, the most noticeable characteristic which the Dark Knight, the Puppet Master and the Golden Era share is the purity of purpose which they bring. Each myth comes with a sense of just conflict, after which everything will be better: goodies versus baddies; the people versus 'the establishment'; the good old days versus a bleak future.

What would the populist left do, after all, if we fulfilled the goals of a philosopher like Rawls? The lesson of history, from times when we have been closer to this situation than we are now, is that they do not simply toast the progress made. The myths remain prevalent, and if an oppressor or dystopia does not exist, one is created. Hence, the array of phantom menaces currently on offer – be it 'transphobes', 'centrists', 'neoliberals' or 'Blairites'.

In this respect, the myths conjure not the possibility of utopia, but a mirage of one – an oasis we can't get to. This condemns the left to a future of being alternative rather than radical. Like goths or punks or hard-core football ultras, we are defined by what we're against and become a niche and exclusive subculture as a result. If everyone started dressing like us or supporting the same team, our identity would be lost. Hence, the populist left doesn't just oppose the status quo; it's reinforced by it and, in a sense, needs it.[1]

This explains why the 1994–2010 Labour project was doomed to split the left. As ex-Blair aide Peter Hyman notes, the New Labour aim wasn't to be merely 'a good opposition party' but to attain 'political hegemony: winning power and locking out the Tories, to ensure that the twenty-first century was a Labour century with Labour values, in contrast to a Tory-dominated twentieth century'.[2] This would have required the far left to become comfortable with the political mainstream being a left-of-centre one, and with the establishment being progressive. It would have involved engaging realistically with the challenges of government. The power of the myths meant that this could never happen. Hence, rather than being constructive critics of the Blair–Brown premierships, the approach was to disown these governments entirely and to construct ways of believing that all of those involved were closet Tories.

TRUTH AND USEFULNESS

Upon once explaining the Puppet Master myth to someone, they came back with a surprising response. 'But even if it's not true, isn't the myth still helpful: to get people to embrace good causes?' This was an interesting point, and suggests there are two tests the myths need to be judged by: truth and usefulness. So far, we have been switching between these, but let's separate them out.

Some beliefs are both true *and* useful, and some are neither. Yet between these points are beliefs which are useful but not true, and others that are true but not useful.

For example, it is true that most leaders would never, if the moment came, have the stomach to press the nuclear button. But, in the interests of preventing nuclear weapons from being deployed, it is not useful to say so.

Conversely, a faith in God isn't backed up by scientific 'truth'. But it is still useful for many people, building community support structures and helping individuals through trauma or grief. Forcing people to concede that their faith is groundless would achieve nothing.

With each of our myths, differentiations between truth and usefulness exist. With the Dark Knight, for example, we might privately doubt that Tories are 'scum' but conclude that it is expedient, in mobilising towards a fairer society, to pretend they are.

The Dark Knight is, in fact, the most flawed myth when it comes to truth. It is hard to find a true example of political distinctions being underpinned by moral binaries. This certainly applies to classifying groups of citizens: individuals with certain politics are not inherently 'bad', even if they are myopic or misguided. And it goes for institutions, causes and policies too. Would it be 'true' to say that the private sector, the army, Israel or nuclear multilateralism are in themselves immoral? Even on issues like war versus peace there are times – e.g. Britain's decision to go to war in 1939 – where conflict is necessary and right.

With this said, the Dark Knight is useful in crystallising

arguments and mobilising blocs of support. Yet this usefulness can also unleash huge collateral damage, and should be used sparingly. In the modern world, strident moral binaries are increasingly unhelpful.

The Puppet Master and the Golden Era are different, as both are based on an overestimation rather than a falsehood. The powerful *do* actively and cynically oppress the populace at certain points. And there *are* periods of decline. A citizen in Stalin's Russia who thought they lived under the yoke of totalitarianism would be very much in touch with reality. And an American who felt, in the aftermath of the Wall Street Crash, that things were getting worse, would be the clear-thinking one. The problem occurs when these myths become the default.

In 2020 Britain, the idea that we are being oppressed by 'elites' is really quite a long way from the truth, even compared to a few decades ago. In reality, most of our problems relate to organic and anarchic forces. The 'useful' spirit which the Puppet Master mobilises – of freedom, unshackling, the proximity of utopia and the overthrow of tyranny – leads to disillusionment and cynicism if it is based on a flawed premise. Nick Clegg's promises on tuition fees showed this. And the wins for Trump and Brexit, which were premised on insurrection, will also, ultimately, disappoint those who backed them. 'Useful' Puppet Master narratives bring diminishing returns if they're untrue.

Of the three myths, the Golden Era currently contains the most truth. We have inequality, climate change, automation and urbanisation on the horizon – not to mention new forms of terrorism and the fallout from COVID-19. This does not make the Golden Era any 'truer' as a psychological default. But it does mean that, right now, fears about the future are not unfounded.

Yet the Golden Era is also the least 'useful' myth. It has become a cliché to point out that successful Labour leaders have a vision for the future – e.g. Harold Wilson's 'white heat of technology' – but history does show that Golden Era thinking offers little by way of electability or policy formation, even in times of genuine deterioration. Indeed, the more risk there is of a change for the worse, the more Golden Era narratives accelerate that decline. As we saw in the 1980s, when the left dug its heels in and refused to adapt to globalisation, the myth cedes the agenda to those who do have a vision for the future.

I have referred at points to all three myths as dangerous. The question of the harm each one does is an extension of the 'truth and usefulness' discussion. The effect of the myths, if exploited for their usefulness without being true, is often to direct venom at those who don't deserve it. Is it really fair to falsely claim that a Tory prime minister relishes the suffering of the vulnerable, just because it's rhetorically useful?[3]

Rawls coined a term for this approach: 'telishment'. This describes punishing someone for a crime of which they're innocent, because the punishment provides a social good. Rawls's objection to telishment separated his philosophy from the utilitarian one. For example, if your aim was to deter racial attacks, and you had a defendant wrongly accused of attacking an ethnic minority person, would it be okay to jail them anyway, to set an example? The utilitarian answer would be yes – if there was evidence that future attacks would be prevented. The Rawlsian answer would arguably be no: if you were forming the world from the original position, you wouldn't want there to be a chance you could be imprisoned for a crime you hadn't committed, even if the wider population would benefit.

If the populist left makes arguments which it knows to be untrue but feels to be useful, I would argue that it is engaging in telishment. And, as the murder of Jo Cox showed, there will always be unhinged individuals around who take at face value the narratives used for expediency by populists.

POLITICS WITHOUT THE MYTHS

In criticising the myths which prop up left populism, I am advocating pluralism. Some call this 'centrism'. I have chosen not to use that term, because the way it assigns an ideological position – a mid-point on the spectrum – is unhelpful. It allows right and left populists to claim that 'centrists' stand for a particular set of policy positions (usually a blend of cosmopolitanism and 'neoliberalism'), whereas what we are really describing here is a mindset. This mindset strives for objectivity and reason, rather than dealing in conspiracy theories or seeking to dominate and destroy opponents.

It is thus possible to be a left pluralist or a right pluralist; even to be a communist pluralist or an isolationist/nationalist pluralist – if your politics are democratic, flexible and based on persuading rather than condemning. It is true that our populist myths are most prolific at the furthest ends of the spectrum, where politics tends to be more instinctive or sentimental. But there is no reason why you couldn't be a far-left pluralist. I myself support ideas that are a long way left of centre – e.g. 90 per cent or 100 per cent taxes on unearned wealth – while remaining a pluralist.

Whereas populists pride themselves on emotional authenticity, pluralism is founded on intellectual integrity. Pluralists have the integrity to know that what we think is not what everyone thinks; that our values don't automatically come from a place of greater morality; that we cannot attack a policy without having an alternative; that there is no perfect solution, held back by elites; that we cannot cherry-pick only the aspects of the past that overlap with our values.

Populists regard this as a careerist devotion to public opinion. Tony Benn, for instance, distinguished between authentic 'signposts' and opportunistic 'weathercocks'.[4]

But this is not remotely what pluralism is. Instead, it's a position which attempts to achieve perspective and to be honest with itself. Indeed, when you look at those presently posing as authentic 'signposts', what they all share is a dishonesty about the choices on offer. Tories on the Brexiteer right, for example, may be acting in ways that are true to some deep, 'authentic' sense of sovereign pride. But the 'pro-cake and pro-eating it' answers which they advance lack integrity. What kind of 'signpost' points to a destination that doesn't exist?

The same goes for those on the populist left who rely on the idea that you can wish a socialist idyll into existence. Using the myths, they claim that anyone who asks how you will do this is a stooge or a sell-out, who opposes equality and fairness in principle.

Without the three populist myths, we would have a politics based on this pluralism. This goal has been closer and further away at certain points. But it has rarely, since the Second World War, felt more distant than it does today. Indeed, Britain seems to be descending into a full-on culture war.

A truly pluralist politics would deliver the things that British politics is crying out for: a grown-up and consensual climate; respect for the range of needs and values running across the population; a debate based on argument and persuasion; the ability to address the challenges of the future (and the deeper factors underlying populism). On the left, we would gain the rationality and impartiality to be taken seriously. We would be able to promote ideals based on Rawlsian fairness and policies designed to deliver egalitarian internationalism.

However, a question remains: do we *lose* something by dispensing with the myths? What would politics look like without them? One of the arguments made by populists is that the only alternative to their approach is a technocratic and passionless form of decision-making – the end of democracy itself, even. The fear is that, by expunging the myths, we hand the keys to the bean-counters.[5]

It could even be argued that British party-political democracy is reliant on the Dark Knight, Puppet Master and Golden Era. The two sides, red and blue, sit facing each other, as if in combat. They seek to play up the goodness of their own position and the badness of the other side's. The opposition is explicitly given the role of insurgent, developing lines of attack which pretend the government's job is easier than it is. This relies on suggesting that the country is getting worse under the incumbent.

The cut and thrust that this creates can drive change, helping to avoid a politics which is inaccessible and designed by committee. Maybe, by eliminating the myths, we reduce democracy to cost-benefit deductions and SWOT analyses – reliant only on the expert witness and the professional technician. Perhaps, some might say, we had reached this point by 2010 and it was this which triggered the rise of populism over the subsequent decade.

The attitudes of populists towards Tony Blair are an interesting example here. The references to Blair throughout this book have generally been positive, for the reason that – although I do not share all of his views on policy – he was among the most pluralist prime ministers the country has seen. Blair eschewed the populist myths, presenting an approach which was consensual, comfortable with change and serious about the challenges of government.

This created a formula which was electorally successful for a time, and which has significant policy achievements to its name. Yet the anger now directed at Blair cannot be dismissed. Among left and right populists alike, he prompts near-hysterical fury – a pantomime-villain status best summed up by George Galloway's small-budget film, *The Killings of Tony Blair*. Blair himself refers to this as an 'unholy coalition' of the *Guardian* left and the *Mail* right.[6]

Given that Blair's politics are fairly 'moderate', the strength of feeling is striking. Opponents of course have their stated reasons for the hatred, be it Iraq or immigration. But you cannot help wondering if part of it is a reaction to Blair's ostentatiously pluralist approach. By refusing to engage with the myths, he gave nothing whatsoever to those who wanted tribal politics or anti-establishment rhetoric. He appeared dismissive of identity politics and made little pretence of being 'on your side'. He would rather be 'right' than 'good'.

He has therefore become an aloof and isolated figure – respected by some but loved by few. People identify with Blair far less than they agree with him. And the agreement – when it comes – is grudging. His belief that there could be a politics without attrition or sentimentality led the left to regard him as an unprincipled 'weathervane', and the right to view him as a detached globalist.

Maybe we see, in the response to Blair, a risk inherent in plural-ism: that it appears clinical and devoid of feeling. That it ignores key aspects of human nature, even.

There are three things to say about this concern.

The first is that it is partly true. As a press officer for Labour can-didates, I often slipped into using the narratives without thinking. The problem with the Dark Knight, the Puppet Master and the Golden Era is that they have become articles of faith for populists. But the myths have always, necessarily, played a small role in the political toolkit – to underscore a point or invoke a sense of jeopardy.

As former New York governor Mario Cuomo famously put it, 'We oppose in poetry, we govern in prose.' By eliminating the myths altogether, we would potentially take all feeling out of politics, promoting head over heart and science over art.

The second thing to say, however, which directly counters this, is that encouraging the myths means making peace with irrationality. It means accepting that decision-making might be wrong or counterproductive – formed on the basis of falsehoods. The myths are the enemy of an honest and accurate form of politics.

This may seem unimportant. Better, perhaps, to have a spirit of romance which engages people, if the alternative is a bloodless pluralism. Yet policy decisions have genuine meaning and impact. Getting them wrong harms the population – especially the most vulnerable. To allow the myths in is, potentially, to say we will tolerate more unhappiness and suffering in return for a livelier debate.

I do not know how completely we must remove the populist instincts. But it seems like there is a balance to be struck between the visceral and mindless populism we are currently seeing and its potentially over-clinical counterpoint.

However, beyond this, there is a third, larger thing to be said about the fear of the technocrats taking over, which is that pluralism still allows, by its very nature, differences in values. This is why pluralism does not equal 'centrism', 'neoliberalism' or any other populist caricature.

It is true that a genuinely pluralist debate would more quickly filter out dishonest arguments. The Brexit right, for instance, would not – when challenged on the facts – have Puppet Master 'saboteurs' to fall back on, or halcyon myths about a Golden Era. They would have to be honest about the pros and cons of EU membership, weighing up the things they do not like (loss of sovereignty, higher migration) against the things they do (prosperity, security) and conclude that its worth jeopardising the latter to stop the former. It seems likely that fewer would do this than currently support Brexit. But if they did, then that diversity of opinion is to be welcomed.

The same goes for Bennite policies. If these could be proposed in a genuinely pluralist way – honestly advocating siege economics or blanket non-intervention, for example, without resorting to the populist myths every time the questions got too hard – then so much the better.

The point is that a pluralist politics wouldn't stop a range of values from existing, or funnel all policies in a single direction. In this hypothetical world, left pluralists would be openly championing progressive values (community, social justice, equality, and so on), and right pluralists would be advocating conservative ones (self-reliance, personal responsibility, tradition, and so on). Pluralist supporters of other ideals – e.g. green values – would also be making their case.

The debate would therefore contain the friction necessary for a dynamic democracy. All sides would be arguing for different goals, but doing so with integrity, presenting genuine choices about realistic courses of action.

The British party system is a massive, complicating factor in getting to a pluralist politics. First Past the Post rewards tribalism, not pluralism. And this means that our politics has struggled to accommodate globalisation, a process which asks existential questions of both main UK parties. As we saw in the *isolationism to interconnectedness* shift, this creates tensions between isolationist Golden Era believers and interconnected non-Golden Era believers in both camps, especially in light of Brexit. During the debates about how to leave the EU, you had four main groupings when it came to where loyalties instinctively lay (not counting smaller parties): Brexiteer Tories, globalist Tories, 'siege economy' Labourites and internationalist Labourites.

In the midst of the Brexit negotiations, temporary common ground established itself between globalist Tories and internationalist Labourites – the sides of the respective parties who are most supportive of 'open' policies. Both opposed leaving the EU and tended to represent the pluralist wings of their parties – being suspicious of the narratives which feed isolationism. Change UK was an effort to build a bridge between the two.

A centre party like Change UK is in many respects a flawed concept, thanks to the different core values of the internationalist Labour and globalist Tory groupings. It was noticeable, for instance, that Anna Soubry defended austerity during the first week of the TIG's formation, creating a divide with her new colleagues. As the final diagram in the *isolation to interconnectedness* chapter (replicated below) suggested, the ideological questions for a centre party will only get trickier once the issue of Europe (and, by implication, the question of isolation versus interconnectedness) retreats. COVID-19 may alter this as well, and may even throw into disarray the assumptions of globalisation for a period. But, ultimately, fundamental questions about openness are not going anywhere.

A centrist party could also be at odds with the pluralism that feeds it. Pluralist objections are the true basis for opposing populism, after all. (The Change UK MPs' grievances with their former parties were at least as much about a style of politics as about a set of policies.) But, were a centrist party to be as successful as its supporters hope, it would amalgamate much of the political spectrum – from the views of David Lammy through to those of Ken Clarke – into a single movement obeying a single whip. This is not an especially pluralist ideal.

Ultimately, while pluralism points towards openness and realism, which in turn often point to certain policies, it is a mindset, not a value system. A mindset may create a better environment for cooperation between value systems. But it is not the foundation for a party of its own. The true aim should be for several pluralist parties, all with different values – able, between them, to represent with integrity the diversity of opinion across the country.

Even *within* these parties, there must remain policy differences. Within Labour, for example, the dynamic between far left and centre left has often been based on a productive interplay between different interpretations of the same values.[7] Figures like Robin Cook robustly asked if the compromises of Labour were the right ones, without succumbing to populism.

Yet, for all of this, those on the left who supported a new party of some sort were correct to feel that the situation under Corbyn was untenable.[8] It was clear from the beginning that Corbynism could not be a pluralist movement; that it could not even permit a broad church within Labour, let alone govern a diverse country in a complex world. By 2019, Labour had sunk so far into dishonest and

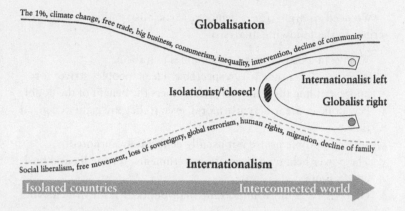

The 1%, climate change, free trade, big business, consumerism, inequality, intervention, decline of community

Globalisation

Isolationist/'closed'

Internationalist left

Globalist right

Social liberalism, free movement, loss of sovereignty, global terrorism, human rights, migration, decline of family

Internationalism

Isolated countries — Interconnected world

extreme populism that for some a Conservative government was barely considered any worse.

Ultimately, it took the catastrophic loss of their traditional heartlands for Labour to even consider changing course – with the party electing the more mainstream Keir Starmer. However, Labour's much-derided 'period of reflection' in early 2020 only served to showcase quite how pervasive the three myths are. From Corbyn's claim that Labour had 'won the argument' to the idea that Brexit was to blame, many Corbyn supporters discounted every piece of evidence which countered their world view.

The leadership election saw all of the prospective candidates tiptoe around the fortress of cognitive biases which the three myths instil within Labour thinking. The moment of reckoning needed – to drive out the falsehoods, folklore and dogma underpinning left populism – still looks some way off.

To make the argument against these myths, those of us who are left pluralists should make our case in an unapologetically egalitarian way.[9] We should point out that left populism undermines Labour's social justice credentials, taking the movement into reactionary territory. We should state that Labour needs to be a genuinely progressive non-populist force. Faced with accusations that they're 'Red Tories' or 'Conservative lite', those who make this case should retort that they're the true left-wingers.

We need to argue for a democratic socialist politics which subscribes to the following analysis:

1. We live in a democracy – this implies pluralism.
2. There are a range of respectable ideas people strive for – understanding this relies on giving others the benefit of the doubt.
3. Few policies are inherently moral, even if they are right at a given time.
4. Society's problems are not usually deliberately authored.
5. The power held by democratic governments, the media and business is finite.
6. Objectivity is more important than political faith in achieving our objectives.
7. There have been advances and setbacks, but there was no moment of 'original socialism' which was innately superior to today.
8. Cooperation with other countries is part of the modern world.
9. If we derive our passion solely from fighting an enemy, an elite or a looming dystopia, then we stand for nothing.
10. Accepting the above makes us more likely, not less, to achieve progressive goals.

What a left-pluralist movement stands for – in terms of substance – is the next question. Free of Corbyn's leadership, the Labour Party has a chance to think about this seriously. I obviously don't claim to have all the answers to this, but an emphasis on equal rights, equal opportunities and fair outcomes offers a firm philosophical basis. In particular, Rawls's focus on 'justice as fairness' is important. The concept of fairness isn't just a by-word for equality in this context (although high inequality blights fairness), but a proxy for a broader, more sustainable, socialist vision. A fair society is one where there is no prejudice, where opportunities are equal and where economic relationships are reciprocal.

The idea of fairness also offers a platform that could appeal beyond Labour's base. A sense of fairness stops some from voting Labour on economic grounds, because they feel that Labour rewards freeloaders. Meanwhile, many traditionalists avoid voting for left-wing parties, which they see as unjustly privileging marginal or minority groups.

We may think these right-of-centre voters are working on a false premise and, indeed, their ideas of fairness are not my own. But one version or another of fairness nevertheless governs their politics – and fuels their aversion to the left. By establishing a platform which made the case for a truly just, Rawlsian society – and which debated what fairness really means – many essentially fair-minded people could be persuaded of the left's merits.

In policy terms, there must be two focuses in particular, as discussed earlier. The first is to embrace multilateral and transnational platforms, seeking to enlarge global institutions and bend them in a progressive direction – and aiming to do this more radically than Labour has managed in the past. The primary routes to a Rawlsian world are the egalitarian internationalist, multilateral methods that someone like Piketty advocates. In the aftermath of a hard Brexit, we obviously approach this from a position of real weakness.

The second step is to champion approaches which are competent on security and confident in celebrating Britain's identity. A sense of pluralism underpins this, because it is about accepting that others care deeply about these things, and that there is nothing right-wing about reassuring people who are worried about change. But so too does a sense of community and shared values. In part this is about progressives avoiding the temptation to wade into zero-sum 'culture war' disputes.

These policy emphases build on the ideas of someone like Clement Attlee, who supported aspects of world government, while embracing the parts of British patriotism which give us confidence and a positive connection with others. A combination of security, social contract and sustainability can create an ethos which appeals to fair-minded voters everywhere.

Another part of this is about democratic engagement. So far, we have seen lower levels of deference without – partly thanks to the timidity of decision-makers – greater involvement and participation in the hard choices that exist. Brexit, for example, was plainly not a grown-up evaluation of pros and cons, because politicians never allowed it to be.

Engagement could be supported by policies seeking transparency about decisions, including measures like hypothecation or ID cards, to build trust in the tax and immigration systems, respectively. This would create faith in government and the social contract, which is a prerequisite for many progressive things (i.e. raising taxes or taking more refugees).

After the coronavirus crisis, meanwhile, there is a strong case for a new, post-COVID-19 social settlement. This could maintain, for a set period, certain measures – such as high levels of economic intervention and state support (as the Attlee government did after the Second World War). However, even if this transpires, we need to be careful to learn the right lessons from the pandemic, and to think seriously about what we would have done had it *not* occurred. Progressive parties must consider what they look like during peacetime; we cannot depend on crisis events to make our arguments for us.

The wishlist above is a sketch, not a blueprint. I don't pretend it's that original. But the point is that even these policies cannot be debated or enacted while the left remains in the thrall of populist narratives. The myths must be dispensed with so that Labour is seen as a just arbitrator: competent, forward-looking, and impartial.

A final point is about right pluralism. Left pluralists should welcome anything which brings British Conservatism back to a pluralist place. When we look at the behaviour of Boris Johnson and Dominic Cummings or the queues to watch Jacob Rees-Mogg speak, the urgency of this is obvious. The right is at least as poisoned by populism as the left.[10]

It isn't that we necessarily need a pro-EU, 'One Nation' or liberal conservative movement (although it is true these stances would be easiest to accommodate with pluralism). You could have a Leave-leaning, socially conservative or Thatcherite form of pluralism. Rather, right pluralism needs to promote values which are different to left pluralism but which can still be held up as a thought-through, transparently presented ideal. This would require right-wingers of whatever hue to accept the legitimate existence of differences of opinion and to make their goals correspond with reality.

Thus, right pluralism does not have to be philosophically perfect. But it needs to be coherent and constructive enough that it stands for more than the ragtag set of utopias, gut instincts and wistful recollections which comprise right populism.[11] This was part of the reason that some on the pluralist left welcomed Rory Stewart's run at the 2019 Tory leadership. Despite having different values, Stewart's emphasis on the realities of government at least offered the hope that one wing of British politics might return to a pluralist footing. His politics aspired to Michael Oakshott's famous definition of conservativism as a tendency to prefer 'fact to mystery, the actual to the possible' – rather than to the right populism of Boris Johnson or the Brexit Party.

My stress on the need for right pluralism is partly self-interested. I believe that left-of-centre values are most likely to succeed if they are competing on a playing field governed by logic, not instinct. I tend to think that left pluralism beats right pluralism, but that left populism loses to right populism.

But beyond this, a right-pluralist party is essential in a democracy as an alternative to left pluralism. For much of the past five years we have not had anything close to this creative tension. Instead we have had two discrete populist entities, neither seeking to genuinely engage had the other.

Times columnist Daniel Finkelstein, one of the strongest anti-populist voices on the right, argues that 'cults, populists and revolutionaries' all fail in the end because

> they keep purging themselves until there is no one left . . . They die having never identified the voice of the people, because there isn't such a thing . . . The people live varied lives, and have varied interests, and have conflicting beliefs and competing rights.[12]

Within Finkelstein's acknowledgement lie the clues about how Conservatives can drag their politics back from the brink.

Political scientist Robert Reich identified four defining political parables:[14] 'the rot at the top', 'the mob at the gates', 'the benign community' and 'the triumphant individual'. The matrix below plots these on to a grid of right and left populism and pluralism. It identifies the parables with which each are most comfortable.

There is major overlap, of course. Politicians of all four leanings

	Left	Right	
Populism	'The rot at the top'	'The mob at the gates'	Fear
Pluralism	'The benign community'	'The triumphant individual'	Hope
	We	Me	

use all four parables at points. But the matrix depicts the 'home turf' of each political strain. For example, Clement Attlee's emphasis on 'winning the peace' was a near-perfect instance of the left pluralist, 'benign community' parable. And much of Thatcher's language evoked 'the triumphant individual'.

The core difference between the populist and pluralist parables is about conflict. Both 'the rot at the top' and 'the mob at the gates' rely on an enemy to be overthrown or driven away – after which the parable will, in theory, no longer apply. 'The benign community' and 'the triumphant individual', by contrast, are sustainable as a long-term ideal. Of course, both latter narratives could become unsustainable – if triumphant individuals pulled the ladder up behind them, for example. But the narrative premises of both are workable on a permanent basis. They do not rely, for their existence, on a 'rot' or a 'mob'.

The benign community and the triumphant individual would, in an ideal world, be the respective defaults of left and right pluralism. And the two populist parables could be retired, except for rare moments when a specific event rendered one of them true.

There is, after all, a creative interplay between 'the benign community' and 'the triumphant individual'. Both explain how different people see the world and themselves within it. And both operate as a brake on the other, guaranteeing that a benign community does not suffocate innovation and that a triumphant individual does not trample the rest.

Looking at the four parables also helps the pluralist left to think about the questions raised in Chapter Three (to do with 'grand

CONCLUSIONS

narratives' and what Macron calls 'democratic heroism'). The problem we have consistently faced is that, when it comes to populism
and pluralism, the devil has the best tunes. The Dark Knight, the
Puppet Master and the Golden Era may be flawed explanations of
the world, but they remain seductive. Without alternatives to them,
we on the pluralist left become the technocrats.

But in the parable of the 'benign community', we start to see a
narrative which might replace the three myths and underscore left-
pluralist policies. A 'benign community' account of things could
focus on stories of personal redemption and rehabilitation; on cama-
raderie and democratic respect for others; on shared history and
connection to place and people; on the bridgeability of divides; on
bravery, second chances, potential, opportunity and indifference to
background; on fairness, tolerance, rejuvenation, teamwork, the
enjoyment of the good times and much else besides. These narratives
may sound vacuous. But they are no more so than the myths I have
spent this book critiquing. And they have the advantage of not
demonising others. They correspond better to the complex societies
of twenty-first – century Britain than anything populists offer.

By looking at issues in these ways, we on the pluralist left can
start to see a way out of our present rut. We can demonstrate that
there is greater fulfilment in constructing something good than in
agitating against something bad. And we can show that there is a
richness in human society, and in its people, stories and ideals, which
goes beyond the crusader mentality which the myths invite. British
Labour appears, at the time of writing, to have become a pluralist
party once again, under Keir Starmer. A figure from the traditional
'soft left', Starmer won over many left-wingers during the leadership
election of 2020. He looks set to retire the Dark Knight approach, in
favour of a broader electoral coalition – and to ditch the Puppet Master, too, so as to engage with the realities of power. You can imagine
him reuniting the left, and perhaps even winning office sooner than
expected – a prospect which would delight most Labourites.

But we should approach this bright future with caution. The historical pattern suggests that, as soon as some fudge or failure
provides the opening, a left populist movement is likely to emerge in

opposition to Starmer's Labour – be it in 2030 or 2035. This move-ment will dismiss whatever progressive achievements Labour has to its name, accusing those who have delivered them of being right-wingers and cynics, unfit to speak the name of Keir Hardie or Clement Attlee or even of Gordon Brown. The risk is that their easy, Puppet Master slogans will be appealing to some; that gradually the whole project will be destroyed after a few short years, and Con-servative rule will return.

This is the future that the British left faces, unless the populist narratives are challenged: a slow, generational rotation, with Labour holding power for just five or ten years in each thirty-year cycle, and with the Tories always in the driving seat.

Many social democrats have made their peace with this three-decade pilgrimage – this 'long road back to power'. But it is not inevitable. Perhaps, if we get to the root of the populist narratives once and for all, we can find a quicker and more permanent way.

Ultimately, history is littered with romantic and sometimes vio-lent left populists, from Robespierre to Che Guevara, who have believed in the Dark Knight, the Puppet Master or the Golden Era. They have mistaken struggle, uprising and loss for egalitarian pro-gress, and in the process they have done harm – or, at least, done less good than they could have.

Their populist approach represents not the fulfilment but the deferral of a utopian dream: a style of politics which offers purpose and struggle but does little to make things better for ordinary people. To move towards pluralism is to decide that, rather than it being a mirage we enjoy the prospect of, we want to see a benign community achieved in the flesh – and are willing to recognise it when it arrives. This society can never be perfect. But it can be as equal and fair as is possible – a meaningful achievement, instead of an entity at the end of a rainbow.

Notes

1. LEFT POPULISM AND LEFT PLURALISM

1. Some, such as David Runciman, have pointed out that fears of a return to the 1930s (which often use the quote from Auden's poem) are over-blown. While true, this doesn't change the fact that the debate is currently 'low' and 'dishonest', even if it's less likely to spiral in the direction of all-out totalitarianism.

2. The Edelman Trust Barometer found in 2017 that 'Trust in the UK is at a historic low [with] an accelerating spiral of decline . . . Attitudes to institutions are no longer defined by left and right, but by a political realignment around those who have "faith in the system" and those who don't.'

3. 74 per cent of UKIP voters, for example, believed politicians are out for themselves, compared with 48 per cent of the public as a whole. *Populist Signal*, Policy Network, pp. 14–16.

4. One YouGov poll explicitly tested this, finding that the *Canary*'s explanations for Labour's unpopularity – continued anger about Iraq, 'spin' and ID cards – were some way off those of the public, which tended to relate to immigration and the financial crash.

5. Russell Brand wondered, in 2013, why a 'genuinely popular left-wing movement to counter UKIP, the EDL (English Defence League) and the Tea Party' had not emerged. In the aftermath of Trump's victory, meanwhile, Labour strategists sought to present Corbyn as a 'Trump of the left', and tried to position him as a straight-talking anti-establishment demagogue. 'Last night compounded a growing feeling: Jeremy Corbyn's time is either now, or he does not have one,' one reportedly said, the morning after Trump's victory. Maya Goodfellow declared, 'There is no reason why populism should be anti-immigrant, particularly when it is the elites (economic, social and political), not

migrants, who are the cause of this country's problems.' And Corbyn himself framed things very much in this way.

6. Jeff Sparrow describes a 'splendid foundation of hate' for the left to take advantage of. Momentum activist Michael Chessum called for Labour to 'go hard or go home' and adopt a 'heads on sticks' approach. Commentator Abi Wilkinson argued that abusing Senator John McCain on the basis that he had cancer was justifiable because his voting record rendered him a mass murderer: 'Approaching policy debates as an intellectual exercise isn't evidence of moral superiority – it's a function of privilege. Increasingly, I'm coming around to the idea that incivility isn't merely justifiable, but actively necessary.'

7. 'Why Socialists Should Talk about Aspiration', Grace Blakeley, *Tribune*, January 2020.

8. Examples include rape threats sent to Jess Phillips, dead-baby photos delivered to Peter Kyle, and the suggestion that an MP involved in the 2016 coup would be 'Coxed'. Claire Kober's resignation from Haringey Council followed threats of stalking, and Laura Kuenssberg had to take bodyguards to the 2017 Labour conference. Meanwhile, Conservatives arrived at their own 2017 conference to find effigies of themselves hanging from a nearby bridge.

9. *The Road to Wigan Pier*, George Orwell, Penguin, 1937, pp. 104–5.

10. *The Righteous Mind*, Jonathan Haidt, Penguin, 2012, pp. 333–4.

11. 'Perceptions Matter', Common Cause Foundation, 2016 (full report), p. 38. See also research by Rob Ford and Phil Cowley, which shows that Labour voters would be three times as likely to object to their child bringing home a Tory partner as the Tories would if it was the other way round. Journalist Jane Merrick describes the Corbynite response to her dad not voting Labour, with people declaring that he had 'blood on his hands' and wanted 'children to starve'.

12. According to YouGov, Corbyn voters in the 2016 leadership contest were five times as likely as Owen Smith voters to believe MI5 were plotting against Corbyn – and twice as likely to say they knew no one who voted Tory. These, respectively, suggest that Puppet Master cynicism and Dark Knight partisanship runs much deeper among far leftists than among centre leftists.

13. 'Never mind Churchill, Clement Attlee is a model for these times', Adam Gopnik, *New Yorker*, 2018. Other articles have also pointed out Attlee's pragmatism and pluralism. Attlee, for instance, wrote a critical note to Nye Bevan, calling his famous suggestion that Tories were 'lower than vermin' a 'singularly ill-timed' intervention.

14. 'Obama, in Podcast Interview, Appears to Agree that Britain's Labour Party Has "Disintegrated"', Adam Taylor, *Washington Post*, December 2016.

15. See 'The Real Lesson from Corbyn's Victory? You Can't Hold Back History', Paul Mason, *Guardian*, 2016. Elsewhere, in Mason's world, the post-referendum resignations by Labour MPs were engineered by 'Blairite nabobs', desperate to re-convert the 'Labour machine' into a 'safe tool of the global elite'. Readers are invited to 'join the dots', with Mason pointing to coordinated efforts by pollsters and tabloid newspapers, and to 'undercover surveillance' by right-wingers in the party. These are presented as the 'propaganda arm' of neoliberals. Subsequently, when covering Labour's internal NEC elections, Mason describes 'elite panic', writing that the establishment has 'line after line of trenches with which to defend their privilege', of which 'the right of the Labour Party' is the last. Their eventual goal, he explains, is 'enforced poverty and ignorance for the rest'.

2. WHAT DO WE WANT?

1. Chuka Umunna has pointed out, in exchanges with Corbynites, that the type of regulated capitalism he supports is fairly similar to that advocated by the likes of Paul Mason. Other commentators have noted that the policy differences between Corbyn's manifesto and Ed Miliband's were minimal. Columnist Phil Collins complained of one Corbyn speech: 'Where ... was the intention to shift the tax burden away from income and towards wealth? The leader of the Labour Party sounds less radical than the governor of the Bank of England.'

2. There are exceptions to this, such as journalist John Rentoul, who has provocatively sought to play Corbyn supporters at their own game, criticising the populist left for being right-wing. Similarly, the academic Glen O'Hara criticises Corbyn's Labour for giving up on redistribution.

3. The 1978–91 magazine *Marxism Today*, for example, explicitly set out to avoid binary thinking, opposition for its own sake and narratives which denied that change was happening. Most authors were self-proclaimed communists, but took an approach which was more consistent with pluralism than with populism. In a famous essay republished by the journal, Eric Hobsbawm argued: 'We, as Marxists, must do what Marx would certainly have done: to recognise the

novel situation in which we find ourselves, to analyse it realistically and concretely, to analyse the reasons, historical and otherwise, for the failures as well as the successes of the labour movement, and to formulate not only what we would want to do, but what can be done.' He was 'far left' in policy terms, but nevertheless sought clear analysis over conspiracy theories and war metaphors. 'The Forward March of Labour Halted?' Eric Hobsbawm, *Marxism Today*, September 1978.

4. 'Shared agreement ... would produce a well-ordered society,' Norman Daniels explains, 'governed by principles guaranteeing equal basic liberties, fair equality of opportunity, and the requirement that inequalities be arranged to make those who are worst off as well off as possible.' 'Reflective Equilibrium', Norman Daniels, *The Stanford Encyclopedia of Philosophy* (Winter 2013 edition), Edward N. Zalta (ed.).

5. Daniels explains: 'Groups sharing [competing] comprehensive views modify the content of their comprehensive views over time in order to cooperate within shared democratic institutions.' 'Reflective Equilibrium'.

6. To give one example, Rawls's theory says less talented people shouldn't mind more talented people – doctors, for example – being paid more, as long as the less talented benefited most. He argued that 'the main psychological root of our liability to envy is a lack of self-confidence in our own worth combined with a sense of impotence'. How consistent this is with how people really feel and behave is debatable.

7. Haidt claimed that Rawls was 'creating clever justifications for moral intuitions' (*The Righteous Mind*, Penguin, 2012, p. 38). Similarly, Drew Westen noted that advocates of liberalism 'tend to be intellectual. They like to read and think. They thrive on policy debates, arguments, statistics, and getting the facts right. All that is well and good, but it can be self-destructive politically.'

8. Most notable here is Michael Sandel's *Liberalism and the Limits of Justice*. More recently, Sandel has emphasised the role of a 'good life' ideal in tackling right-wing populism: 'Liberal neutrality flattens questions of meaning, identity and purpose into questions of fairness. It therefore misses the anger and resentment that animate the populist revolt.'

9. Rawls wrote that 'One of the deepest distinctions between political conceptions of justice is between those that allow for a plurality of opposing and even incommensurable conceptions of the good and

those that hold that there is but one conception of the good which is to be recognized by all persons.' See 'Justice as Fairness: Political not Metaphysical', John Rawls, *Philosophy and Public Affairs*, Vol. 14, No. 3 (summer 1985), p. 248.

10. 'The Left and Reciprocity', Stuart White, *Labour's Future*, 2010, pp. 36–41.

11. 'The State of Trust', Simon Parker, Phil Spires, Faizal Farook and Melissa Mean, DEMOS, 2008, pp. 25–7.

12. Rawls was keen to point out that his theory was not a set of 'comprehensive moral ideals', and complained that, too often, 'liberalism itself becomes a sectarian doctrine'. 'Justice as Fairness: Political not Metaphysical', p. 246.

13. 'Power is Fragmenting. But What is the True Cost to Democracy?' Will Hutton, *Guardian*, 2013.

14. This righteous clarity is a big problem with activists' preference for 'direct democracy' over 'representative' democracy. As academic Armine Ishkanian has pointed out, the activist conception of democracy involves a 'more demanding idea of what democracy should mean'. In its current form, it often means privileging the most passionate voices. Hence, 'direct democracy' is often undermined by a failure to see that the goals of activists are not always the goals of the population at large.

15. Research undertaken in 2017 looked at framing fairness in three ways: on the basis of a) charity, b) reciprocity and c) impartiality. It explored which of these made people most willing to embrace redistributive policies, and found that impartiality 'stood apart'. 'A policy that exhibits impartial even-handedness in a caring way – that aims to bring everyone up to a level playing field and doesn't intend to leave anybody in the dust – may be most effectively understood as "fair", and importantly, "good", by the broadest audience.' See 'What Counts as "Fair" and What Makes People Care?' Laura Niemi, *Psychology Today*, June 2017.

16. 'Justice as Fairness: Political not Metaphysical', p. 226.

17. 'Justice as Fairness: Political not Metaphysical', p. 244.

18. Rawls wrote that 'citizens are to recognize that the weight of their claims is not given by the strength and psychological intensity of their wants and desires (as opposed to their needs and requirements as citizens), even when their wants and desires are rational from their point of view'. 'Justice as Fairness: Political not Metaphysical', p. 246.

19. 'Justice as Fairness: Political not Metaphysical', p. 238.

3. DISTORTING MYTHS

1. 'Politics and the English Language', George Orwell, *Horizon*, April 1946.
2. *The Origins of Totalitarianism*, Hannah Arendt, Meridian Books, 1950, p. 474.
3. Janan Ganesh made this argument most directly in a 2015 *FT* article, 'Cosmic Justice for Labour Moderates', arguing that Labour 'centrists' were 'frying in the fat of their own sanctimony'. Meanwhile, Theo Bertram points out that both 'Tony and Gordon used to slop this stuff out too . . . on special occasions.'
4. 'Rise of the Golems', Allen Simpson, *The Fabians*, October 2017.
5. 'One Step Beyond', Hopi Sen, 2015.
6. Macron asks in the same interview: 'Why is a portion of our youth so fascinated by extremes, jihadism for example? Why do modern democracies refuse to allow their citizens to dream?' Speechwriter Phil Collins has written, similarly, of the need to reclaim stories of 'extraordinary hope' about the 'wonders of democracy'.

4. WHAT IS THE DARK KNIGHT?

1. Rob Ford points out that those who complain about 'smears' against Corbyn are willing to share similarly unsubstantiated information about the Tories. Likewise, the 1988 Bennite coup against Neil Kinnock – in which Corbyn played a central role – is tolerated or celebrated by left populists, while the 2016 coup against Corbyn is seen as an act of high treason.
2. 'The Way out of the Wood', Phil Collins, *The Argument*, 2016.
3. The blogger goes on to complain about the 'unimaginable callousness' of right-wingers, writing: 'Our disagreement is not merely political, but a fundamental divide on what it means to live in a society, how to be a good person, and why any of that matters . . . I can't debate someone into caring about what happens to their fellow human beings.'
4. Research by Pew before the 2016 US election showed that Democrat voters were half again as likely as Republicans to say they couldn't respect those voting for opponents.
5. Some on the left, to their credit, were critical of this. Yet many online were not. 'She's ignorant. She voted for what's now happening to her. She deserves it,' said one. 'She was OK with Tories when they killed

people cutting off disabled benefits. She would still support them if she hadn't suffered,' said another. 'She is getting exactly what she deserves for voting Tory. Zero sympathy,' proclaimed a third.

6. An example of this is journalist Joseph Harker's endorsement of Laura Pidcock, when she described the Tories as an 'enemy' she'd avoid being friends with: 'I simply can't imagine having a close relationship with a person who believes the strong have no obligation to help the weak,' Harker wrote, adding that he'd avoid friendship with Blairites and Lib Dems too: 'It may leave me with a smaller social circle, but then, it's always good to know who your friends really are.'

7. This emphasis on morality massively accelerated Labour's civil wars. The pitch from Corbyn-backers was, from day one, that Labour 'moderates' were immoral or self-interested. 'The general public are sick of vacuous, mealy-mouthed and self-serving politicians. It is lovely to have someone who is highly principled, moral and who speaks their mind,' said one *Guardian* letter-writer. Danny Dorling, meanwhile, wrote that Corbyn has the 'moral clarity of a priest' and an appeal 'based on conviction, love and compassion. Just how cynical do you have to be not to see the hope and possibility in that?'

8. Mason adds, in the thread, that this would help get rid of 'the neo-liberals, gentrifiers and Blairite stay-behinds'.

9. 'The Ghost of Social-Fascism', Theodore Draper, *Commentary*, 1969.

10. 'The International Situation', Joseph Stalin, *International Press Correspondence*, 23 October 1924, pp. 838–9.

11. In the UK, Harry Pollitt, the head of the Communist Party, wrote that 'The Labour party is the most dangerous enemy of the workers because it is a *disguised* party of capitalism.'

12. 'For a Workers' United Front against Fascism', Leon Trotsky, December 1931.

13. 'The Austrian Crisis and Communism', Leon Trotsky, November 1929.

14. Wilhelm Pieck reportedly told a friend in early 1933: 'If the Nazis come to power, they will be at the end of their rope in two months, and then it will be our turn!'

15. The Communist International declared in 1933 that 'The establishment of an *open fascist dictatorship, by destroying all the democratic illusions among the masses and liberating them from the influence of Social-Democracy, accelerates the rate of Germany's development* toward proletarian revolution.'

16. John Pilger's support for Donald Trump ahead of Barack Obama and Hillary Clinton is a modern example of how this way of thinking

continues to infect left-wing thought. This is similarly true when we look at some left-populist criticism of the 2017 French election. For example, the left-wing Slovenian intellectual Slavoj Žižek suggested Macron and Le Pen were interchangeable.

17. 'Hitler wasn't Inevitable', Marcel Bois, *Jacobin*, November 2015.

18. Impossibilism and Transitional Demands: the deliberate setting of unachievable goals, so as to prove the impossibility of cooperating with capitalism. Accelerationism: the idea that capitalism 'should be deepened or "accelerated" in order to prompt radical change'. Opposition to charity: an objection 'on the grounds that such organisations as charities are merely trying to deal with the symptoms of capitalism rather than capitalism itself'.

19. *Things Can Only Get Better*, John O'Farrell, Random House, 1998, p. 33.

20. *The Establishment*, Owen Jones, Penguin, 2014, p. 78.

21. *Chavs*, Owen Jones, Verso, 2016, p. 96.

22. *Chavs*, p. 88.

23. *Chavs*, p. 94.

24. *Chavs*, p. 91.

25. The 1998 New Deal – a ten-year work programme to invest in opportunities for eighteen- to twenty-four-year-olds, funded through a £5 billion tax on public utilities companies – isn't mentioned by name once in *Chavs*, despite being one of the most obvious policies to look at in relation to Jones's chosen topic.

26. *The Establishment*, p. 78.

27. There is an important conversation to be had about the Labour record on economic inequality, which is fairly good compared to overall global trends, but nevertheless mixed. Significant inequality reductions in the gap between the richest 10 per cent and the poorest did take place. But a failure to address the top 1 per cent undermined much of this. Yet Jones proposes no policy solution to high pay, focusing throughout on the ill intentions of those who have failed.

28. David Miliband is described as a 'profiteering politician ... not known for his lack of self-regard', who was indifferent to 'the concerns of [his] deprived North East constituency'. Unsurprisingly, there is no mention of Miliband teaching politics unpaid at a comprehensive school while on the backbenches.

29. While Ken Livingstone is relied upon as a character witness in both books, the former London mayor's complicated tax arrangements are never spoken of. Len McCluskey, meanwhile, is described as a 'proud

Scouser' who could 'hardly look or sound less Establishment'. There is no mention of the £400,000 paid by Unite to help McCluskey buy a £700,000 flat in London Bridge. Likewise, behaviour of others on the far left, such as Ian Lavery, are not mentioned. Similarly, Jones has attacked the 'nepotism' of centre-left MP Angela Smith, while never commenting on the fact that Corbyn's son was given a job within his inner circle.

30. Elsewhere, for instance, Jones implies that the likes of Alan Milburn are not just centre leftists or even 'centrists', but that they are interchangeable with the likes of Melanie Phillips and Peter Hitchens. 'Peter Hitchens got me thinking: do lefties always have to turn right in old age?' Owen Jones, *Guardian*, 2015.

31. *The Establishment*, p. 73.

32. Tony Benn reportedly gave a multimillion-pound inheritance to his children via tax loopholes, but left nothing to the Labour Party.

33. 'Questions All Jeremy Corbyn Supporters Need to Answer', Owen Jones, *Medium*, 2016.

34. Trade unionist Manuel Cortes wrote a *Huffington Post* article riven with Dark Knight rhetoric: 'I would not like to be in a trench alongside Owen under heavy shelling . . . It is a moment for solidarity, not back-stabbing.'

35. For Jones, centrism combines 'social liberalism and anti-Brexitism with support for cuts, privatisation and a pro-corporate agenda' – alongside an appetite for 'murderous, never-ending bloody chaos in Iraq'. Meanwhile, *Red Pepper* magazine describes centrism as 'the belief that in the great battle between good and evil, both sides make some valid points'. And a prominent pro-Corbyn blogger tweets 'When you say "I'm a centrist" I hear: . . . 'Fuck disabled people, fuck young people, fuck the poor, because I'm comfortable; I'm a right-winger who pretends not to be right-wing." '

36. BBC election coverage, 12 December 2019, 11.48 p.m.

37. This may sound provocative. But it is exactly the sort of question which is raised by events such as the campaign in Birmingham against LGBT rights being on the school curriculum.

38. Tube drivers do a thirty-six-hour working week, with forty-three days' annual holiday. The strikers were being asked to cover the night tube, meaning more antisocial hours because of a rota which was spread over twenty-four hours rather than twenty. In return they were offered a 2 per cent pay rise, a £500 one-off bonus each, and an additional £2,000 on the salary of affected drivers.

39. 'The Corbyn Identity', Fred Jarvis, 2016.

40. Ken Loach argues that 'The idea of breaking through and leaving everybody else behind is a deeply divisive concept, isn't it? So we've got to reject that notion altogether.' And Giles Fraser, a pro-Lexit commentator who initially supported Corbyn, characterises social mobility as 'Get on. Get out of your community. Find a job anywhere you please. Undo the ties that bind you,' adding, 'this same philosophy . . . encourages bright working-class children to leave their communities to become rootless Rōnin, loyal to nothing but the capitalist dream of individual acquisition and self-advancement.'

41. For instance, when Gordon Brown celebrated the number of people doing middle-class jobs as a sign of rising socio-economic prospects for those from poorer backgrounds, it was interpreted by the populist left as 'rampant sneering at working-class Britain'.

42. As one contributor at a 2016 focus group put it, 'Since the '50s living standards have changed [and] people's expectations have changed . . . Below 30k I suppose is on the state line kind of thing. And then above 30k, 30–60k is kind of middle ground and then above that high earners. So I think the class system's probably gone as a term, but I think the salary banding is still relevant.' GQQR focus groups about the Labour Party, male, working class, Nuneaton, 2016.

43. Margaret Thatcher boasted that she had 'replaced the old, class-based Labour order' with one based on 'merit, ability and effort'. And John Major, a working-class Conservative, said Labour never attracted him because its ethos was that 'You must stay where you are.'

44. The survey concludes that the 'traditional working class' now makes up just 14 per cent of the UK population. 'A New Model of Social Class? Findings from the BBC's Great British Class Survey Experiment', Mike Savage et al., 2013, pp. 245–6.

45. As historian Glen O'Hara puts it, 'Whose thinking is really, really "Labour"? The seventy-year-old ex-factory worker in Lincolnshire who owns his own house outright, or the thirty-year-old graduate mortgage broker renting out a tiny room in South-East London?'

46. 'Antisemitic Violence in Europe, 2005–2015', Johannes Due Enstad, University of Oslo Centre for Research on Extremism, June 2017, p. 17. See also Stan Anson, *Labour and the Jews*, Medium, 2018.

47. Momentum's controversial ex-organiser Jackie Walker deployed this exact approach, creating a hierarchy of deserving and undeserving groups, which culminated in the binary between 'victims' (Africans) and 'perpetrators' (Jews).

48. This is muddied by the fact that the global Jewish community was 'stateless' before Israel was established. Hence, the situation fails one key test of 'imperialism' – namely that a country is 'extending' its territories.

49. Novelist Howard Jacobson points out that Zionism is both an idea which exists within many Jewish people (a 'longing for a homeland . . . or to find a place of safety') and a political project (bound up in the 'cruel exigencies of statehood').

50. A cross-party report into racism against Jews and the political left concluded something quite similar, explaining the 'distinct nature of post-Second World War antisemitism' as follows: 'Unlike other forms of racism, anti-Semitic abuse often paints the victim as a malign and controlling force rather than as an inferior object of derision, making it perfectly possible for an "anti-racist campaigner" to express anti-Semitic views.' 'Antisemitism in the UK', House of Commons Home Affairs Committee, Tenth Report of Session 2016–17, p. 44.

51. As David Hirsh puts it, 'Some on the left are not as exercised . . . by the oppression of [Jewish] groups because it is carried out by forces which they think of as broadly on the progressive side.' 'The politics of position and the politics of reason', David Hirsh, *Fathom Journal*, 2015.

5. THE APPEAL OF THE DARK KNIGHT

1. Social Identity Theory was first set out in 1979. Its creators describe how the 'pressures to evaluate one's own group positively through in-group/out-group comparisons lead social groups to attempt to differentiate themselves from each other'. 'The Social Identity Theory of Intergroup Behaviour', Henri Tajfel and John Turner, in J. T. Jost and J. Sidanius (eds.), *Political Psychology: Key Readings (Key Readings in Social Psychology)*, Psychology Press, 1979, pp. 276–93.

2. 'The Role of Threat in Intergroup Relations', Walter G. Stephan, C. Lausanne Renfro, Mark D. Davis, 2008.

3. 'The Integrated Threat Theory and Politics: Explaining Attitudes toward Political Parties', Danny Osborne, Paul G. Davies and Anne Duran, *Personality and Social Psychology Research*, 2008, p. 71.

4. 'Union Chief Says Christmas Strikes "Co-ordinated to Bring Down This Bloody Tory Government"', *Independent*, 2016.

5. In the 2016 leadership contest, Corbyn supporters were three times as likely as Smith backers to say, 'The motives of our leaders matter just as much as what they achieve.' And polling found that only 56 per cent of Corbyn backers thought he could win an election.

6. YouGov finds that 31 per cent of self-proclaimed centrists say they're morally above average, compared to 39 per cent of self-identifying left-wingers and 47 per cent of right-wingers.

7. Appearing on Facebook, the quote is an illustration of 'expressive voting'. This is the term, used in contrast to 'instrumental voting', to denote political action which is about expressing who you are. Other Corbyn supporters espouse similar sentiments: 'If the voters reject [Labour], that is a price that has to be paid if you want a party that you can believe in,' wrote one, in a letter to the *Independent*.

8. A literature review of 'moral self-regard' by academics identifies a cause, a consequence and an effect of high 'moral self-regard'. The cause (which they call 'moral compensation'), describes the fact that 'moral self-regard' often arises to make up for failure in other areas. The consequence (called 'moral credentials') is that people with high 'moral self-regard' become overly secure in their morality. And the effect (called 'moral resentment') is that those with increased 'moral self-regard' are disliked rather than admired. 'The Dynamic Moral Self: A Social Psychological Perspective', in *Personality, Identity, and Character*, Cambridge University Press, January 2009, D. Narvaez and D. Lapsley, (eds.) pp. 341–54.

9. 'When Do Moral Arguments Facilitate Political Influence?', Matthew Feinberg and Rob Willer, *Personality and Social Psychology Bulletin*, 41, 12, 2015, p. 15.

10. 'Why I've Become Tory Scum', Tony Parsons, *GQ*, 2015. (Laurie Penny defended the perpetrators, explaining, 'I don't have a problem with this . . . What's disgusting is that some people are more worried about a war memorial than the destruction of the welfare state').

11. The study concludes that 'people needing to demonstrate their morality to themselves or to others may exert effort beyond a point that would be considered economically rational because exerting effort on prosocial initiatives boosts their moral self-regard, regardless of whether their efforts actually are helpful. Consequently, a desire for a positive moral self-regard can lead people to generate fewer benefits for people in need.' 'Desire for a Positive Moral Self-regard Exacerbates Escalation of Commitment to Initiatives with Prosocial Aim', Rebecca Schaumberg and Scott Wiltermuth, *Organizational Behavior and*

Human Decision Processes, 123, 2014, pp. 110–23. Elsewhere, findings show that anti-prejudice messages often make the problem worse, through being too staunch or didactic. 'Ironic Effects of Anti-prejudice Messages: How Motivational Interventions Can Reduce (but Also Increase) Prejudice', Lisa Legault, Jennifer Outsell and Michael Inzlicht, Psychological Science, November 2011.

12. Alan Bennett, Diary for 2015, entry on 8 May.

13. 'The Double-edge Sword in Social Judgments', Xiaowei Lu, University of California, 2012, pp. 47–8. See also 'Making It Moral: Merely Labelling an Attitude as Moral Increases Its Strength', Andrew Luttrell et al., Journal of Experimental Social Psychology, 65, April 2016.

6. THE CASE AGAINST THE DARK KNIGHT (PEOPLE)

1. Nick Cohen has long complained about the use, by the left, of language suggesting collective punishment: 'Google the number of times "straight white males" are denounced by public-school-educated women in the liberal media and think how that sounds to an ex-miner coughing up his guts in a Yorkshire Council Flat.'

2. Maajid Nawaz makes the point that, by seeing things through the prism of struggle between rival groups, the left lets down the minorities within the minority ('every feminist Muslim, every gay Muslim').

3. Identity and Violence, Amartya Sen, Penguin, 2006, pp. 19–26.

4. Identity and Violence, p. 26.

5. One account from the 2017 election describes the sheer multiplicity of the electorate, following canvassing in Peterborough: 'We knocked on doors along a monotone Victorian terrace, which in a bygone decade would have been home to an equally monotonous set of voters, but now we found a different universe behind every door: white guys with bellies and tattoos; shy Muslim teenagers in religious dress; nurses who were sleeping off a night shift; recent graduates angry at tuition fees; and families with two kids, two jobs and two cars.' Meanwhile, the conventional Dark Knight emblems are a dying breed. Figures like Mr Birling in An Inspector Calls – white, male, straight, upper class, pro-business, Tory-voting, patriarchal, and so on – were always rarer than is imagined. But they're now even less common.

6. These accusations were aimed at MPs like Sajid Javid and James Cleverly, and came from Kerry Mendoza, Ash Sarkar and Clive Lewis MP

respectively. Chuka Umunna, meanwhile, was accused of not being 'politically black' by members of his local constituency Labour Party.

7. *Tony Blair: A Journey: My Political Life*, Vintage, 2011, p. 135.

8. Post-election surveys in 2015 found that 14 per cent of *Mail* readers voted Labour, 5 per cent Lib Dem and 4 per cent Green. Among *Sun* readers, meanwhile, the percentages were 24 per cent, 4 per cent and 1 per cent respectively.

9. 'Ken Livingstone Stands by Dan Jarvis Hedge Fund Comments', *Guardian*, 2016.

10. Taylor goes on, 'I was born into and love the Labour party. I believe wealthy people, such as myself, should pay higher rates of tax to help fund the NHS, our public services, the armed forces and reduce inequality.'

11. 'Of Course All Men Don't Hate Women. But All Men Must Know They Benefit from Sexism', Laurie Penny, *New Statesman*, 2013.

12. In the article, Penny concludes: 'The idea that nobody can really be a socialist if they were lucky enough to go to a private school is wilful stupidity.'

13. When it comes to gender and sexuality, for example, Penny writes that 'My identity is more complex than simply female or male, but . . . I'm still on the girls' team.'

14. 'For the Record: "We Beat Fear with Hope"', Justin Trudeau, *Macleans*, 2015.

15. 'Text of Obama's Speech: A More Perfect Union', *Wall Street Journal*, 2008. Elsewhere, Obama emphasised the importance of understanding 'the reality of people who are different than us'. Bill Clinton, similarly, built his 2012 Democratic National Committee speech around consensus rather than conflict: 'Though I often disagree with Republicans, I actually never learned to hate them the way the far right that now controls their party seems to hate our president.'

16. Lawson adds: 'The tent was too big and you spent the next 10 years trying to keep the wrong people in it.' 'Dear Tony Blair, Maybe It's Your Fault if the Electorate Hasn't Shifted to the Left', Neal Lawson, *Guardian*, 2015.

17. 'Blair in Assault on Old Labour', Andrew Grice and Colin Brown, *Independent*, June 1999.

18. Labour MP Jon Ashworth spells this out: 'Just because someone voted Conservative the last time, it doesn't mean they're bad people. It doesn't mean their values or their instincts are not respectable . . . If

you speak to people who voted Conservative, it's because they thought at the time the Conservatives were offering them security for their family and local community . . . I don't think they voted Conservative because they want to see the NHS undermined, or more zero hours' contracts or widening inequality.'

19. Just as with the London riots – where deprivation and unemployment was high among those who took part – EDL members were significantly worse educated than average and, in the case of twenty-five- to sixty-four-year-olds in the 'movement', almost six times as likely to be unemployed as the average person.

20. Corbyn supporters in 2016 were nearly twice as likely as Smith backers to say that 'People who don't like immigration are bigoted' and that 'Patriotism inevitably leads to jingoism.'

21. The research finds six attitudinal tribes when it comes to immigration: Confident Multiculturalists, Mainstream Liberals, Identity Ambivalents, Cultural Integrationists, Latent Hostiles and Active Enmity. Identity Ambivalents are described as being 'less financially secure and less optimistic about the future. They are more likely to live in social housing and to view immigration through the prism of its economic impact.' Cultural Integrationists, meanwhile, are 'older, less deprived voters . . . with concerns about the impact of immigration on national identity'. The final groups – those who feel 'latent hostility' or 'active enmity' – tend to be 'older, not university-educated, and more than likely working-class'.

22. Thirty-nine per cent of Asian respondents in 2011 said we should either 'stop all immigration' or 'stop all immigration until the economy improves' – compared to 34 per cent of white respondents (although, within this, white respondents were more likely to say 'stop all immigration').

23. For instance, one commentator asks if, in analysing the Brexit vote, we're putting too much of the referendum outcome down to 'left behind' voters: 'What about the smug late-middle-aged man propping up the Home Counties pub in his check jacket, having driven there in his Audi 4x4, complaining about the "foreigners" and the country going to the dogs?'

24. Coined in 2018, 'gammon' is a pejorative left-populist reference to baby-boomers who are lower middle class, male, non-university educated, pro-Brexit and socially conservative.

25. *Political Change in Britain*, David Butler and Donald Stokes, Palgrave Macmillan, 1974, p. 36.

26. The research concluded that 'Voting intentions are still largely inherited from parents.' 'Young People's Attitudes towards Politics', Nestlé Family Monitor, Number 16 report, July 2003, pp. 49–50.
27. Gallup's 2005 Youth Survey in America found that 71 per cent of thirteen- to seventeen-year-olds' politics are 'about the same' as their parents on the political spectrum. And a study looking at the Scottish referendum revealed that the children of 'Yes' voters were four times as likely to vote 'Yes' as to vote 'No'.
28. 'Accounting for the Child in the Transmission of Party Identification', Christopher Ojedaa and Peter K. Hatemia, *American Sociological Review*, 2015.
29. 'Why Does the Apple Fall Far from the Tree? How Early Political Socialization Prompts Parent–Child Dissimilarity', Elias Dinas, *British Journal of Political Science*, 44, 4, October 2014, pp. 827–52.
30. As Isaiah Berlin puts it, 'I do not regard the Nazis, as some people do, as literally pathological or insane, only as wickedly wrong ... I see how, with enough false education, enough widespread illusion and error, men can, while remaining men ... commit the most unspeakable crimes.'
31. Steven Pinker writes that 'we have to be prepared, when putting on psychological spectacles, to believe that evildoers always think they are acting morally.' Even Hitler's crazed point of view 'was a highly moralistic one' in his own mind, in which 'heroic sacrifices would bring about a thousand-year utopia'. *The Better Angels of Our Nature*, Penguin Putnam, 2011, pp. 494–5.

7. THE CASE AGAINST THE DARK KNIGHT CONTINUED (POLICY)

1. 'Are Right-wingers Evil? Yes', Sunny Hundal, Liberal Conspiracy, July 2013. Other examples – and they're not hard to find – include Clive Lewis's view, in advance of the 2017 election, that people vote Tory because they 'don't care about other people'.
2. Labour activist Conor Pope describes Corbyn's rapid rhetorical shift, during the Grenfell disaster, from talking about immediate solutions to talking about core morals – the effect being to 'move public issues from a question of practicality to one of values'. Indeed, some have argued that to be a 'centrist' is in essence to distinguish between these layers. See 'The Spirit of Centrism', Bo Winegard, Quillette, October 2017.

3. 'Labour MP Jo Cox's Maiden Speech to Parliament in June 2015', *Guardian*, June 2016.
4. Barack Obama emphasised this in his eulogy to political opponent John McCain, writing that McCain 'did understand that some principles transcend politics, that some values transcend party . . . They give shape and order to our common life, even when we disagree.'
5. Haidt uses African fieldwork to emphasise that societies with a strong link between morality and authority have characteristics which 'are more like those of a parent and a child than those of a dictator and fearful underlings'. This comes at the expense of autonomy, but is built on the idea of a benevolent hierarchy which benefits everyone. *The Righteous Mind*, Penguin, 2012, pp. 167–9.
6. An example of this was 'Sachsgate', the 2008 incident when Jonathan Ross and Russell Brand called up a veteran actor and claimed to have had sex with his granddaughter. The event sparked a fallout between older conservatives and younger liberals. On one side were those using an Authority/Subversion or Sanctity/Degradation moral compass ('It's disgusting. Jonathan Ross has got a mouth like a sewer,' complained one older woman.) On the other were those operating on a Liberty/Oppression or Care/Harm basis, who saw a freedom of speech issue, with no damage done.
7. Haidt writes that, through getting his head around the Sanctity/ Degradation foundation, he 'began to understand why the American culture wars involved so many battles over sacrilege'. 'When an artist submerges a crucifix in a jar of his own urine, or smears elephant dung on an image of the Virgin Mary, do these works belong in art museums? Can the artist simply tell religious Christians, 'If you don't want to see it, don't go to the museum'? Or does the mere existence of such works make the world dirtier, more profane and more degraded? If you cannot see anything wrong here, try reversing the politics. Imagine that a conservative artist had created these works using images of Martin Luther King Junior and Nelson Mandela . . . Could such works be displayed in museums in New York or Paris without triggering angry demonstrations? *The Righteous Mind*, pp. 122–4.
8. 'Isaiah Berlin on Pluralism', *New York Review of Books*, XLV, 8, 1998.
9. Lakoff adds that 'Moderates have both political moral worldviews, but mostly use one of them. Those two moral worldviews in general contradict each other.' 'Why Trump?', George Lakoff, March 2016.

10. 'The worst source of confusion is the tendency to use the word [social-ism] to describe, not a certain kind of society, or certain values which might be attributes of a society, but particular policies which are, or are thought to be, means to attaining this kind of society.' *The Future of Socialism*, Jonathan Cape, 1956, p. 75.

11. As James Purnell argues, 'We believed in [education] reform, not least because it reduced inequality . . . Far from choice vying with equality, a set of reforms that included choice had reduced one of the worst causes of inequality in Britain.'

12. David Wearing wrote in the *Guardian*, during Labour's 2016 leader-ship contest, that 'We assume that the dividing line between conservatives and progressives falls between the two main parties – but it now runs through Labour's heart . . . This is the real struggle taking place in the party now: . . . between conservatives and progressives.'

13. See 'Free to Dream, I'd be Left of Jeremy Corbyn', Polly Toynbee, *Guardian*, August 2015. The weaknesses of this were encapsulated by another Toynbee article: 'The unpalatable answer is that policies mat-ter less than the personality, performance and persuasiveness of leaders . . . Corbyn's image may by now be sealed for ever with too many. He's honest – but he's no prime minister.'

14. 'In Conversation with Tony Blair', *Progress*, July 2015.

15. Blair's article 'In Defence of Blairism' makes this point. He sets out the values he sought to promote – 'community, society, family, com-passion and social justice' – but says his disagreement was with the policies and electoral strategies the left relied on, which spoke for interests rather than values: 'Yes . . . we celebrated London as a finan-cial centre. But we did this because we knew that without a growing economy life would be harder for those at the bottom.'

16. Kendall spelled this out very clearly in a *Newsnight* interview in July 2015, explaining that while she agreed with Corbyn on the 'outcomes', she had a different view on the way of achieving them.

17. McDonnell argued, upon becoming Shadow Chancellor, that 'There's nothing left-wing about excessive spending, nothing socialist about too much debt.'

18. Liam Byrne, for instance, proposed in 2015 that Labour add a com-mitment to reduce inequality to the Labour constitution. Tristram Hunt said that 'The task of helping communities like Stoke-on-Trent to thrive in an era of intense global competition and rapid technologi-cal change requires a clear and unambiguous focus on reducing inequality.' Sadiq Khan, who was similarly demonised for his

criticism of Corbyn, made the same point about inequality in 2014, referring to the issue as a 'stain'.

19. 'Hilary Benn's Speech in Full', *Independent*, 2015.

20. 'Jeremy Corbyn Reveals He was "Appalled" by MPs' Reaction to Hilary Benn's Pro-intervention Syria Speech', *Independent*, 2015.

21. Nick Pearce and Gavin Kelly point out that 'Trade unions are already invisible across large swathes of the mass-employing private service sector. Among low-paid workers, membership rates are just 9 per cent.'

22. Corbyn's 2017 claim that EU membership would prevent Labour fulfilling its manifesto, for example, had little basis in reality – unless he was pursuing policies like nationalisation interminably, at the expense of all else.

23. Hopi Sen writes that 'The easiest political technique in the Labour party is to imply someone one step to your right is a Tory or not one of our tribe. It's so simple to question their grasp of what it is to be truly, really Labour and to use that to box them in and cut them off', 'One Step Beyond', 2015.

24. Corbyn argued in 2015 that nuclear weapons are 'immoral', as he has done over twenty times in Parliament before.

25. Nawaz described in 2015 how this sort of viewpoint can mutate: '[The regressive left] have come to the view that . . . if you're to challenge Islamist theocracy you're supporting neo-conservative foreign policy. So, in their minds they've prioritised. They've said neo-conservative foreign policy is the bigger evil . . . In doing so they make alliances with some of the most regressive, theocratic fascist, totalitarian, barbaric, murdering regimes across the world.' Stop the War Coalition claims, for example, that Hamas and Hezbollah represent 'a legitimate part of [our] movement' – and that the French were 'reaping the whirlwind' of Western foreign policy during the 2015 Paris attacks.

26. 'Only the Foolish Would Allow Themselves to be Swayed Solely by Jeremy Corbyn's Sincerity', Howard Jacobson, *Independent*, August 2015.

27. See, for example, 'The 9 Charts That Show the "Left-wing" Policies of Jeremy Corbyn the Public Actually Agrees With', Matt Dathan and Jon Stone, *Independent*, 2015.

28. TUC polling after the 2015 election showed this. The main doubts about Labour were around the idea that Labour would spend money they didn't have. This was couched in terms of basic competence; people didn't feel Labour was too radical, but they wanted to know

radicalism would be limited by common sense. The 2016 'Cruddas Review', meanwhile, demonstrated an appetite for policies which were 'economically radical [but] fiscally prudent'. See 'Labour's Future: Why Labour Lost in 2015 and How It Can Win Again', Jon Cruddas, Nick Pecorelli and Jonathan Rutherford, 2016, p. 9. In 2019, meanwhile, 40 per cent of Labour defectors said they 'did not believe Labour would be able to deliver the promises it was making' and 24 per cent were worried Labour would 'spend and borrow too much'. Michael Ashcroft, *Diagnosis of Defeat: Labour's Turn to Smell the Coffee*, Biteback Publishing, 2020.

29. A good parallel with this is the difference between support for feminism and for gender equality. Opinion research in 2018 found that 81 per cent of Brits support feminist ideas (equal rights, status and treatment for women), but that this falls to 27 per cent once people are asked if they support feminism itself. The reasons for this hostility, polling finds, relate to inexorability, with many people believing that feminists 'want women to be better than men'. This perception may be wrong (and no doubt some genuine prejudices are involved), but it's interesting all the same. It suggests that, for potential recruits to a cause, a fear of unwavering partisanship can be a major barrier to signing up.

8. WHAT IS THE PUPPET MASTER?

1. 'What I Learned from Podemos', Owen Jones, Medium, 2015.
2. Corbyn said in a 2017 speech, for example, that 'The people who run Britain have been taking our country for a ride. They've stitched up our political system to protect the powerful ... They've rigged the economy and business rules to line the pockets of their friends.' Elsewhere he has stated that he does not believe we live in a democracy.
3. Introduction to *Post-Capitalism*, Paul Mason, Allen Lane, 2015.
4. This is according to polling from YouGov in 2015, which found that 28 per cent of Corbyn supporters strongly agree with the sentiment, compared to 19 per cent of Burnham supporters, 16 per cent of Cooper supporters, and 7 per cent of Kendall supporters. The national average was 13 per cent. The subsequent 2016 campaign showed that this type of feeling hadn't diminished, with 55 per cent of Corbyn backers believing that security services like MI5 were working to undermine him, compared to 19 per cent of the population at large. Separate

polling found that 61 per cent of Corbyn supporters believe politicians don't care about the poorest, compared to 28 per cent of Smith backers.

5. Alex Tsipras of Syriza in Greece, for example, criticised as avoidable the package of cuts planned by the previous administration, telling voters 'the future has now begun' and pledging an end to austerity. Yet the deal he himself brokered was equally severe, causing a backbench revolt and anger from the far left. The same goes for Nick Clegg's 2010 promise to 'scrap tuition fees for good', which Clegg later discovered was an 'unwise commitment'. Meanwhile, Corbyn and McDonnell reneged on countless life-long commitments after taking command of Labour, from welfare cuts, nuclear energy and defence spending to freedom of movement and taxation. Even without getting into Number 10, these concessions became electorally necessary.

6. The University of Oxford's vice-chancellor, Louise Richardson, points out that even when populists enter government they still 'manage to convey themselves as victims. Right-wing Erdoğan in Turkey blames Gulen and his domestic supporters, while left-wing Hugo Chavez in Venezuela blamed foreign enemies. On some occasions, faced with the reality of governing, populists moderate and lose their appeal as outsiders ... In others, they take aim at the institutions of the state.' 'Fulbright Lecture: Universities in an Age of Populism', King's College London, Edinburgh, Oxford, June 2017, p. 7.

7. Long-running research, for example, found that, among the top reasons for low trust, the chief complaints were that politicians didn't do what they said they would, didn't set out the real choices, weren't open about real problems and would rather win than govern. The issue was with a lack of honesty about the limits of power, more than with corrupt plutocrats blocking the popular will. *More Sex, Lies and the Ballot Box,* eds. Philip Cowley and Robert Ford, 'Neither Loved nor Trusted: British Political Parties', Harold Clarke, in Biteback Publishing, pp. 111–14.

8. 'Revealed: The Rise and Rise of Populist Rhetoric', Paul Lewis et al., *Guardian*, March 2019.

9. 'Hard Labour', Ben Jackson, *Political Quarterly*, January 2016.

10. One example is the government's 'Ricu' department and its communications work. This includes the production of online content to create better understanding of the British Islamic community and reduce alienation and polarisation. It represents an essentially liberal and inclusive approach. Yet in May 2016 a *Guardian* journalist launched

an exposé of the programme, portraying it as a 'shadowy' propaganda machine and a source of 'covert' control.

11. This was John McDonnell's claim in 2017. Other Puppet Master narratives about Labour infighting include the Portland Communications conspiracy in 2016.

12. *The Establishment*, Penguin, 2014, p. 70.

13. John Bew, *Citizen Clem: A Biography of Attlee*, RiverRun, 2017, pp. 400–401.

14. David Runciman defines a conspiracy theory as 'a view about the world in which the surface story is never the real story. It's a view without any limits to its scepticism or doubt. It's a mindset in which nothing that contradicts the theory is taken as anything other than evidence that the theory is true.' The boundary between conspiracy theory and justified scepticism is the point at which the suspension of disbelief is required. For instance, if there is no evidence of MI5 tinkering in the Labour leadership coup of 2016, then believing that there was defies the Occam's razor principle.

15. According to the 2017 Corruption Perceptions Index, the UK is the eleventh least corrupt out of 181 countries – a couple of places behind New Zealand, Canada and the Scandinavian nations.

16. The notion of 'neoliberalism' is especially reliant on the Puppet Master. Paul Mason describes 'neoliberal' efforts to 're-arm the police, security services and jail system to suppress dissent'. He defines 'neoliberalism' as 'a set of ideas that justifies the economic dominance of a ruling group . . . propagated through the ruling group's control of the media and education'.

17. Corbyn himself has repeatedly claimed that a media conspiracy is at hand. His speech on the topic in August 2018 attacked 'print barons' and 'establishment gatekeepers', who are 'wedded' to the Tories and 'corporate interests': this 'tightening oligopoly' exert a 'stranglehold of elite power and billionaire domination'.

18. 'The Jeremy Corbyn Story That Nobody Wanted to Publish', Crispin Flintoff, *Independent*, 2016.

19. 'Celebrities to Tour Britain in "Jeremy Corbyn for Prime Minister" Musical Show', Michael Wilkinson, *Telegraph*, 2016.

20. 'Capitalism in One Family', Jan-Werner Müller, *London Review of Books*, 2016.

21. 'Journalistic Representations of Jeremy Corbyn in the British Press: From Watchdog to Attackdog', Bart Cammaerts et al., London School of Economics and Political Science, July 2016, p. 12.

22. 'Should He Stay or Should He Go? Television and Online News Coverage of the Labour Party in Crisis', Justin Schlosberg, Media Reform Coalition in association with Birkbeck, University of London, 2016.

23. For example, Paul Mason describes how the right-wing press 'run fake stories about the Labour Party to stop it winning the next election'.

24. The Chomskyite site Media Lens refers to George Monbiot as 'a corporate lightning rod conducting the raw energy of outrage and dissent down to the safe little "box" of *The Guardian* website [where] his readers are regaled with state propaganda, corporate adverts and assailed by the poisonous, system-supportive beliefs of his corporate colleagues'.

25. Blair described the press as obsessed with 'impact': 'it is like a feral beast, just tearing people and reputations to bits, but no one dares miss out ... A vast aspect of our jobs today ... is coping with the media, its sheer scale, weight and constant hyperactivity.'

26. The same arguments apply to other areas. The book *Bluffocracy*, for instance, by James Ball and Andrew Greenway (Biteback Publishing, 2018), points to a culture of chancers, 'all-rounders' and broad-brush generalisers winging it to the top of our institutions. This is a different critique to that made by the populist left, but is no more sympathetic.

27. '5 Myths about Corbyn Media Bias', Media Reform Coalition, August 2016.

28. 'You are What You Read?' Bobby Duffy and Laura Rowden, Ipsos MORI, 2005, p. 9.

29. 'Call Me Illegal: The Semantic Struggle over Seeking Asylum in Australia', Ben Doherty, Centre on Migration, Policy and Society, Working Paper, no. 126, University of Oxford, 2015, p. 11.

30. If we look at net migration levels, mentions of migration in the press and public preoccupation with migration over time in the UK, we see the same self-perpetuating process. 'Shifting Ground: Report 1', Ipsos MORI, 2012, p. 5.

31. 'Journalists in the UK', Neil Thurman, Alessio Cornia and Jessica Kunert, Reuters Institute for the Study of Journalism, University of Oxford, 2016, pp. 12–13.

32. 'It's the Clunking Fist School of Conspiracy', Hugo Rifkind, *The Times*, June 2012.

33. 'The Battle against Irrelevance', Gaby Hinsliff, *Progress*, March 2016.

34. NewsWorks, Market Overview, Readership (Multiplatform), PAMco 3: July 2018–June 2019. Note: the *Evening Standard* and *FT* are not

included, due to the subtler lines these publications take – left-wing socially and culturally, and right-wing economically in both cases. Similarly, the *Metro* is not included, as it doesn't have an overt editorial line.

35. As of summer 2019, the proportion who said they would vote for right-of-centre parties was close to the proportion who said they would vote for left-of-centre parties. Electoral Calculus put the combined Tory, Brexit Party and UKIP vote at 47 per cent and the combined Labour, Lib Dem and Green vote at 48 per cent, based on opinion polls from 30 August 2019 to 7 September 2019.

36. Polling by the Social Market Foundation, from around the time that Corbyn came to power, showed that only 10 per cent identified as far left. Fifteen per cent identified as centre left, meanwhile, with 45 per cent centre, 17 per cent centre right and 13 per cent far right.

37. 'How to Talk about Immigration', Sunder Katwala, Steve Ballinger and Matthew Rhodes, British Future, 2015, pp. 10–24.

38. See, for instance, the *Sun*'s hostile depiction of Bob Diamond or the *Mail*'s coverage of the Fred Goodwin case.

39. Owen Jones writes of a 'concerted attempt to re-direct people's anger . . . away from the powerful'. He explains that 'elite politicians' and the media have worked 'hand in glove' to 'vilify' immigrants and benefit claimants. *The Establishment*, Penguin, 2014, p. xi.

40. 'You are What You Read?', p. 9.

41. The Chomsky explanation is that 'The smart way to keep people passive and obedient is to strictly limit the spectrum of acceptable opinion, but allow very lively debate within that spectrum – even encourage the more critical and dissident views.' The problem with this is that, in a spectrum which ranges from Katie Hopkins to Aaron Bastani, it's hard to see what 'limits' are being put on this range.

42. The authors of Audit of Democracy found that 'political affiliations of the UK's national newspapers have become significantly more fluid . . . There is a powerful rationale for the press to follow [the public], if only to avoid alienating their own readers.'

43. 'Newspaper Support in UK General Elections', https.//www.theguardian.com/news/datablog/2010/may/04/general-election-newspaper-support.

44. 'Tax Credits Cut Bonkers: We Launch Campaign to Aid Low-pay Workers', Craig Woodhouse and Ben Griffiths, *Sun*, October 2015.

45. The *Mail* led the charge against the Windrush Scandal. They were central to the media hunt for the killers of Stephen Lawrence, and splashed similarly in 2017, on an attack on an asylum-seeker in

Croydon. During the Olympics, meanwhile, the *Sun* lauded 'marvellous modern Britain' as an odyssey of multiculturalism and opportunity. More recently they exposed the mistreatment by the car insurance industry of people called Mohammed. In each case, they decided that their readerships were more likely to be piqued by the left-wing angle than by the right-wing one.

46. Once papers' reach is factored in, 48 per cent of all referendum-focused articles were pro-Leave and 22 per cent pro-Remain. 'UK Press Coverage of the EU Referendum', David A. L. Levy, Billur Aslan and Diego Bironzo, Reuters Institute, 2016, pp. 5–8.

47. Lakoff explains: 'Direct causation is dealing with a problem via direct action. Systemic causation recognizes that many problems arise from the system they are in and must be dealt with via systemic causation.'

9. THE APPEAL OF THE PUPPET MASTER

1. 'The "False Consensus Effect": An Egocentric Bias in Social Perception and Attribution Processes', Lee Ross, David Greene and Pamela House, Stanford University, 1976.

2. 'Voters on the Extreme Left and Right are Far More Likely to Believe in Conspiracy Theories', Jan-Willem van Prooijen, LSE Politics and Policy blog, February 2015.

3. *Manufacturing Consent: The Political Economy of the Mass Media*, Edward S. Herman and Noam Chomsky, Pantheon, 1988, p. 1.

4. *Manufacturing Consent,* pp. xi–xii.

5. 'College Faculties a Most Liberal Lot, Study Finds', Howard Kurtz, *Washington Post*, March 2015. See also 'Professors Moved Left since 1990s, Rest of Country Did Not', Sam Abrams, Heterodox Academy, January 2016.

6. 'College Students' Commitment to Activism, Civic Engagement Reach All-time Highs', UCLA, February 2016.

7. 'Rebuilding Labour Britain', Jonathan Rutherford, *Fabian Review*, January 2016.

8. 'Analytic Thinking Reduces Belief in Conspiracy Theories', V. Swami et al., *Cognition*, 133, 3, December 2014, pp. 572–85.

9. 'Materialism and Post-materialism', Our World in Data.

10. 'Voters on the Extreme Left and Right are Far More Likely to Believe in Conspiracy Theories', Jan-Willem van Prooijen, LSE Politics and Policy blog, February 2015.

11. 'It's No Accident: Our Bias for Intentional Explanations', Evelyn Rosset, *Cognition*, 108, 3, September 2008, pp. 771–80.
12. *The Tower*, 'IV, The Narrative', Andrew O'Hagan, *London Review of Books*, 2018.
13. For instance, musicians Akala and Lily Allen advanced the idea that the true Grenfell death toll was being hidden by the authorities.
14. 'Omission and Commission in Judgment and Choice', M. Spranca, E. Minsk and J. Baron, *Journal of Experimental Social Psychology*, 27, 1991, pp. 76–105. This relates to a wider debate about the merits of 'doing' versus 'allowing' harm.
15. Iraq is a good example here. Norman Geras, a defender of the war, refers to the 'two modes of opposing' the conflict. One group acknowledged that both courses of action were imperfect, but concluded that 'the reasons stacked against the war [were] overriding'. A second group saw it as a violent and gratuitous intervention, the alternative to which was peaceful non-intervention.
16. The 'Nirvana fallacy' means, according to Ian Leslie, that when populists are 'faced with a series of complex, imperfect options', they 'overleap them to reach the sunlit uplands of an ideal scenario'.
17. 'Wanted: A Tax and Spend Policy that Makes Sense', Patrick Diamond, *Guardian*, 2014.

10. THE CASE AGAINST THE PUPPET MASTER (GOVERNMENT)

1. 'Donald Trump and the Age of Rage', Ed Smith, *New Statesman*, April 2016.
2. Monbiot adds that 'the numbers [are] on our side. Most people are socially minded, empathetic and altruistic. Most people would prefer to live in a world in which everyone is treated with respect and decency ... We know that if we can mobilise such silent majorities, there is nothing this small minority can do to stop us.' Russell Brand, meanwhile, talks of 6 million like-minded citizens, controlled by a 'tiny, greedy, myopic sliver of the population'.
3. Chris Floyd of Stop the War describes 'those gilded figures who have strode the halls of power for decades in the high chambers of the West'. And Corbyn himself writes that 'The wars of the twenty-first century are crude fights for oil or power, and emanate from glittering boardrooms in Western capitals.'

4. *The Establishment*, Penguin, 2014, p. 14.
5. For instance, in reviewing *Wasted* – a book about politics and young people by Labour councillor Georgia Gould (daughter of New Labour pollster Philip) – Jones describes it as a 'marketing pitch', devised in a boardroom by a 'sharp-suited management consultant'. Similarly, Jones writes that David Miliband saw politics as 'a launchpad', providing 'networks and prestige that made him attractive to members of the economic elite'. He describes Miliband 'scanning the room for someone more powerful or useful' to talk to.
6. *The Establishment*, p. xi.
7. 'The Establishment Uncovered: How Power Works in Britain', Owen Jones, *Guardian*, 2014.
8. Studies in the US using OCEAN (see https://en.wikipedia.org/wiki/Big_Five_personality_traits) find that politicians score higher for conscientiousness, agreeableness and extraversion. Meanwhile, UK research also reveals that extraversion is more common among those who become councillors.
9. In the long run, this attitude leads not to a better democracy but to more apathy. Social psychology professor Karen Douglas points out that belief in conspiracy theories 'threaten[s] the social systems that people rely upon, and encourage[s] inaction where it cannot be afforded'.
10. 'Propaganda and the *Guardian*', Darren Allen, January 2017.
11. In describing how Labour governments deal with competing priorities, the academic Ben Jackson writes that 'To each of these . . . constraints New Labour had a clear answer, based on conceding some ground to the right in order to focus on other fronts where recognisably left-of-centre policy goals could be advanced. This is not to say that New Labour politicians judged these compromises correctly in every case – they did not – but it is to note that the architects of the Blair and Brown government had at least thought about the politics of power in some depth.' 'Hard Labour', Ben Jackson, *Political Quarterly*, January 2016.
12. Leo Baresi writes that Corbyn performed balancing acts on Brexit and the economy in 2017, signalling 'internationalist values . . . while adopting EU and immigration policies that did the opposite'. Baresi adds that 'Labour's help to graduates and richer pensioners has to be seen as a choice – the party promised to protect them before it offered to protect much poorer people.'
13. Ed Smith refers to populism as 'A delayed consequence of the end of deference, in part fuelled by the emergence, especially on social media,

of a strong, hard-edged and almost daily picture of "the will of the people". Maybe this is what real democracy looks like?'

14. Brexit is an obvious case in point. John Curtice's polling found that 'It would appear that the debate about whether the public would prefer a "soft" or a "hard" Brexit has been at risk of being based on a false premise. Rather than wanting one or the other, a majority of voters apparently want both.' 'What Do Voters Want from Brexit?' NatCen, November 2016.

15. For instance, as Rob Ford has pointed out, failure to address off-shore tax avoidance is not the consequence of an electoral strategy but of other policy constraints.

16. 'Now We are Fifty', *Times Higher Education*, 2013. Other figures suggest that, between the 1960s and the 2010s, there was a tenfold increase in the proportion going into higher education.

17. In Scotland social mobility has stalled and educational attainment for the poorest has worsened, thanks to ten years of the SNP's flagship policy of free tuition. Indeed, the SNP is in many ways the perfect example of a political party that has never engaged with prioritisation, thanks to the perennial safety valve of blaming Westminster. Nicola Sturgeon's party has a poor record on poverty, centre-right policies on tax, and regressive policies on austerity and public services. They're in the unique position of being able to adopt anti-establishment mood music whilst rarely, in their capacity as the Scottish establishment, engaging in the 'language of priorities' enough to do anything radical.

18. Collins adds that 'Power is elusive, even in the West Wing . . . Not even the clever politicians at the head of the world's most powerful democracy can predict what will happen.'

19. In the 2017 election Labour refused to increase the overall tax burden, raising taxes only on the very richest, yet claiming that this would be sufficient to buy back nationalised industries and backdate the cancellation of student fees. This led to the accusation from the IFS that Labour – along with the Conservatives – was not providing an 'honest set of choices'. Elsewhere, the IFS has pointed out that raising the top rate of tax only gets you a quarter of the revenue that raising the level overall would achieve. The rich would actually pay much more according to the latter policy, but it's a far harder electoral sell.

20. Umunna wrote, 'We need a serious debate about what we want the NHS to provide and what we are willing to pay for it.' He advocated

a 'hypothecated Health Tax to specifically help fund the NHS'. This prompted accusations that he was a 'neoliberal'.

21. Philip Collins writes that it's 'worrying for the Labour Party that so much of its moral fervour still derives from images of struggle. Implicit in the very idea . . . is that power is held elsewhere.'

11. THE CASE AGAINST THE PUPPET MASTER CONTINUED (SOCIETY)

1. 'Are cities more liberal? Of course: all your liberal mates moved to one,' writes Jonn Elledge. The claim is backed up by evidence that certain 'Big Five' personality types predominate in different areas – and that this is becoming more extreme over time. Similarly, work by the Centre For Towns finds that smaller settlements have become older in the past four decades, and larger cities have become younger. These changes come thanks to a steady accumulation of everyday decisions.

2. Jonn Elledge describes the growth and over-funding of London in precisely these terms. He shows how, once the capital had gained a small advantage, the gap steadily grew. 'Here's Why London Gets so Much of Britain's Transport Funding', Jonn Elledge, City Metric, 2015.

3. Inheritance tax is a particularly acute example, showing how an infinity of tiny choices rack up. Raising inheritance tax significantly would be the right thing to do, but is immensely unpopular (described by the Fabians as 'toxic') even among those not affected. There is no omnipotent Puppet Master, but rather a steadily growing advantage, driven by day-to-day gut instincts.

4. Tony Blair writes that newspapers are a shrinking market, 'only feeling [they] can survive by capturing a core constituency of support and keeping it in a permanent state of anger'.

5. 'Hard Labour', Ben Jackson, *Political Quarterly*, January 2016.

6. 'Corbyn's Posh Boys Can't Crush "the Elite"', Camilla Long, *Sunday Times*, April 2017.

7. Tim Bale suggests that Corbyn's support is concentrated among 'younger, more educated urbanites' and, specifically, a group which he calls 'educated left-behinds'. These voters have reasonable prospects but feel a sense of relative deprivation compared to their expectations and to the situations of their peers.

8. The Institute for Fiscal Studies demonstrated the long-term impact of Labour's 2017 manifesto on different income groups, with the highest-earning future graduates benefiting the most.

9. The Economic and Social Research Council Party Members Project finds that 'objective' ideological difference between pre-Corbyn and post-Corbyn Labour members is small, but that the 'subjective' difference (e.g. how people position themselves) is much bigger. In the US, meanwhile, there was little evidence that Bernie Sanders's supporters were more left-wing than Hillary Clinton's. But, again, they thought they were. Something similar is true among students. While more culturally left-wing, they're less egalitarian on questions like the top rate of tax and redistribution of wealth. 'Today's Students are Left-wing, but Less So on Economic Issues', Anna-Elizabeth Shakespeare, You-Gov, August 2015.

12. WHAT IS THE GOLDEN ERA?

1. Writing about US politics, Jonathan Chait describes the 'nostalgic' premise on which the accusation of 'neoliberalism' is based: 'Its basic claim is that, from the New Deal through the Great Society, the Democratic Party espoused ... social democracy or socialism. Then, starting in the 1970s, a coterie of neoliberal elites hijacked the party and redirected its course toward a brand of social liberalism targeted to elites and hostile to the interests of the poor.' Jonathan Chait, 'How "Neoliberalism" became the Left's Favorite Insult of Liberals', *New York* magazine, July 2017.

2. 'Alan Bennett: Tories Govern with Totalitarian Attitude', Aisha Gani, *Guardian*, October 2015.

3. 'Inside the Mind of an Optimist', Will Dahlgreen, YouGov, May 2015.

4. Brand says we should reject 'quaint, old-fashioned notions like nation, capitalism and consumerism' and turn our backs on 'myopic' and 'outmoded' ideas.

5. The Webb quote in full is as follows: 'What were the chances, in the course of human history, that you and I should be born into an advanced liberal democracy? That we don't die aged 27 because we can't eat because nobody has invented fluoride toothpaste? That we can say what we like, read what we like, love whom we want; that nobody is going to kick the door down in the middle of the night and take us or our children away to be tortured? The odds were vanishingly small.'

6. Corbynite MP Emma Dent Coad, for example, wrote in the *Guardian* that the wedding showed all that was wrong with contemporary society: 'How far we have travelled away from the compassion shown by Diana.' Centre-left commentator Ayesha Hazarika, by contrast, saw the event more optimistically: '[Meghan Markle]'s African-American roots infused the occasion in a way which no diversity campaigner would have dared to dream about ... My favourite moment was the black American pastor Michael Curry, who boomed Martin Luther King ... not far from where Henry VIII was buried. It doesn't get more modern than that.'

7. *The Imagined Past: History and Nostalgia*, (ed.) Christopher Shaw, Manchester University Press, 1989, p. 28.

8. Ken Loach on post-war Britain, *Start the Week*, BBC Radio 4, March 2013.

9. *Chavs*, Verso, 2016, pp. 49–57.

10. 'Materialism: A System That Eats Us from the Inside Out', George Monbiot, *Guardian*, December 2013.

11. 'Unchallenged by Craven Labour, Britain Slides towards Ever More Selfishness', George Monbiot, *Guardian*, June 2014.

12. As one young Labour supporter put it in 2016, Corbyn 'has been on the right side of history for the last thirty years, and dares to make the case against the widely accepted – yet failing – neoliberal economics we live under'.

13. 'Beyond Blair', Phil Collins, *DEMOS Quarterly*, September 2015.

14. Maiden speech by Zarah Sultana, Labour MP for Coventry South, 15 January 2020.

15. Corbyn voted against the Anglo-Irish agreement, for example, and has consistently supported a victory for the republican side over a peaceful settlement. 'Jeremy Corbyn Reiterates Support for United Ireland', *Irish Times*, September 2015. McDonnell, meanwhile, opposed the creation of a power-sharing assembly during the Good Friday agreement, on the basis that 'an assembly is not what people have laid down their lives for over thirty years ... the settlement must be for a united Ireland'. Indeed, as recently as 2003 he praised the 'bullets, bombs and sacrifice' of the IRA.

16. 'The only Labour government these people will ever defend is the Attlee administration of 1945,' writes Phil Wood, having spent time analysing Corbyn supporters on social media.

17. 'Clement Attlee Detested Faddish Radicalism – You Couldn't Say that Jeremy Corbyn is His Heir', John Bew, *New Statesman*, July 2015.

18. Full text: Blair's Fabian speech (part 1), 2003.
19. *Nye: The Political Life of Aneurin Bevan*, Nicklaus Thomas-Symonds, L. B. Tauris, 2014, p. 254.
20. Benn wrote that the post-war Labour government wanted to 'use the wartime planning powers to plan for full employment and welfare. There was no real socialism in it, I think – it was consensus politics born during the war. The Labour Party as a party played only a marginal part.' *The End of an Era: Diaries 1980–90*, Tony Benn, Random House, 1994, Friday 30 July entry.
21. *The Attlee Governments 1945–1951*, Kevin Jefferys, Routledge, 2013.
22. 'Welcome to the NATO-fest', Jeremy Corbyn, *Morning Star*, 2014.
23. The case with Harold Wilson is similar, if less stark. Wilson became unpopular within the left after office, despite achievements including the Race Relations Act. Yet by the 2010s the Wilson administrations were held up as an example of redistributive socialism (see *Chavs*, p. 156).
24. 'We are Many', Tom Crewe, *London Review of Books*, 38, 16, August 2016, pp. 13–18.
25. Historian Dominic Sandbrook traces left-wing nostalgia back as far as it will go and points out the myopia at its core. He writes that even the much-eulogised Peasants Revolt involved the killing of foreigners on the streets.
26. 'Jeremy Corbyn Warned of "European Empire" and Said EU Treaty Would Create "a Military Frankenstein"', Benjamin Kentish, *Independent*, February 2019.
27. Corbyn called for British products to be made on home soil again, post-Brexit, rather than by 'cheap foreign labour'. As he put it: 'What there wouldn't be [post-Brexit] is wholesale importation of underpaid workers from central Europe in order to destroy conditions, particularly in the construction industry. You prevent agencies recruiting wholescale workforces like that; you advertise for jobs in the locality first.'
28. 'Filmmaker Loach Wins Palme D'Or for Second Time', ITV, May 2016.
29. 'Should Britain Leave the European Union?' *New Internationalist*, May 2016.
30. Brexit: 'Ex-WTO Chief Pascal Lamy in "No Deal" Warning', Joseph D'Urso, BBC, March 2017.
31. 'EU Law is No Barrier to Labour's Economic Programme', Andy Tarrant and Andrea Biondi, *Renewal*, September 2017.

32. David Marquand predicted that, once outside Europe, Britain's pros-perity would 'depend, even more than it does now, on the competitiveness of her financial sector'. And just days before the refer-endum the French economic minister said Britain was headed for 'Guernseyfication'.

33. 'Labour: Now It's Kind of Blue', Allegra Stratton, *Guardian*, 2009.

34. 'Maurice Glasman: Why Should Labour Support the Undemocratic EU? The Case to Leave', LabourList, June 2016.

35. 'Family, Faith and Flag', Dominic Sandbrook, *New Statesman*, 2011.

36. 'Miliband Speech to Engage with Blue Labour Ideals', Patrick Win-tour, *Guardian*, April 2011.

37. 'The Conditions for Labour's Previous Successes are Falling Apart. Where Do We Go from Here?' Bridget Phillipson, *New Statesman*, November 2016.

38. 'Owen Jones on the Condition of Britain: Where is the Left's Trans-formative Programme?' Owen Jones, *New Statesman*, July 2014.

39. 'Thatcherism was a National Catastrophe That Still Poisons Us', *Independent*, Owen Jones, April 2013.

40. Corbyn proposed that we 're-industrialise' the north in his 2015 Lead-ership campaign.

41. Richard Angell made this point when reviewing a 2016 Party Political Broadcast by Labour: 'Optimists, not Miserablists, become Labour Prime Ministers.'

42. 'Back to the Future: Nostalgia Increases Optimism', Wing-Yee Cheung et al., *Personality and Social Psychology Bulletin*, 398, August 2013, pp. 1484–96.

43. *Broken Windows: The Police and Neighbourhood Safety*, George L. Kelling and James Q. Wilson, Wadsworth Publishing, 1982.

44. *Lady Chatterley's Lover*, D. H. Lawrence, Penguin Books, 1960, p. 5.

45. *A Shrinking Island: Modernism and National Culture in England*, Jed Esty, Princeton University Press, 2004, p. 49.

46. In *Lady Chatterley's Lover*, for example, a servant who educates herself is ridiculed as 'pining to be superior'. *Lady Chatterley's Lover*, p. 85.

47. *Lady Chatterley's Lover*, p. 148.

48. *The Politics of Cultural Despair: A Study in the Rise of the Germanic Ideology*, Fritz Richard Stern, University of California Press, 1961, p. xi.

49. One poll from before the 2016 Presidential election suggested that 22 per cent of Sanders supporters planned to vote Trump, with a further 18 per cent choosing Libertarian Gary Johnson.

50. 'Bernie Supporters Should Vote Trump because Hillary Will Reinforce Dynastic Globalism', Christopher Willard, *Federalist*, October 2016.

51. Christopher Achen and Larry Bartels report that Sanders's supporters were 'more pessimistic than Mrs Clinton's about "opportunity in America today for the average person to get ahead" and more likely to say that economic inequality had increased. However, they were less likely than Mrs Clinton's supporters to favour concrete policies that Mr Sanders has offered as remedies for these ills, including a higher minimum wage, increasing government spending on health care and an expansion of government services financed by higher taxes.'

52. This quote, used by Obama, was originally coined by Martin Luther King. In a 2016 outgoing essay, Obama made a similar point, arguing against a 'crude populism that promises a return to a past that is not possible to restore – and that, for most Americans, never existed at all'.

53. 'Analysis: The Curious Link between Prosperity and Pessimism', Peter Kellner, YouGov, November 2015.

54. 'The Most Important Thing, and It's Almost a Secret', Nicholas Kristof, *New York Times*, October 2015. See also Our World in Data.

55. 'Is the World Really Better than Ever?' Oliver Burkeman, *Guardian*, July 2017.

56. *The Future of Socialism*, Jonathan Cape, 1956, p. 405.

57. Polling found that 43 per cent of 2016 Corbyn backers agreed with the statement 'Gradual change is not enough; we need to smash the system', compared to 11 per cent of those supporting Owen Smith.

13. THE APPEAL OF THE GOLDEN ERA

1. 'Britain's Nostalgic Pessimism', Peter Kellner, YouGov, February 2012.

2. Research finds that 'Older adults show more emotionally gratifying memory distortion for past choices and autobiographical information than younger adults.' 'Ageing and Motivated Cognition: The Positivity Effect in Attention and Memory', Mara Mather and Laura L. Carstensen, *Trends in Cognitive Sciences*, 9, 10, October 2005 pp. 496–502.

3. Just 33 per cent of eighteen- to thirty-five-year-olds believe they've had a better life than their parents – compared to 41 per cent of thirty-six- to forty-nine-year-olds, 67 per cent of baby-boomers, and 81 per

cent or those over seventy. The controversial Momentum video 'They Just Don't Get It', which shows smug baby boomers mocking the plight of future generations, plays on precisely this anxiety.

4. This is Richard Wilkinson and Kate Pickett's argument in *The Spirit Level*. They identify a correlation between mistrust of others (which they see as innately bound to pessimism) and inequality. *The Spirit Level*, Allen Lane, 2009, pp. 55–6.

5. 'Shopkeepers at War', George Orwell, in *The Lion and the Unicorn*, Secker and Warburg, 1941.

6. Journalist John Harris attributes the rise of populism to 'ever-increasing complexity, and the diminishing returns it now creates'.

7. Erica Seifert's research pinpoints the early 1970s as the point when 'authenticity gained currency', with a growing expectation that 'public life would become more personal, speech patterns would become less formal and artificial [and] the structures of public debate would become reshaped'. *The Politics of Authenticity in Presidential Campaigns, 1976–2008*, Erica J. Seifert, McFarland & Co., 2020, p. 21.

8. Hillary Clinton was heavily criticised by one journalist for being 'super stilted, very cautious, very scared of the press, and being very calculated about how much of her real self she lets show'.

9. As Liam Byrne put it, Corbyn 'is the craft ale of the labour movement. He is authentic, he has got strong flavours, he is seen as something very different to the bland mediocrity of politics.'

10. 'Keeping It Real? Corbyn, Trump, Sanders and the Politics of Authenticity', Mathew Humphrey and Maiken Umbach, University of Nottingham, February 2016.

11. The proportion agreeing was almost four times lower in the richest country – the US (14 per cent) – than in the poorest, India (51 per cent). Only 19 per cent of Brits agreed. See 'Analysis: The Curious Link between Prosperity and Pessimism', Peter Kellner, YouGov, November 2015.

12. 'Chinese People are Most Likely to Feel the World is Getting Better', Will Dahlgreen, YouGov, 2016.

13. *An Inspector Calls*, Heinemann, 1947, pp. 6–7.

14. 'Steven Pinker's Book is a Comfort Blanket for the Smug', Andrew Brown, *Guardian*, November 2011.

15. The review claims that *The Better Angels* is 'a snow job', and that Pinker 'ignores the kind of violence that is built into the structure', by

overlooking 'the increasingly savage global class war of the 1 per cent against the other 99 per cent'.

16. *The Better Angels*, Penguin Putnam, 2011, p. 47.

17. Pinker writes that you cannot 'lump [inequality, poverty, climate change, and so on] together with rape and genocide ... It's not that these aren't bad things, but you can't write a coherent book on the topic of "bad things".'

18. 'My mood is not so much one of optimism as of gratitude ... As a scientist, I must be cautious of any mystic force or cosmic destiny that carries us ever upwards.' *The Better Angels*, p. 671.

19. *The Better Angels*, p. xxii.

20. 'Jeremy Corbyn's Supporters aren't Mad – They're Fleeing a Bankrupt New Labour', *Guardian*, Owen Jones, August 2015.

21. *The Establishment*, Penguin, 2014, p. 23.

22. *Look Back in Anger*, John Osborne, Faber, 1957, Act 3, Scene 1, p. 89.

23. William Wordsworth's Romantic poetry lauds figures like 'The Old Cumberland Beggar' who were authentic, connected to nature and untainted by modernity. In contemporary Britain, similarly, the story of gentrification in London – characterised by Dave Hill as 'The Grand Narrative' – is one of clinical luxury replacing the hearty communities of the past.

24. 'We No Longer Have the Luxury of Tradition', Russell Brand, *New Statesman*, October 2013.

25. Brand also attacks the 'all-encompassing total corruption of our political agencies'. Positive values, he says, have been 'aborted and replaced with nihilistic narratives of individualism'.

26. Yeats was an Irish nationalist, less on ideological grounds than on aesthetic ones. His poems about figures from Irish folklore were used as propaganda during the Easter Uprising in 1916 (an event which Yeats hoped would restore the country's tradition of heroic sacrifice). As well as leading him to take pleasure in the aesthetic of political violence in poems like 'The Second Coming', and to search for what he called the 'great moment', it bred a sympathy with feudalism (*Essays and Introductions*, Springer, 1961, pp. 250–60).

27. *Essays and Introductions*, p. 259.

28. *Explorations*, Macmillan, 1962, p. 392.

29. *Essays and Introductions*, p. 210.

30. Having seen the reality of political violence, Yeats admitted, in 'Easter 1916', that 'Too long a sacrifice, Can make a stone of the heart.'

14. THE CASE AGAINST THE GOLDEN ERA
(GLOBAL ECONOMY)

1. The average number of hours worked annually by the average UK worker has fallen from over 2,000 throughout the 1950s to around 1,650 hours today. Child labour fell by over a third between 2000 and 2012. The percentage of the global population living in extreme poverty has reduced by two thirds since the start of the 1980s. Smoking has halved. There are many less war deaths. There are many more fully functioning democracies, and the global nuclear stockpile is around a fifth of what it was a few decades ago. Life expectancy in developed countries increased by around four years over the course of the 1990s and 2000 – and by twice that in the least-developed places. In the UK recycling has increased massively and homophobia has halved since the early 1980s.

2. Janan Ganesh points out that populists 'credit elites with an omnipotence that makes them culpable for all failures . . . but gradual overall enrichment, falling crime and international peace are all fatherless achievements somehow'.

3. Increasingly, 'neoliberalism' is a 'buzz-word'. Academics complain that the term has 'become a means of identifying a seemingly ubiquitous set of market-orientated policies as being largely responsible for a wide range of social, political, ecological and economic problems. The term is frequently used somewhat indiscriminately and quite pejoratively to mean anything "bad" . . . Such lack of specificity reduces its capacity as an analytic frame.' *The Handbook of Neoliberalism*, (eds.) Simon Springer, Kean Birch and Julie MacLeavy, Routledge, 2016, p. 2.

4. Professor Colin Talbot argues that the true definition of 'neoliberalism' would mean a 'reversion to roughly what the state did in . . . the nineteenth century'. It would feature a 'Night Watchman' government, 'providing for property rights, contracts, markets and personal and national security and not much else'.

5. 'New Labour's Domestic Policies: Neoliberal, Social Democratic or a Unique Blend?', Glen O'Hara, Institute for Global Change, November 2018.

6. As has been pointed out, the individuals seen as exemplifying neoliberalism – i.e. the version put forward in Charles Peters's 1982 'Neoliberal Manifesto' – are not conservatives in the mould of Reagan. 'Peters's neoliberals are liberals (in the US sense of the word) who

have dropped their prejudices in favor of unions and big government and against markets and the military.'

7. Extracts from Gordon Brown's 2017 book describe efforts 'to swim against the neoliberal tide'. This was taken by some as a validation of the term, ignoring the fact that Brown was clearly using it to describe a set of unavoidable conditions, not an 'ideology'.

8. This took place in a Twitter exchange with Hugo Rifkind.

9. For instance, one *Guardian* long read defines neoliberalism as a 'bloodless paragon of efficiency'.

10. An example here is George Monbiot's frequent inclusion of climate change in the 'neoliberal' canon, despite our desire and ability to tackle it improving steadily in recent decades.

11. This in turn causes us to shy away from the methods which might help to tame globalisation. The 'Lexit' argument, for instance, with its suspicion that the EU is a 'neoliberal club', prevents us from seeing that pan-European approaches are the best way of reducing inequalities.

12. Hitchens has made this claim both in interviews and in print, writing, for example, that 'Labour has a real lefty . . . so can we have proper conservatives?'

13. Dominic Sandbrook, in an RSA lecture, reminds us that the 1970s was a time where coal, rail, telecoms, gas, electricity and transport were nationalised, but also one where Alf Garnett told TV audiences that we should 'put the coons down the pits'.

14. Richard Carr argues that the populist left's stance is based on a paradox between openness and closedness: a pretence that we can be socially open but economically closed. This was demonstrated by the surprise – and disappointment – among some supporters of Corbyn when it comes to the Labour leadership's anti-migration proposals.

15. Labour's protectionist policies under Corbyn resulted in opposition to freedom of movement, with the 2017 manifesto representing Labour's most anti-immigrant policy in a generation. Many left populists backed this, with Paul Mason initially advocating a '10-year, temporary suspension'.

16. As left-wing Democrat and historian Allan Lichtman points out, protectionism would harm those on low incomes and make it much harder to deal multilaterally with climate change. Meanwhile, Paul Krugman, while sceptical about the need for ever more free trade, presents a realistic forecast of what reversing it involves in the US: 'If Sanders were to make it to the White House, he would find it very hard to do anything much about globalization – not because it's

NOTES

technically or economically impossible, but because the moment he looked into actually tearing up existing trade agreements the diplomatic, foreign-policy costs would be overwhelmingly obvious. In this, as in many other things, Sanders currently benefits from the luxury of irresponsibility.'

17. The countries which have embraced true socialist isolationism – like North Korea or Cuba – are also countries with high levels of social conservatism, poorly travelled populations and inadequate civil rights.

18. As the academic Jan Rovny writes, 'transnationalism effectively shatters the old electoral coalition of the left. The naturally protectionist workers are pulled away from the naturally cosmopolitan intellectuals.'

19. Macron was a socially liberal, pro-EU, pro-migrant, free-trade global capitalist, whereas Le Pen was Eurosceptic, statist and nativist.

20. Research by Bright Blue shows the markedly different attitude of subsets of Tory voters. 'A Balanced Centre-right Agenda on Immigration: Understanding How Conservative Voters Think about Immigration', Ryan Shorthouse and David Kirkby, Bright Blue, 2015.

21. Labour, for example, finds its broad church divided: between cosmopolitans and communitarians; between liberals and authoritarians; between supporters and opponents of immigration; between Remain- and Leave-leaning voters, and so on. As Will Brett puts it, 'The new social cleavage runs clean through [Labour].' YouGov polling corroborates this, revealing a divide between those who want to see Labour as a socially conservative 'workers' party' and those who want to see Labour become a liberal-left party based on worldwide equality.

22. Forty years ago, in a world less interconnected than today's, the mobility of wealth was already an issue. Labour spent years attempting, unsuccessfully, to introduce a wealth tax unilaterally. Howard Glennerster, the author of an LSE study into why it failed, asked: 'How far is any radical change in the pattern of economic rewards feasible in a modern mobile interdependent economy? The archives show how much this exercised the Treasury in 1974, long before capital, human and financial, was as mobile as it is today.' Indeed, a few years later, in 1981, French President François Mitterrand saw several billion dollars leave the French economy when he attempted to introduce a wealth tax. Evidence from 2006 France and 2009 Britain suggests that even modest tax increases can lead to departures.

23. The UK corporation tax main rate fell from 28 per cent in 2010 to 19 per cent by 2017. It had previously fallen from 40–50 per cent in the

mid-1960s to 31 per cent in the mid-1990s. Most OECD countries in Europe have corporation tax rates of 20–25 per cent. These rates have fallen dramatically since the early 2000s.

24. A May 2017 Robert Peston article summed up this dilemma, writing that the question would be 'whether Labour's programme would in practice harm the private sector, which ultimately pays for our public services, and lead to a significant increase in the indebtedness of a relatively highly indebted state, well beyond what Labour forecasts, believes and hopes'.

25. The EU was already doing this in some cases, such as with its Anti-Tax Avoidance Directive, AIFMD regulations, plans for an EU-wide transaction tax and the Regional Development Fund.

26. Tony Blair made the point as he left office, and as early as 2005 the 'drawbridge up versus drawbridge down' distinction was proposed.

27. In 2013 data showed that British eighteen- to twenty-four-year-olds are the most socially and economically liberal generation there has been.

28. If we look at two of the most 'centrist' Labour figures, Tony Blair and David Miliband, we see a desire to bend the interconnected world towards social democratic values. Blair champions interconnectedness in addressing climate change and creating regulatory frameworks for global finance. He points out that Brexit 'will not mean more money for the NHS, but less . . . It will not mean more protection for workers, but less.' Meanwhile, David Miliband argues that the EU is a potential vehicle to 'protect citizens from the risk of market excess'.

29. Thomas Piketty makes this argument more forcefully and specifically, and has long advocated a progressive global wealth tax.

30. Eduardo Porter, for instance, uses the analogy of footballers' pay to describe the 'superstar effect' – where globalisation increases the scale at which success accumulates: 'Ronaldo is not better then Pelé. He makes more money because his talent is broadcast to more people.'

31. Marx and Engels, for instance, praised the Industrial Revolution for having 'rescued a considerable part of the population from the idiocy of rural life'. *The Communist Manifesto*, Marx and Engels, Penguin, 1967, p. 84.

32. Milanović adds that 'there are similarities to the first upswing of the Kuznets Wave in the past, because you can actually argue that it was the result of the Industrial Revolution. The bottom line is that technological revolutions lead to an increase in inequality.'

33. Some may note that there are actually four technological revolutions – not two. The World Economic Forum describes the key dates as: 1784 for steam, water and mechanical production; 1870 for division of labour and mass production; 1969 for electronics, IT and automated production; and the present day for intelligent robotics. But from the point of view of my argument, 1870 and 1969 seem like the key turning points, as these most obviously changed the scale at which capitalism operates.

34. *The Future of Socialism*, Jonathan Cape, 1956, pp. 87–8.

35. For instance, in 1970 countries were arranged into two basic groups – rich and poor. They have gradually merged since this point. See Our World in Data.

36. Milanović says that we're moving towards a situation where both the US and China are less internally equal than they once were – but where the differences in wealth between the two are smaller.

37. 'Taxation and the International Mobility of Inventors', Ufuk Akcigit, Salomé Baslandze and Stefanie Stantcheva, NBER Working Paper No. 21024, issued in March 2015, revised in October 2015.

38. A 2011 qualitative study of high earners' attitudes, produced for the High Pay Commission, describes high earners' ability to compare themselves with equivalents in other countries. For these individuals there is 'a worldwide "culture of plenty"' and a corresponding view that to 'keep the UK professionally competitive', salary packages have to match those around the world.

39. In focus groups with 2015 Labour–UKIP swing voters, findings concluded that local people ostensibly 'welcomed immigrants who worked'. Welfare rather than immigration was described as 'the main target of their anger', with talk of 'feckless UK youngsters' stirring up more anger than that of immigrants from abroad.

40. 'Don't blame poverty. Africa knows poverty. UK has free education, healthcare, school meals, benefits,' the tweet read. 'Starving malnourished children dying in Somalian refugee camps is something to riot about. Not getting a free 42inch Plasma TV,' wrote another. A third suggested we should 'round those kids up and put them on a plane to Africa to see what real deprivation is'.

41. Older people, for instance, are more hostile to international aid but often more progressive on welfare. Demos research with older, 'left behind' voters reflected this, with many arguing that 'charity begins at home'. 'It's 0.7 per cent of the GDP, so you know that could be put to the NHS,' said one respondent.

42. Work by Lancaster University takes this back as far as 1801, showing a five-fold increase, up until 1951, in the proportion of people in larger cities. It also reveals a significant increase, after 1920, in how many kilometres people migrated from their home towns. 'Migration and Mobility in Britain from the Eighteenth to Twentieth Centuries', Colin G. Pooley and Jean Turnbull, *Local Population Studies*, 57, autumn 1996, pp. 50–71.

43. There were no cities with more than 10 million people at the end of the Second World War, but there will be forty-one by 2030. Overall population growth contributes to this. But larger settlements are, as a proportion of the population, growing quicker than smaller ones. Globally, the number of urban dwellers surpassed the number of rural dwellers for the first time in 2007. See 'World Urbanization Prospects', United Nations, New York, 2014, pp. 7–13.

44. For instance, in 2017 London Mayor Sadiq Khan came out against an international financial transaction tax. Khan is on the left of Labour, yet called the idea 'madness' that would threaten 'growth and jobs'. Even a politician as progressive as Khan will struggle to unilaterally address regional inequality while so many of his constituents benefit from it.

45. The meat industry left Chicago thanks to advances in transport and refrigeration technology. The car industry left Detroit due to the attractiveness of countries where production was cheaper and wages were lower.

46. Will Jennings and Gerry Stoker write that 'In cosmopolitan areas we find an England that is global in outlook; relatively positive about the EU; pro-immigration; comfortable with more rights and respect for women, ethnic communities and gays and lesbians; and generally future-oriented.'

47. Research prior to the 2016 US election revealed a significant relationship between how far people had moved from home and their voting intentions. The more transient people were, the more likely they were to vote Clinton.

48. Brexit is described by IPPR as a rejection of the 'networked world'. This was evident right down to the brands that Remain and Leave voters preferred, with the former citing LinkedIn, the London Underground and Airbnb.

49. David Goodhart, *The Road to Somewhere: The Populist Revolt and the Future of Politics*, Chapter Two: 'Anywheres and Somewheres', Oxford University Press, 2017.

50. Piketty's essay on the 'Brahmin Left versus the Merchant Right' argues against both the pro- and anti-globalisation positions taken by leftists (i.e. against the approaches of both Blair and Corbyn). It champions an 'egalitarian-internationalist' platform, but acknowledges the compromises required to achieve this, when operating in a situation of 'multi-dimensional inequality'.

51. Tony Hockley writes that 'The same old tactics of skewed resource allocation in state grants and heavy-handed intervention will not improve the feelings of inadequate self-determination and threatened social identities.'

52. Leave-voting Wales received £2.4 billion from the EU in the 2014–20 funding cycle. A *Guardian* profile of Ebbw Vale found that the town – where 62 per cent voted Leave – was effectively kept alive by EU funding following a steelworks closure. Other analyses confirm that the regions most vulnerable to Brexit are also those which voted most heavily for Leave.

53. A trivial example, highlighted in the 2016 Casey Review, was a council's renaming of a Christmas tree as a 'festive tree' so as not to offend minorities. Minor decisions like this, often more than substantive policies, alienate those who have been 'left behind'.

54. 'Corbyn's Sect betray Labour's Proud Foreign Policy Tradition', John Bew, CapX, May 2017.

55. 'Q&A on the Entry into Force of the Anti-Tax Avoidance Directive. European Commission Fact Sheet', December 2018. See also Macron's proposed EU-wide corporation tax.

15. THE CASE AGAINST THE GOLDEN ERA CONTINUED (POLITICS)

1. The letter argued that the comparison between Jeremy Corbyn and Michael Foot is 'misleading because ... policies that would in 1981 have seemed "loony right" are now viewed as mainstream, and formerly social-democrat positions are commonly reviled as somehow Marxist'.

2. As Luke Akehurst points out, if the Corbyn movement is just 'social democratic "Old Labour", [then] why did Benn and Corbyn and McDonnell attack Wilson and Callaghan so much in the 1970s? ... Why do they look for overseas models in authoritarian Venezuela and Cuba, not social democratic Sweden and Denmark?'

3. Owen Jones argues that 'Advocates of privatisation, deregulation, lower taxes on the rich and anti-trade unionism have dramatically shifted the window . . . over the last generation or so.'
4. Winston Churchill, speech to the Peel Commission, 1937.
5. *This Boy*, Bantam, 2013, pp. 89–94.
6. *The Future of Socialism*, Jonathan Cape, 1956, pp. 402–8.
7. Reflecting on his legacy, Blair said that 'One of the things that I think is good about the country today is that there are not – between the main political parties, at any rate – any real rows about race or sexuality; things that . . . in the 1970s and 1980s were very prominent political issues.'
8. The list of New Labour achievements is familiar, and we will avoid going into it at length. Detailed appraisals come in the form of *The Verdict* by Polly Toynbee and David Walker, or reviews by think tanks such as the JRF and IPPR. Shorter checklists include the Progress 'Bedtime' edition (and their '100 list').
9. Anthony Seldon, *Blair's Britain, 1997–2007*, Cambridge University Press, p. 552.
10. 'A war of the generations is not a solution – hope is', Owen Jones, *Guardian*, March 2016.
11. 'There was a genuine preoccupation with increasing social justice [within the New Labour governments] – a notion alien to Margaret Thatcher, Keith Joseph and their guru Milton Friedman,' writes New Labour supporter and architect of the 'third way' Anthony Giddens.
12. If we're to use the size of the public sector as a proportion of GDP as our metric, for example, one analyst concludes that 1997–2010 Labour was the most 'socialist' ever.
13. See, for further examples, the Employee Relations Act, the flattening of the Gini-coefficient, the big redistributions from the richest 10 per cent to the poorest, the two-thirds reduction in rough sleeping and, towards the end of Labour's tenure, increases in the top rate of tax and legal duties to tackle inequality.
14. Osborne's claim came in 2007, and Cameron's statements on poverty were a year before: 'I want this message to go out loud and clear – the Conservative Party recognises, will measure and will act on relative poverty.' The then Tory leader also repeatedly emphasised that the NHS was safe in his hands. Indeed, although many supporting services were cut thanks to austerity, school spending by 2015 remained 50 per cent up on levels at the end of the Major premiership, thanks in some part to the ringfencing of education.

15. Writing in 2007, Cameron accused grammar-school supporters of 'clinging on to outdated mantras that bear no relation to the reality of life'.

16. 'A Poverty of Information: Assessing the Government's New Child Poverty Focus and Future Trends', David Finch, Resolution Foundation, October 2015.

17. Hope Not Hate's Nick Lowles predicted that a Hard Brexit would offer 'fertile ground for right-wing demagogues'.

18. This obviously applies to Corbyn's siege-economy policies, but also to the Tories'. In the wake of Brexit, Theresa May implied that she would shift to the right from a social and internationalist perspective – on aid, for example – and to the left when it came to the economy.

19. 'Jeremy Corbyn is No Interloper – He is Part of Labour's DNA', Geoffrey M. Hodgson, New Politics blog, May 2016.

20. 'The Values Ratchet', George Monbiot, June 2014.

21. Cameron's claim, made shortly before becoming the Conservative leader, is used by Owen Jones as evidence that Blair did not represent a 'real alternative' to Thatcherism.

22. Blair himself makes this point: 'As a result [of Labour being in office for thirteen years] the Tories, to win, had to start borrowing from us, not [us] from them. That is a sign of our success.'

23. It is surely no coincidence that Labour prime ministers tend to age worse in the public memory than their Tory equivalents. Labour's failure to defend its record damaged its chances in 2015, and each of the most recent three Labour leaders – Brown, Miliband and Corbyn – have got mileage out of condemning their predecessors. Likewise, in the US Obama is now attacked by left-wingers for 'passing up' the chance to help the working classes and for proving 'not capable of the most basic task: keeping black children alive'.

24. Even Margaret Thatcher promised from opposition to expand nursery education, build more polytechnics and raise the school-leaving age – only becoming a fully-fledged ideologue while in power.

25. 'Olympic Britain: Social and Economic Change since the 1908 and 1948 London Games', Gavin Thompson et al., House of Commons Library, p. 153. See also the Life Peerages Act and the removal of hereditary peers on the parliament.uk website.

26. 'Leading People 2016: The Educational Backgrounds of the UK Professional Elite', Dr Philip Kirby, Sutton Trust, February 2016.

27. See *Balfour*, p. 78.

28. As late as 1949, the nation's most prominent poet, T. S. Eliot, stated that 'In our headlong rush to educate everybody, we are lowering our

standards, and . . . [making] ready the ground upon which the barbarian nomads of the future will encamp in the mechanised caravan.'

29. Education Secretary Edward Boyle, a liberal Conservative, wrote that '[working-class children's] potentialities are no less real, and of no less importance . . . The essential point is that all children should have an equal opportunity . . . of developing their talents and abilities.' *Newsom Report*, p. iv. The 'Crosland Circular' was distributed by the Labour government two years later, advocating the phasing out of grammar schools.

30. This is demonstrated by policies to level the playing field: the Future Jobs Fund, the Education Maintenance Allowance, Child Trust Funds, family and working tax credits, access courses, the Child Poverty Act, the learning and skills council, and so on. Even tuition fees, which were controversial on the left, were motivated by evidence that it was more important for social mobility to invest in early years.

31. OFFA, the new 'access regulator', looked into ways of helping state-educated pupils with lower grades to be accepted. In response, a joint statement by independent schools called for a process which was 'fair, objective, transparent and consistently applied'. Hodge, on the other hand, said it should be 'merit, not class and background, that determine who gets a place at the university'.

32. In 2015 Cameron centred his conference speech on the equal opportunities theme: 'Our belief is in equality of opportunity . . . Not everyone ending up with the same exam results, the same salary, the same house – but everyone having the same shot at them.'

33. A 2012 study by Oxford sociologist John Goldthorpe distinguishes between 'absolute' and 'relative' social mobility – the former being 'the simple percentage of individuals who are found in the same or in a different class to that in which they originated' and the latter being 'the relative chances of individuals starting in two different classes of origin ending up in two different classes of destination'. He said that the three decades after the war had seen an increase in absolute mobility, but not in relative mobility. As Phil Collins puts it, 'social mobility in Britain has been a case of more room being found at the top' – as opposed to people from poorer backgrounds replacing those from richer ones.

34. Tim Wigmore writes that 'because the number of the best jobs is finite, the lack of downward social mobility is a roadblock to the upward social mobility beloved by all'.

35. 'Understanding – and Misunderstanding – Social Mobility in Britain', John Goldthorpe, Oxford Institute of Social Policy and Nuffield College, University of Oxford, 2012, p. 19. Meanwhile, Richard Wilkinson and Kate Pickett point out how strong the correlation between economic equality and social mobility is (*The Spirit Level*, Allen Lane, 2009, pp. 157–72).

36. 'Living Standards, Poverty and Inequality in the UK', Jonathan Cribb et al., IFS Report R81, 2013.

37. 'Why Did the Post-war Welfare State Fail to Prevent the Growth of Inequality?' Howard Glennerster, Institute of Historical Research, 2008.

38. Thatcher famously made this argument in 1990, claiming that socialists were happy to make the poor poorer in order to stop the rich from getting richer.

39. The LSE's Howard Glennerster concludes that 'Technological change and the UK's dependence on international trade were to powerfully widen the distribution of earned income and this was very difficult [for Labour] to reverse.' He adds that 'welfare state benefits in cash and kind have significantly cushioned the impact of both the big structural changes that took place in the British economy in the 1980s and have had to work harder to contain the growing income inequality that took place afterwards.'

40. 'What Do People Think about Government Action?' blog by the Equality Trust. Figures based on NatCen data collected since 1983. Other polling corroborates this. For instance, the public oppose a 'maximum wage', according to YouGov – even if it's as high as £1 million a year.

41. There is a connection of sorts between high inequality and a desire to see it reduced. But, as the academic Márton Medgyesi explains, the correlation is minimal: 'A huge increase is needed in the Gini index to modify societal judgment about the level of inequality to a significant extent.' 'Increasing Income Inequality and Attitudes to Inequality: A Cohort Perspective', Márton Medgyesi, GINI Discussion Paper 94, August 2013, pp. 15–17.

42. Stephen Bush puts Labour's improved result in 2017 down to 'the person sleeping rough in every alcove around the conference centre late at night' – i.e. the visibility of poverty at the bottom. He adds that it's no coincidence that 'the demand for more spending started to tail off once the Blair government had got us to the European average in health and education'.

NOTES

43. 'There is no separate equality foundation. People don't crave equality for its own sake.' *The Righteous Mind*, p. 211. See also 'Why People Prefer Unequal Societies', Christina Starmans, Mark Sheskin and Paul Bloom, Department of Psychology, Yale University, 2017.

44. From behind a 'veil of ignorance', research suggested, people would 'maximiz[e] the average with a floor constraint'. 'Choices of Principles of Distributive Justice in Experimental Groups', Norman Frohlich, Joe A. Oppenheimer and Cheryl L. Eavey, *American Journal of Political Science*, 31, 3, 1987, pp. 606–36.

45. Branko Milanovič, for example, describes inequality as 'a totally new topic [in the early 2000s], entirely ignored in economics'. According to some analysis, the use of the word 'inequality' in writing trebled between 1950 and the early 2000s.

46. Similarly, the IMF's Christine Lagarde argued strongly for the need to tackle inequality in 2015, marking a significant step.

47. Piketty says: 'The sharp reduction in income inequality that we observe in almost all the rich countries between 1914 and 1945 was due above all to the world wars and the violent economic and political shocks they entailed (especially for people with large fortunes).' He concludes 'We are now emerging from this exceptional period.' *Capital in the Twenty-first Century*, Harvard University Press, 2014, pp. 15 and 402.

48. 'Coronavirus: Jeremy Corbyn Says He was Proved "Right" on Public Spending', BBC, March 2020.

49. The wedding was condemned in Britain by both Church and state, with the Secretary of State for Commonwealth Relations writing of the 'difficult problem it threw up'.

50. 'Statistics on Race and the Criminal Justice System 2010: A Ministry of Justice Publication under Section 95 of the Criminal Justice Act 1991', October 2011, p. 11.

51. BME groups remain under-represented in senior management and in parliament – with black students less likely to go to top universities and BME graduates liable to earn 24 per cent less.

52. Corbyn's 2016 speech 'Five Ills of Twenty-first-century Britain' set out two of the most pressing contemporary problems as prejudice and discrimination – the implication being that these things had become more severe since Beveridge initially set out his 'five ills' in 1942.

53. Racism roughly halved in the thirty years from 1983 to 2013, for instance. And findings show a big shift towards liberal values in the wider population during the 1990s.

54. This is the reverse of the post-war years, which had more upward mobility but deeper class distinctions. David Lodge's introduction to *Lucky Jim* explains that 'To many young people who grew up in the post-war period, and benefited from the 1944 Education Act . . . the old pre-war upper classes still maintained their privileged position because they commanded the social and cultural high ground.'

55. The London housing campaigner Anna Minton, for example, refers to the 'social cleansing' of the capital by elites.

56. For instance, protesters staged a Black Lives Matter demonstration on the runway at City Airport in 2016, on the basis that climate change is the consequence of deliberate racism. As the events of 2020 proved, Black Lives Matter campaigns are vital in raising the profile of the overt and covert institutional racism that continues to exist. But it is important to distinguish between those issues that are the result of active, wilful discrimination and those that are not.

57. Max Hastings wrote in the *Daily Mail* that 'Those at the bottom of [contemporary] society behave no better than their forebears, but the welfare state has relieved them from hunger and real want. When social surveys speak of "deprivation" and "poverty", this is entirely relative.'

58. The *Guardian*'s Gary Younge argued that: 'This tinder in the box was lit at least as much by the long arm of the law as the invisible hand of the market.' He suggested that the riots should be categorised alongside the Arab Spring.

59. 'I don't think the producers take a position at all. They just hope for a few laughs and maybe the odd flood of tears,' wrote Rachel Cooke, in reviewing the show.

60. Often, doing this leads us to miss the real, structural issues. As Stephen Bush points out, 'The biggest educational gap is between children in the first year of compulsory education – and in most cases, it is one which is never closed . . . But the truth is that fixing this is expensive and in some cases politically difficult, where it is neither expensive or politically difficult to say Oxbridge could do more, although of course they should.'

16. THE CASE AGAINST THE GOLDEN ERA CONTINUED (PSYCHOLOGY)

1. Left-wing academic Jeremy Gilbert describes how 'neoliberalism' provided a 'convenient set of discursive tools' for responding to the 'rising tide of democratic demands'.

2. George Monbiot's basic analysis is that Margaret Thatcher changed the country's 'soul' and that no one has had the courage to change it back: 'values and baselines keep shifting, and what seemed intolerable before becomes unremarkable today. Instead of challenging the new values, [New Labour] adjusted . . . When a party reinforces conservative values and conservative ideas . . . what outcome does it expect, other than a shift towards conservatism?'

3. This is based on a model developed by Common Cause foundation, which argues that social change must be framed in terms of 'compassionate' values: 'selling people green behaviours and products on the basis of appeals to status, image, and money values' will not change attitudes, they claim, and can be 'corrosive'. Rather, you should frame it as a social good in itself.

4. Although the model is not bound by demographics – there are many with groupish values in social grade AB, for instance – values do correlate with affluence and education. Populations are generally moving towards post-material values across all classes, with the highest social grades often making this transition quickest. 'The Myth of Deconsolidation: Rising Liberalism and the Populist Reaction', Christian Welzel and Amy Alexander, *Journal of Democracy*, March 2017, p. 11.

5. 'The New Electorate', Nick Pecorelli, Institute for Public Policy Research, 2013, p. 19. Meanwhile, Christian Welzel describes how, over time, 'fading existential pressures' make people 'prioritize freedom over security, autonomy over authority, diversity over uniformity, and creativity over discipline'. *Freedom Rising: Human Empowerment and the Quest for Emancipation*, Chritian Welzel, Cambridge University Press, 2013, p. xxiii.

6. The 1968 Ford machinists strike saw a bitter struggle for women to be paid the same as men. The strikers' male counterparts – and the male-dominated unions representing them – were in many cases obstructive in the battle for equal pay, their groupishness extending to gender as well as to class. Other examples include the 1972 Mansfield hosiery strike, the 1974 Imperial Typewriters dispute and the 1977 Grunwick dispute.

7. Following a visit to a centre for young, working-class people starting businesses, journalist Jason Beattie reflects on the attitudes of what he calls the 'Uber generation': 'It is more fluid, beholden to neither the state nor past ideologies . . . They will care little who provides their schools or collects their taxes, still less whether that service is provided by staff who are unionised or wedded to particular ideology.'

8. The think tank British Future notes that hostility to interracial marriage has fallen by 20 per cent since 1993. *How to Talk about Immigration*, Sunder Katwala, Steve Ballinger and Matthew Rhodes, British Future, 2014, pp. 52–5.

9. 'Social Attitudes of Young People: A Horizon-scanning Research Paper by the Social Attitudes of Young People Community of Interest', HM Government, December 2014, p. 8.

10. A TUC report into Britain's 'young core workers' – that is, working non-graduates in their twenties – finds that they are 'status-driven and optimistic – and less loyal to causes or traditions'. Their value systems are individualistic – in both progressive and non-progressive ways. *Living for the Weekend*, TUC, 2016, pp. 29–32.

11. This helps to explain Labour's curious performance in the 2017 General Election – winning post-materialist university towns like Canterbury but losing heartlands like Mansfield. The 2017 result was 'simultaneously Labour's highest middle class support since 1979, and the Conservatives' best score among C2DEs since then', according to the Chief Executive of MORI, Ben Page. The 2019 result was, of course, the savage denouement of this process – especially when it comes to the C2DE vote.

12. Lampton says in the novel: 'The salary I'd been so pleased about, an increase from Grade 9 to Grade 10, would seem a pittance to him. The suit in which I fancied myself so much – my best suit – would seem cheap and nasty to him . . . That was the most local government had to offer me; it wasn't enough.' *Room at the Top*, Eyre and Spottiswoode, 1957, p. 29.

13. *Room at the Top*, p. 85.

14. *Room at the Top*, pp. 94–5.

15. *Room at the Top*, p. 197.

16. *Saturday Night and Sunday Morning*, W. H. Allen & Co., 1951, p. 35.

17. This transition was common to many of the Angry Young Men authors. John Braine, Kingsley Amis, John Osborne and John Wain all began by attacking the conformity and deference of class-bound post-war communities but ultimately tacked towards individualism.

18. An interesting example here is the fact that the number of young people with driving licences has halved since 1994 – while the popularity of endurance sports has grown exponentially among the same cohort. As George Eaton points out, 'Just as the car's rise reflected an era of Conservative hegemony, so its fall marks the fracturing of the Thatcherite settlement.' The love of running and endurance sports, meanwhile,

offers 'temporary relief from the burdens of self-awareness', according to sociologists.

19. Geodemograpic experts highlight a turning point in the rise of post-materialism as the 1966 election, when Hampstead returned its first ever Labour MP: 'In an earlier era, it would have been unthinkable that Labour could win so middle class a seat ... During the 50 years since 1966 there has been a huge growth in the size, confidence and influence of this particular geodemographic group. A radical minority, once fabled for its eccentric habits ... has now come to dominate large swathes of inner London and significant parts of the high status Victorian inner suburbs of Britain's provincial cities.' Richard Webber and Roger Burrows, *The Predictive Postcode*, Sage, March 2018, pp. 141–63.

20. In *Saturday Night and Sunday Morning*, Arthur predicts that within five years we will have put a man on the moon, an idea he has read in the paper but which his father scoffs at. *Saturday Night and Sunday Morning*, p. 29.

21. The decline of racism in football is an example. This was partly due to intense campaigning. But it also came from rising number of foreign and non-white players as television money raised the status of the Premier League. Football is based on definable individual talent, with a single player able to win or lose you a game, and the illogicality of racism was steadily exposed.

22. John Gray writes that, despite being more divided and unequal, post-Thatcher Britain is also 'less fixed in its hierarchies and notably less ready to defer to authority'. TV characters in the 1980s like Harry Enfield's 'Tim Nice-But-Dim' showed the growing disdain for unearned privilege in Thatcher's Britain.

23. 'Changing Values among Western Publics from 1970 to 2006', Ronald Inglehart, *West European Politics*, 31, 1–2, 2008, pp. 130–46, p. 138.

24. 'Materialism and Post-Materialism', Max Roser, Our World in Data, 2017.

25. Pippa Norris identifies the rise of Trump as the consequence of a failure to do this, with 'a long-term generational shift threaten[ing] many traditionalists' cultural values'. She argues that the move towards post-materialist values has led to a gradual rise in authoritarian populism since the 1970s.

26. Bragg claims that this is the reason for the rise of the BNP in east London, and Momentum's Jon Lansman has said that Labour's loss of the working-class vote was the result of 'centrists' driving working-class voters away. Meanwhile, the RMT union endorsed Corbyn so as

to 'keep building a Labour Party that fights for the interests of the working class'. In response to this, Peter Kellner makes the following observation: 'Half a century ago, two thirds of voters were working-class ... Today, Britain has six million more middle-class than working-class electors. Of course the profile of Labour support has become more upmarket since 1997. That's because Britain's economic structure has changed, not because a disproportionate number of the party's historic core voters have rebelled.'

27. This is according to work by the academic Tim Bale and colleagues, and to leaked internal data showing Labour becoming more middle class under Corbyn. See also 'The Copeland Test: Labour's Core Vote', Theo Bertram, Medium, February 2017.

28. Accusations about croissants were according to Lord Watts. Elsewhere, Sarah Ditum has critiqued the 'heritage, heirloom leftism' of Corbyn's supporters, comparing his appeal to the 'retro pleasures you find at the farmers' market'.

29. The proportion doing ABC1 jobs surpassed the proportion doing C2DE jobs in 2000.

30. Thirty-four per cent of ABC1 voters see themselves as 'working class' and 26 per cent of C2DE voters consider themselves 'middle class', according to YouGov polling. Peter Kellner writes that 'As far as I know, no equivalent data exists for the Fifties or Sixties, but it is hard to believe that the equivalent cross-over figures would have been anything like as high.' Likewise, it is notable that the percentage identifying as working class has remained the same since 1983, despite the proportion doing working-class jobs shrinking significantly.

31. This group are, according to NatCen, 'in middle-class occupations [but] still think of themselves ... as working-class, and especially so if their family background was working-class or they have never been to university.' Politically speaking, they are not the same as downwardly mobile post-materialist graduates. Rather, their sense of working-class identity 'means that they are less libertarian and less pro-immigrant, but not necessarily more left-wing'. 'The New Electorate', p. 8.

32. The Tories led among ABC1 voters by 37 per cent back in 1974, for instance. This had dropped to 12 per cent by 2010. Labour's lead among DE voters fell from 38 per cent to 9 per cent over the same period.

33. 'Social Class: The Role of Class in Shaping Social Attitudes', Anthony Heath, Mike Savage and Nicki Senior, British Social Attitudes 30, 2013, p. 178.

34. Those with groupish values, for example, deserted Labour some time before the 2015 election – whereas those with more individualistic values were more likely to be the shy Tories who abandoned Ed Miliband on polling day. *The Cruddas Review* (Labour's Future), Independent Inquiry, One Nation Register, 2016, pp. 41–2.

35. Over successive generations the proportion who see British identity in purely civic terms has trebled, and the proportion who don't attach any meaning at all to national identity has risen from 2 per cent to 10 per cent. 'National Identity and Exploring Britishness', Zsolt Kiss and Alison Park, British Social Attitudes 31, NatCen, 2014, p. 7. Similar trends apply to church attendance and trade union membership.

36. Claudia Chwalisz points out that 'With almost everyone having access to the internet . . . the concept of unassailable authority is a notion of the past.' *Populist Signal*, Rowman and Littlefield International, 2015, p. 27.

37. A positive example of *innocence to awareness* can be seen in the residual racial tolerance that exists in parts of Britain where black American GIs were stationed in the Second World War. Contact with others increased understanding and tolerance in the long term. 'Shocking Racial Attitudes: Black G.I.s in Europe', David Schindler and Mark Westcott, CESifo, 6723, November 2017.

38. In 1986, for example, 38 per cent trusted the government to put the country first. By 2013 this was down to 17 per cent.

39. *More Sex, Lies and the Ballot Box*, Biteback Publishing, 2016, pp. 143–7.

40. Ipsos MORI finds that people overestimate the scale of countless problems – be it terrorism, the murder rate or the safety of vaccines. Elsewhere, Our World in Data reveals that trust and optimism have fallen, despite education and democracy being in the ascendant. These things are, in a sense, linked: a more informed and transparent society is a more sceptical one.

41. Other studies find that evaluations of issues remain the same, even as standards change. 'Most of the people in the 1850s who thought slavery was an abomination would have rejected the idea of inter-racial marriage. Wife beating wasn't considered a violent crime in just the very recent past. What racism and sexism mean has changed over time. Are these examples of concept creep or progress? . . . [The trick is to] not be fooled into thinking that progress hasn't been made just because our identifications have changed.' 'Why Sexism and Racism Never Diminish – Even When Everyone Becomes Less Sexist and Racist', Alex Tabarrok, *Marginal Revolution*, June 2018.

42. Overall crime rates fell for two decades from the early 1990s onwards – effectively halving. Yet two thirds continue to believe crime is rising. UCL research finds that perceptions and reality are barely related on this question: even when people acknowledge local reductions in crime, they assume their area is an anomaly.
43. *The Better Angels*, Penguin Putnam, 2011, p. xxii.
44. Amartya Sen, *The Idea of Justice*, The Belknap Press, 2009, pp. 164–5.

17. STRENGTHS, WEAKNESSES AND ADMISSIONS

1. A photo of the T-shirt was tweeted by J. K. Rowling. One Corbyn supporter wrote an impassioned defence of the wearer, based on the idea of Rowling as a Puppet Master figure, crushing dissent. 'Rowling – with net worth $1 billion – in front of her enormous Twitter following criticised this man, who is unlikely to have had access to such resources to promote his viewpoint. All he had was a T-shirt. But even that seemed too much.'
2. Tony Blair, for instance, intervened personally to stop the deselection of Corbyn in the early 2000s, and defended Diane Abbott when she sent her son to private school.
3. 'How We Uncovered Labour's Quinoa Quandary', Deborah Mattinson and Max Templer, *Total Politics*, September 2018.
4. Polly Billington writes that 'We are the Labour Party. We are for those who labour. This isn't just about electoral viability: it is a moral question about the role and purpose of our party.'
5. Ian Leslie pointed out in 2015 that the centre left did a poor job of persuading people to vote for their leadership candidates – telling Corbyn backers, for instance, to 'grow up'. By making the argument about interpretation and understanding, perhaps this book falls into the same trap.
6. 'Authority and the Individual', Bertrand Russell, Reith Lecture 1: Social Cohesion and Human Nature, transmitted on the Home Service, 24 December 1948.

18. CONCLUSIONS

1. In an article on the use of intellectual language by the left, campaigner Ellie Mae O'Hagan admits that the far left's fondness for 'functioning as a counter-culture' is 'intentional'. Although she concedes that this can lead to exclusivity, she also says that 'the whole point of the left is

to oppose the mainstream and shift society in a new direction, and in that respect we want to be different from the ordinary'.

2. Peter Hyman adds, 'If Labour could be in power for a serious amount of time, then the country would, we believed, change for good; not a burst of socialism for one time (if that), but changed institutions and values . . . for all time.' Similarly, Ben Jackson reminds us that the true aim of New Labour was to 'gain office and hold it for a decade or more, as opposed to the abrupt, short-lived Labour governments of the 1940s and 1960s/70s'.

3. W. B. Yeats, who we mentioned earlier, saw politics very much in this way. He believed that the idea of a common enemy could, regardless of its truth, serve the cause of Irish nationalism: 'I dreamed of enlarging Irish hate . . . All movements are held together more by what they hate than by what they love, for love separates and individualizes and quiets, but the nobler movements . . . hate great and lasting things.' *Essays and Introductions*, Springer, 1961, p. 259.

4. Tony Benn described his famous distinction as follows: 'I admire anyone who speaks their mind whatever their party and divide politicians of all parties into two categories: the signposts who point the way they think we should go and the weathercocks who haven't got an opinion, until they've studied the polls, focus groups and spin doctors.'

5. The truth is that a genuinely rational form of public decision-making is very hard. One study finds that, 'most of the time, the voters adopt issue positions, adjust their candidate perceptions, and invent facts to rationalize decisions they have already made'. 'It Feels Like We're Thinking: The Rationalizing Voter and Electoral Democracy', Christopher H. Achen, Department of Politics and Center for the Study of Democratic Politics, Princeton University, 2006.

6. *A Journey*, p. 274.

7. Tony Blair describes, during his premiership, 'a perpetual drumbeat of opposition from those who thought New Labour was a betrayal of our principles', but clarifies, 'I never resented that debate. I cheerfully engaged in it. I enjoyed it.'

8. One Labour councillor wrote, after the 2017 election: 'I went against my principles and voted for a man who I believe should be a pariah to the liberal-left . . . I was not anti-Corbyn just because I did not think he was electable. I was anti-Corbyn because I hated his politics.'

9. Steve Fielding argues that social democrats need to 'angrily reject the terms "centrist" or "moderate" '. 'For the Many Not the Few: Labour's

Social Democrats and Corbynism', Steven Fielding, Policy Network, June 2018, p. 1012.

10. We can see this in the *Sun* and *Mail*'s fondness for the language of betrayal and sabotage – and in the threats of deselection (and even death) aimed at anti-Brexit Conservatives.

11. Arch-populist Nigel Farage, for instance – whose approach the Conservative Party increasingly apes – has no internally consistent ideal, and no obvious view of what the world should look like post-Brexit. UKIP, the Brexit Party and Vote Leave more generally cannot articulate what they stand for, beyond hostility to a set of imagined enemies and fondness for a hallucinatory past.

12. 'Populist Cults like UKIP Always End in Failure', Daniel Finkelstein, *The Times*, March 2017.

13. 'Political Parables for Today', Robert B. Reich, *New York Times*, 1985.

Acknowledgements

I would like to give a massive thank you to Barry Colfer, Roger Liddle, Patrick Diamond and Josh Newlove at Policy Network, as well as to Dhara Snowden, Karen Ackermann and Sean McDonagh at Rowman & Littlefield, for all of the support in the initial publication and production of this book. I am hugely grateful to Nathan Yeowell at Progress, who was an invaluable support when it came to promoting and launching the first edition.

I would also like to thank Simon Winder, Eva Hodgkin and Richard Duguid at Penguin, who, along with Matthew Hutchinson and Liz Parsons, made possible the subsequent release of the book as *The Dark Knight and the Puppet Master*. A huge thank you also to my agent, Charlie Brotherstone.

I owe a great deal to Ned Pennant-Rea and Daniel Jackson, who gave thoughtful and constructive feedback on a sprawling first draft I showed them, and to others at The Campaign Company who fed back on the book.

Lastly, I want to acknowledge the support of my wife Charlotte and my parents Carol and Charles, who provided feedback and encouragement from beginning to end.

ALLEN LANE
an imprint of
PENGUIN BOOKS

Also Published

Martyn Rady, *The Habsburgs: The Rise and Fall of a World Power*

John Gooch, *Mussolini's War: Fascist Italy from Triumph to Collapse, 1935-1943*

Roger Scruton, *Wagner's Parsifal: The Music of Redemption*

Roberto Calasso, *The Celestial Hunter*

Benjamin R. Teitelbaum, *War for Eternity: The Return of Traditionalism and the Rise of the Populist Right*

Laurence C. Smith, *Rivers of Power: How a Natural Force Raised Kingdoms, Destroyed Civilizations, and Shapes Our World*

Sharon Moalem, *The Better Half: On the Genetic Superiority of Women*

Augustine Sedgwick, *Coffeeland: A History*

Daniel Todman, *Britain's War: A New World, 1942-1947*

Anatol Lieven, *Climate Change and the Nation State: The Realist Case*

Blake Gopnik, *Warhol: A Life as Art*

Malena and Beata Ernman, Svante and Greta Thunberg, *Our House is on Fire: Scenes of a Family and a Planet in Crisis*

Paolo Zellini, *The Mathematics of the Gods and the Algorithms of Men: A Cultural History*

Bari Weiss, *How to Fight Anti-Semitism*

Lucy Jones, *Losing Eden: Why Our Minds Need the Wild*

Brian Greene, *Until the End of Time: Mind, Matter, and Our Search for Meaning in an Evolving Universe*

Anastasia Nesvetailova and Ronen Palan, *Sabotage: The Business of Finance*

Albert Costa, *The Bilingual Brain: And What It Tells Us about the Science of Language*

Stanislas Dehaene, *How We Learn: The New Science of Education and the Brain*

Daniel Susskind, *A World Without Work: Technology, Automation and How We Should Respond*

John Tierney and Roy F. Baumeister, *The Power of Bad: And How to Overcome It*

Greta Thunberg, *No One Is Too Small to Make a Difference: Illustrated Edition*

Glenn Simpson and Peter Fritsch, *Crime in Progress: The Secret History of the Trump-Russia Investigation*

Abhijit V. Banerjee and Esther Duflo, *Good Economics for Hard Times: Better Answers to Our Biggest Problems*

Gaia Vince, *Transcendence: How Humans Evolved through Fire, Language, Beauty and Time*

Roderick Floud, *An Economic History of the English Garden*

Rana Foroohar, *Don't Be Evil: The Case Against Big Tech*

Ivan Krastev and Stephen Holmes, *The Light that Failed: A Reckoning*

Andrew Roberts, *Leadership in War: Lessons from Those Who Made History*

Alexander Watson, *The Fortress: The Great Siege of Przemysl*

Stuart Russell, *Human Compatible: AI and the Problem of Control*

Serhii Plokhy, *Forgotten Bastards of the Eastern Front: An Untold Story of World War II*

Dominic Sandbrook, *Who Dares Wins: Britain, 1979-1982*

Charles Moore, *Margaret Thatcher: The Authorized Biography, Volume Three: Herself Alone*

Thomas Penn, *The Brothers York: An English Tragedy*

David Abulafia, *The Boundless Sea: A Human History of the Oceans*

Anthony Aguirre, *Cosmological Koans: A Journey to the Heart of Physics*

Orlando Figes, *The Europeans: Three Lives and the Making of a Cosmopolitan Culture*

Naomi Klein, *On Fire: The Burning Case for a Green New Deal*

Anne Boyer, *The Undying: A Meditation on Modern Illness*

Benjamin Moser, *Sontag: Her Life*

Daniel Markovits, *The Meritocracy Trap*

Malcolm Gladwell, *Talking to Strangers: What We Should Know about the People We Don't Know*

Peter Hennessy, *Winds of Change: Britain in the Early Sixties*

John Sellars, *Lessons in Stoicism: What Ancient Philosophers Teach Us about How to Live*

Brendan Simms, *Hitler: Only the World Was Enough*

Hassan Damluji, *The Responsible Globalist: What Citizens of the World Can Learn from Nationalism*

Peter Gatrell, *The Unsettling of Europe: The Great Migration, 1945 to the Present*

Justin Marozzi, *Islamic Empires: Fifteen Cities that Define a Civilization*

Bruce Hood, *Possessed: Why We Want More Than We Need*

Susan Neiman, *Learning from the Germans: Confronting Race and the Memory of Evil*

Donald D. Hoffman, *The Case Against Reality: How Evolution Hid the Truth from Our Eyes*

Frank Close, *Trinity: The Treachery and Pursuit of the Most Dangerous Spy in History*

Richard M. Eaton, *India in the Persianate Age: 1000-1765*

Janet L. Nelson, *King and Emperor: A New Life of Charlemagne*

Philip Mansel, *King of the World: The Life of Louis XIV*

Donald Sassoon, *The Anxious Triumph: A Global History of Capitalism, 1860-1914*

Elliot Ackerman, *Places and Names: On War, Revolution and Returning*

Jonathan Aldred, *Licence to be Bad: How Economics Corrupted Us*

Johny Pitts, *Afropean: Notes from Black Europe*

Walt Odets, *Out of the Shadows: Reimagining Gay Men's Lives*

James Lovelock, *Novacene: The Coming Age of Hyperintelligence*

Mark B. Smith, *The Russia Anxiety: And How History Can Resolve It*

Stella Tillyard, *George IV: King in Waiting*

Jonathan Rée, *Witcraft: The Invention of Philosophy in English*

Jared Diamond, *Upheaval: How Nations Cope with Crisis and Change*

Emma Dabiri, *Don't Touch My Hair*

Srecko Horvat, *Poetry from the Future: Why a Global Liberation Movement Is Our Civilisation's Last Chance*

Paul Mason, *Clear Bright Future: A Radical Defence of the Human Being*

Remo H. Largo, *The Right Life: Human Individuality and its role in our development, health and happiness*

Joseph Stiglitz, *People, Power and Profits: Progressive Capitalism for an Age of Discontent*

David Brooks, *The Second Mountain*

Roberto Calasso, *The Unnamable Present*

Lee Smolin, *Einstein's Unfinished Revolution: The Search for What Lies Beyond the Quantum*

Clare Carlisle, *Philosopher of the Heart: The Restless Life of Søren Kierkegaard*

Nicci Gerrard, *What Dementia Teaches Us About Love*

Edward O. Wilson, *Genesis: On the Deep Origin of Societies*

John Barton, *A History of the Bible: The Book and its Faiths*

Carolyn Forché, *What You Have Heard is True: A Memoir of Witness and Resistance*

Elizabeth-Jane Burnett, *The Grassling*

Kate Brown, *Manual for Survival: A Chernobyl Guide to the Future*

Roderick Beaton, *Greece: Biography of a Modern Nation*

Matt Parker, *Humble Pi: A Comedy of Maths Errors*

Ruchir Sharma, *Democracy on the Road*

David Wallace-Wells, *The Uninhabitable Earth: A Story of the Future*

Randolph M. Nesse, *Good Reasons for Bad Feelings: Insights from the Frontier of Evolutionary Psychiatry*

Anand Giridharadas, *Winners Take All: The Elite Charade of Changing the World*

Richard Bassett, *Last Days in Old Europe: Triste '79, Vienna '85, Prague '89*

Paul Davies, *The Demon in the Machine: How Hidden Webs of Information Are Finally Solving the Mystery of Life*

Toby Green, *A Fistful of Shells: West Africa from the Rise of the Slave Trade to the Age of Revolution*

Paul Dolan, *Happy Ever After: Escaping the Myth of The Perfect Life*

Sunil Amrith, *Unruly Waters: How Mountain Rivers and Monsoons Have Shaped South Asia's History*

Christopher Harding, *Japan Story: In Search of a Nation, 1850 to the Present*

Timothy Day, *I Saw Eternity the Other Night: King's College, Cambridge, and an English Singing Style*

Richard Abels, *Aethelred the Unready: The Failed King*

Eric Kaufmann, *Whiteshift: Populism, Immigration and the Future of White Majorities*

Alan Greenspan and Adrian Wooldridge, *Capitalism in America: A History*

Philip Hensher, *The Penguin Book of the Contemporary British Short Story*

Paul Collier, *The Future of Capitalism: Facing the New Anxieties*

Andrew Roberts, *Churchill: Walking With Destiny*

Tim Flannery, *Europe: A Natural History*

T. M. Devine, *The Scottish Clearances: A History of the Dispossessed, 1600-1900*

Robert Plomin, *Blueprint: How DNA Makes Us Who We Are*

Michael Lewis, *The Fifth Risk: Undoing Democracy*

Diarmaid MacCulloch, *Thomas Cromwell: A Life*

Ramachandra Guha, *Gandhi: 1914-1948*

Slavoj Žižek, *Like a Thief in Broad Daylight: Power in the Era of Post-Humanity*

Neil MacGregor, *Living with the Gods: On Beliefs and Peoples*

Peter Biskind, *The Sky is Falling: How Vampires, Zombies, Androids and Superheroes Made America Great for Extremism*

Robert Skidelsky, *Money and Government: A Challenge to Mainstream Economics*

Helen Parr, *Our Boys: The Story of a Paratrooper*

David Gilmour, *The British in India: Three Centuries of Ambition and Experience*

Jonathan Haidt and Greg Lukianoff, *The Coddling of the American Mind: How Good Intentions and Bad Ideas are Setting up a Generation for Failure*

Ian Kershaw, *Roller-Coaster: Europe, 1950-2017*

Adam Tooze, *Crashed: How a Decade of Financial Crises Changed the World*

Edmund King, *Henry I: The Father of His People*

Lilia M. Schwarcz and Heloisa M. Starling, *Brazil: A Biography*

Jesse Norman, *Adam Smith: What He Thought, and Why it Matters*

Philip Augur, *The Bank that Lived a Little: Barclays in the Age of the Very Free Market*

Christopher Andrew, *The Secret World: A History of Intelligence*

David Edgerton, *The Rise and Fall of the British Nation: A Twentieth-Century History*

Julian Jackson, *A Certain Idea of France: The Life of Charles de Gaulle*

Owen Hatherley, *Trans-Europe Express*

Richard Wilkinson and Kate Pickett, *The Inner Level: How More Equal Societies Reduce Stress, Restore Sanity and Improve Everyone's Wellbeing*

Paul Kildea, *Chopin's Piano: A Journey Through Romanticism*

Seymour M. Hersh, *Reporter: A Memoir*

Michael Pollan, *How to Change Your Mind: The New Science of Psychedelics*

David Christian, *Origin Story: A Big History of Everything*

Judea Pearl and Dana Mackenzie, *The Book of Why: The New Science of Cause and Effect*

David Graeber, *Bullshit Jobs: A Theory*

Serhii Plokhy, *Chernobyl: History of a Tragedy*

Michael McFaul, *From Cold War to Hot Peace: The Inside Story of Russia and America*

Paul Broks, *The Darker the Night, the Brighter the Stars: A Neuropsychologist's Odyssey*

Lawrence Wright, *God Save Texas: A Journey into the Future of America*

John Gray, *Seven Types of Atheism*

Carlo Rovelli, *The Order of Time*

Mariana Mazzucato, *The Value of Everything: Making and Taking in the Global Economy*

Richard Vinen, *The Long '68: Radical Protest and Its Enemies*

Kishore Mahbubani, *Has the West Lost It?: A Provocation*

John Lewis Gaddis, *On Grand Strategy*

Richard Overy, *The Birth of the RAF, 1918: The World's First Air Force*

Francis Pryor, *Paths to the Past: Encounters with Britain's Hidden Landscapes*

Helen Castor, *Elizabeth I: A Study in Insecurity*

Ken Robinson and Lou Aronica, *You, Your Child and School*

Leonard Mlodinow, *Elastic: Flexible Thinking in a Constantly Changing World*

Nick Chater, *The Mind is Flat: The Illusion of Mental Depth and The Improvised Mind*

Michio Kaku, *The Future of Humanity: Terraforming Mars, Interstellar Travel, Immortality, and Our Destiny Beyond*

Thomas Asbridge, *Richard I: The Crusader King*

Richard Sennett, *Building and Dwelling: Ethics for the City*

Nassim Nicholas Taleb, *Skin in the Game: Hidden Asymmetries in Daily Life*

Steven Pinker, *Enlightenment Now: The Case for Reason, Science, Humanism and Progress*

Steve Coll, *Directorate S: The C.I.A. and America's Secret Wars in Afghanistan, 2001 - 2006*

Jordan B. Peterson, *12 Rules for Life: An Antidote to Chaos*

Bruno Maçães, *The Dawn of Eurasia: On the Trail of the New World Order*

Brock Bastian, *The Other Side of Happiness: Embracing a More Fearless Approach to Living*

Ryan Lavelle, *Cnut: The North Sea King*

Tim Blanning, *George I: The Lucky King*

Thomas Cogswell, *James I: The Phoenix King*

Pete Souza, *Obama, An Intimate Portrait: The Historic Presidency in Photographs*

Robert Dallek, *Franklin D. Roosevelt: A Political Life*

Norman Davies, *Beneath Another Sky: A Global Journey into History*

Ian Black, *Enemies and Neighbours: Arabs and Jews in Palestine and Israel, 1917-2017*

Martin Goodman, *A History of Judaism*

Shami Chakrabarti, *Of Women: In the 21st Century*

Stephen Kotkin, *Stalin, Vol. II: Waiting for Hitler, 1928-1941*

Lindsey Fitzharris, *The Butchering Art: Joseph Lister's Quest to Transform the Grisly World of Victorian Medicine*

Serhii Plokhy, *Lost Kingdom: A History of Russian Nationalism from Ivan the Great to Vladimir Putin*

Mark Mazower, *What You Did Not Tell: A Russian Past and the Journey Home*

Lawrence Freedman, *The Future of War: A History*

Niall Ferguson, *The Square and the Tower: Networks, Hierarchies and the Struggle for Global Power*

Matthew Walker, *Why We Sleep: The New Science of Sleep and Dreams*

Edward O. Wilson, *The Origins of Creativity*

John Bradshaw, *The Animals Among Us: The New Science of Anthropology*

David Cannadine, *Victorious Century: The United Kingdom, 1800-1906*

Leonard Susskind and Art Friedman, *Special Relativity and Classical Field Theory*

Maria Alyokhina, *Riot Days*

Oona A. Hathaway and Scott J. Shapiro, *The Internationalists: And Their Plan to Outlaw War*

Chris Renwick, *Bread for All: The Origins of the Welfare State*

Anne Applebaum, *Red Famine: Stalin's War on Ukraine*

Richard McGregor, *Asia's Reckoning: The Struggle for Global Dominance*

Chris Kraus, *After Kathy Acker: A Biography*

Clair Wills, *Lovers and Strangers: An Immigrant History of Post-War Britain*

Odd Arne Westad, *The Cold War: A World History*

Max Tegmark, *Life 3.0: Being Human in the Age of Artificial Intelligence*

Jonathan Losos, *Improbable Destinies: How Predictable is Evolution?*

Chris D. Thomas, *Inheritors of the Earth: How Nature Is Thriving in an Age of Extinction*

Chris Patten, *First Confession: A Sort of Memoir*

James Delbourgo, *Collecting the World: The Life and Curiosity of Hans Sloane*

Naomi Klein, *No Is Not Enough: Defeating the New Shock Politics*

Ulrich Raulff, *Farewell to the Horse: The Final Century of Our Relationship*

Slavoj Žižek, *The Courage of Hopelessness: Chronicles of a Year of Acting Dangerously*

Patricia Lockwood, *Priestdaddy: A Memoir*

Ian Johnson, *The Souls of China: The Return of Religion After Mao*

Stephen Alford, *London's Triumph: Merchant Adventurers and the Tudor City*

Hugo Mercier and Dan Sperber, *The Enigma of Reason: A New Theory of Human Understanding*

Stuart Hall, *Familiar Stranger: A Life Between Two Islands*

Allen Ginsberg, *The Best Minds of My Generation: A Literary History of the Beats*

Sayeeda Warsi, *The Enemy Within: A Tale of Muslim Britain*

Alexander Betts and Paul Collier, *Refuge: Transforming a Broken Refugee System*